He Died To Make Men Holy

He Died To
Make Men Holy

Norman Bales

Library of Congress Catalog Number: XXXXXXX
International Standard Book Number: 0-89900-271-4

DEDICATION

To my wife, Sarah Ann Williams Bales, who has given me her love, loyal support, devoted attention and years of personal joy and to the memory of our parents,

Jeff Robert Williams (1909-1964)
Sarah Ann Richardson Williams (1908-1985)
Burl Bales (1906-1988)
Ruby Lois Lane Bales (1908-1980)

this book is fondly and affectionately dedicated.

Table of Contents

INTRODUCTION

In 1989 I was asked to prepare a message on "Restoring the Biblical Doctrine of Holiness" for Restoration Forum VIII in Lincoln, Illinois. Shortly after I submitted the manuscript to College Press for publication, Don DeWelt called and asked if I would consider writing a comprehensive book on the subject of holiness. Without giving too much thought to the immensity of such a task, I accepted the invitation. Researching and writing this book have consumed almost every minute that I could spare away from my ministry and family responsibilities during the last two years.

Getting this manuscript together has been a monumental struggle. It was more than a struggle for time. There was also an awareness of my limitations. God has said, "Be holy, because I am holy" (I Pet. 2:16). To pretend that one has come anywhere close to God's standard of holiness is surely the epitome of egomania. And if that's true, what does it say about any mortal who would dare to think that he can instruct others on the subject. I wrestled with my finiteness throughout the entire project. On a good day, I've felt that I needed to grow some more before attempting to write on such a profound subject. On a bad day I've questioned whether I was really sane the day I so casually told Don I would be willing to write the book.

Now that the manuscript is completed and ready for the appraisal of the reader, I am able to view the project from a different perspective. I am unable to say whether you will profit from reading my insights on the subject of holiness, but there is absolutely no doubt that Norman Bales is much better for having researched and written on the subject. More than ever before I realize that God is transcendent, holy, awesome and full of glory.

Early in my research, it became apparent that getting to know God is the first requirement of following after holiness. Consequently, about half of the book is devoted to the holiness of God. I was frustrated in my attempt to find resource material on God. As strange as it may seem, books on the nature of God are not usually hot ticket items in Christian bookstores. The second great insight for me was the realization Jesus makes us holy through his redemptive sacrifice on the cross. One of the most beautiful expressions of this concept is communicated in brilliant poetic style by Julia Ward Howe's "Battle Hymn of the Republic." She wrote, "He died to make men holy...." The act that saves us and the act that sanctifies us are one and the same. Furthermore, the Savior who gave us holy status at Calvary, also modeled the lifestyle of holiness for us through his personal ministry. He calls us to emulate that high standard. In this book, we call that "progressive holiness."

I am deeply indebted to all those who have made suggestions, loaned resource material and reviewed portions of the manuscript. I am especially grateful for the use of the facilities of the Cedar Rapids, Iowa, Public Library, The University of Iowa Library, and the Abilene Christian University Library. Monroe Hawley of Milwaukee, Wisconsin, offered invaluable historical insights which served as a foundation for chapters 16-18. I am also indebted to Michael Armour of Dallas, Texas, who opened my eyes to the limitless amount of Biblical literature on the subject of God's glory. Dennis Randall, director of Restoration Leadership Ministry in Nashville, is a trusted friend. Dennis has done more to make this book happen than he realizes. He's the one who said to me, "Norman, we're still in the dark ages when it comes to holiness." I have bounced ideas off him from the beginning to the end. He has always been objective and helpful. I could not have written it without his encouragement.

My entire life and ministry has been spent in the fellowship of *a capella* churches. Hopefully this work will be read on "both sides of the keyboard." I'm most grateful for the friendship of Victor Knowles, Phil Scott, Dave O'Grady and Jim Knutson who have helped me to understand perspectives of those in churches who use instrumental music in worship.

The most valuable help of all has come from my wife, Ann. She has read every line and corrected every chapter. When I thought that I had taken leave of my senses in agreeing to write the book, she encouraged me and affirmed her confidence in me. She also deflated my ego when I needed it. The reader will never know how many absolutely brilliant expressions of prose received the death sentence from her dreaded blue pencil. Of all those who have offered suggestions, she's the only one who has the nerve to say, "That idea is off the wall. I never read such a harebrained thing in my life." Admittedly, she has saved me from embarrassment. There have also been moments when we sharply disagreed over the way an idea ought to be communicated and to her credit she has graciously accepted my decision to overrule her proposed changes. She didn't give up without a fight however and there were times when my rationale for retaining a portion of the manuscript was no more coherent than to say, "I'm the author and I say it stays." If the book has any literary merit, much credit goes to her for smoothing out the rough spots. She will always be my most severe and most respected editor.

Norman Bales
Cedar Rapids, Iowa
March 1, 1991

1
Why We Need
to Focus on Holiness

Not long ago, a friend and I travelled together to attend a meeting some distance away. As we rode toward our destination our conversation drifted toward the topic of holiness. My friend was reared in one segment of the Restoration Movement and my spiritual pilgrimage has all been lived out in another. As we compared notes on various aspects of holiness, he shocked me by saying, "When it comes to holiness, we're still in the dark ages. I'm inclined to agree with his candid, if somewhat cynical assessment. The Restoration Movement has treated holiness like an unwanted stepchild.

NEGLECT IN THE RESTORATION MOVEMENT

Thought molders in the Restoration Movement appear determined to wade around in the shallow end of this very deep pool of Biblical truth. Only three articles were published on the subject of holiness during the thirty year life of the *Millennial Harbinger,* according to the subject index. During most of its history the *Harbinger* was edited by Alexander Campbell, perhaps the most influential Restoration Movement leader. The "Sage of Bethany" conducted a search for truth that seldom saw the importance of emphasizing holiness. His energies were consumed with enlightening his readers on other subjects.

It is significant, however, to note Barton W. Stone's response to Campbell when the two men started putting their heads together. Unity was the topic most often associated with these two nineteenth century spiritual giants, but Stone made sure that Campbell realized that unity without holiness would get them nowhere. Stone wrote,

> Oh my brethren, let us repent and do the first works, let us seek more holiness, rather than trouble ourselves and others with schemes and plans of union. The love of God, shed abroad in our hearts by the Holy Ghost given unto us, will more effectually unite than all the wisdom of the world combined.[1]

Stone's commitment to holiness was of no small concern. To him the restoration of the ancient order of things and devotion to a life of holiness fit together like a hand in a glove.

> Till the Church of Christ become so holy, as in Apostolic times, "that of the rest durst no man join himself to them," the truth will not have that universal good effect in converting the world. O, Lord revive us! Amen.[2]

Aside from an occasional mention in a sermon here and a periodical essay there, it would be fair to say that holiness has never gotten a grip on Restorationists. Toward the close of the nineteenth century, W. T. Moore published, *The Living Pulpit of the Christian Church.* The list of contributors reads like a "Who's Who" among nineteenth century preachers. Moore's anthology included Campbell's famous "Sermon on the Law"[3] as well as sermonic essays by Moses E. Lard, J. W. McGarvey, Benjamin Franklin and Isaac Errett. None of them addressed the subject of holiness.[4]

In the early part of the twentieth century, Z. T. Sweeney published three sermon books. Free distribution of these books continued throughout all segments of the Restoration Movement for several generations. The sermons represented the cream of the crop among Restoration preachers of the late nineteenth and early twentieth centuries. In the entire trilogy no one dealt with the subject of holiness.[5]

When Restoration Movement heirs decided to go separate ways in 1906, nobody seemed to have given much thought to holiness. It has not been a major emphasis in any one of the three major branches of Restoration heritage.

Perhaps the best known preaching forum among the *a capella* churches in the twentieth century has been the Abilene Christian University Lectureship in Abilene, Texas. For more than seventy years, church members have gathered inside the cream colored brick buildings on the dust covered West Texas campus of that university to hear the best known preachers of the day address contemporary spiritual concerns. Many people think the lectureship represents the best contemporary thinking in the *a capella* brotherhood. Most of the main speeches in that forum have been published. According to published records, holiness has been addressed twice in seventy years. Jack Bates spoke on "The Holiness of God" in 1958 and James Le Fan addressed the theme, "Be Ye Holy," in 1963.

G. E. Busenburg blames Alexander Campbell for our aversion to holiness.

> Holiness has never been a popular subject in the Restoration Movement due probably in part to Campbell's view of the Holy Spirit and his seeming total reliance on the pragmatism of John Locke.[6]

On those rare occasions when Restoration communicators have dared to address the holiness idea, their emphasis has often been confined to warnings about worldliness. Little has been said about inward transformation. Not long ago a friend of mine decided that he would do some special study on what the Bible has to say about the inner man. He observed, "We don't write on that subject." To find quality published materials on the nature of inward transformation, one must turn to such writers as Henri Nowen – a Roman Catholic priest, Richard Foster – a Quaker, and Andrew Murray – a Scottish Presby-

17

terian who lived more than a hundred years ago.

Homilies on holiness tend to attack negative behavior patterns. Much has been said about abstaining from certain practices which are popular in the world at large, but probing the mysteries of God's holy nature does not attract either the modern preacher, editor, writer or professor. Trying to find books to assist one in his quest for a deeper knowledge of God can be a frustrating experience. That's especially true if one limits his reading to works of Restoration Movement writers.

Too often the concept of holiness is limited to a superficial morality menu. Holiness is said to consist of abstinence from sexual immorality and from activities which promote sexual misconduct. Christians sometimes disagree with each other as to which actions qualify as worldliness. The live issues of the twentieth century have included the propriety of dancing, mixed swimming, attending movies, familiarity in dating and defining the standards of modest dress.

The call to a holy life has also included appeals to abstain from the use of tobacco products, to avoid using all forms of alcoholic drink and to resist the pressures of participating in various popular forms of gambling such as office pools and lotteries. Each individual Christian has his own list of do's and don'ts. No two lists are the same. Sometimes the taboos are supported by the Biblical text, but at other times the recognized standards of holiness are derived from a person's own subjective interpretation. Human wisdom and personal tastes dictate the agenda of holiness.

Sometimes a brother or sister will hold tenaciously to cherished traditions which appear to be ludicrous in the thinking of another Christian. Several years ago, I met a brother who firmly believed that hunters should not be allowed to kill doves. He boldly insisted that shooting a dove is a matter of sin. This is not to suggest that he was an anti-hunting activist. On the contrary he openly espoused National Rifle Association philosophy. He boasted of his prowess in killing other kinds of game birds. To him quail, pheasant, ducks and geese are fair game for the sportsman, but doves are off limits. He reasoned that God's decision to have Noah send a dove out of the ark entitled all succeeding doves to special protection. I think his exegesis of Genesis 8:6-12 is suspect, but I do not question his sincerity.

Sincerely held quirks and peculiarities are often standards of holiness by people who hold them. The Christian who does not share such eccentric scruples may regard the person who does as something of a puritanical extremist. It's hard to conceal the smirk on your face when someone like the anti-dove brother bombards you with his rationale. We need to remember that turning a personal interpretation into a requirement for holy living and making it the basis of fellowship is very serious business according to Romans 14. We draw our own mental pictures of what constitutes the holy life. But that is all the more reason to be careful in our exegesis of scripture and to make sure we are promoting genuine holiness instead of our own personal idiosyncrasies.

We also tend to be somewhat arbitrary in deciding which ethical issues deserve the most attention. One needs only to point to common attitudes toward racial discrimination to observe how narrow our agenda tends to be. Some church members would never drink, smoke, attend R rated movies, gamble or engage in any kind of questionable sexual activity. Nevertheless, they display racist attitudes, enjoy ethnic stories which degrade certain classes of people and discriminate against others on the basis of their social standing. It never occurs to them to consider racial discrimination as an unholy action. A person may crusade against abortion and pornography on the one hand and behave in a rude and insensitive manner in dealing with the opposite sex on the other hand. Such a person may deny kindness to the poor and hold people in contempt who are not in his social class. If taking a strong stand against pornography and abortion constitutes evidence of one's holiness, then it stands to reason that social injustice is just as important. In Isaiah 1 the Lord indicated that the practice of injustice on the part of the nation of Judah provided evidence that the people had ". . . forsaken the Lord. They have spurned the Holy One of Israel and turned their backs on him" (Isa. 1:4). The prophet, Amos, reported that God preferred a people who would ". . . let justice roll on like a river . . ." (Amos 5:24).

While morality, public opinion and holiness often run on parallel tracks, they are not equal to each other. We move in the direction of holiness only when we focus attention on the holy God, when we see life from His point of view, and when we seek to emulate the stan-

19

dards which He demonstrated in sending His son to live on the earth. The issue is set before us in I Peter 1:15, "But just as he who called you is holy, so be holy in all you do, for it is written, 'Be holy, because I am holy.'" Holiness involves greater issues than simply setting limits on modest dress, making prudent choices about recreation and practicing clean habits.

You can observe all the taboos which will make you acceptable to the most conservative church fellowship in the country and still be unholy. You can withdraw from the world and shut out its sinful influences and still not be holy. Vance Havner said it well, ". . . living in a hole does not make you holier!"[7] Prudishness must never be equated with holiness.

R. C. Sproul put that kind of thinking into proper focus when he wrote,

> A superficial style of nonconformity is the classical pharisaical trap. The kingdom of God is not about buttons, movies, or dancing. The concern of God in not focused on what we eat or what we drink. The call for nonconformity is a call to a deeper level of righteousness that goes beyond externals.[8]

If we are really serious about restoring New Testament Christianity, we must find a place for holiness. No group claiming to "speak where the Bible speaks" can afford to neglect the massive amount of Biblical material on this important subject.

HOLINESS IN THE EVANGELICAL COMMUNITY

Sometimes Restorationists grow weary of our shortcomings and assume the grass to be greener in some other ecclesiastical pasture. Evangelicalism may look attractive to Restorationists who become disenchanted with our refusal to come to grips with holiness. If you find yourself leaning that way, I would suggest that you take a visit to your local Christian book store and start searching for contemporary titles which address the holiness theme. You'll find "Christian" books on how to lose weight, how to manage your money, how to have better marriages and even how to play better baseball with the help of the

Lord. You won't find many books telling you how to be holy. There's a very simple explanation. Sanctification doesn't sell. It has been suggested that "anyone who tries to expound on sanctification for discriminating readers should enter a plea for charity."[9]

In the early sixties, A. W. Tozer shook the evangelical world with a stinging indictment. He said,

> We have lost our spirit of worship and our ability to draw inwardly to meet God in adoring silence. Modern Christianity is simply not producing the kind of Christian who can appreciate or experience the life in the Spirit. The words, "Be still and know that I am God," mean next to nothing to the self confident, bustling worshiper in the middle period of the twentieth century.[10]

It's safe to say that little has been done in evangelical circles to alter the bleak picture Tozer painted at mid-century. More recently Donald Bloesch criticized his fellow evangelicals for limiting their concept of holiness to the motto, "let go and let God." He warned, "This ignores the truth that Scriptural holiness entails warfare and struggle in carrying forth the banner of God."[11]

HOLINESS IN MAINLINE PROTESTANTISM

Preoccupation with secular concerns gutted mainline protestantism's emphasis on holiness many years ago. Protestant thought is currently dominated by people who disavow the supernatural origin of the Bible. Consequently, the thought molders in contemporary theology have no base from which to launch a crusade for holiness. How could they relate to Moses taking off his shoes on the holy ground around the burning bush when they do not believe the burning bush incident actually occurred?

When contemporary Protestants address holiness, they inevitably think in terms of political and social responses to the temporal needs of the world community. James C. Fenhagen appealed for holiness among his fellow churchmen, noting that "The call to be a holy person is fundamental to what is implied in our baptism."[12] So far, so

21

good, but Fenhagen's idea of a holy person is someone "whose energies are expended in dealing with the complexities of the world."[13] As one might suspect his candidates for holiness models in the twentieth century are Desmond Tutu and Mother Teresa. He even suggests that his readers look for contemporary holiness in such places as Lebanon, Northern Ireland, Central America and South Africa. To Fenhagen holiness appears to be mainly a matter of social concern. He says nothing about the personal integrity of the individual and ignores the development of the inner person. He bypasses the need for cultivation of fellowship with a transcendent God. One might even wonder if faith is a requirement of holiness from Fenhagen's perspective.

SUMMARY AND CONCLUSION

While other groups have fought entrenched battles over the manner in which holiness is acquired, over the degree of holiness which can be attained in this life and over the Biblical requirements of the holy life, Restorationists have fought few if any battles over holiness. That's probably because our basic response to holiness has been one of indifference.

With a few noticeable exceptions Restoration leaders have treated the subject of holiness as if it were a deadly poison to be avoided at all costs. Some of our reluctance to deal with holiness may stem from the fact that the Age of Enlightenment in the 18th century had a profound influence on the people who molded the thought patterns of the Restoration Movement in the 19th century. As a result many Restorationists were so caught up in the objective study of Biblical facts that they were not able to focus on the emotional and volitional commitment that holiness requires.

The evangelical and mainline protestant perspectives on holiness can hardly be regarded as improvements on the Restoration approaches. Evangelicals have a tendency to avoid the struggle and discipline associated with the holy life; mainline Protestants would confine the holiness agenda to social action, while ignoring ethics and the development of the inner life.

Somehow God's call to holiness must get our attention. Progressing in holiness must be focused more sharply in our thinking. Paul challenges us to make it a priority in II Corinthians 7:1, "Since we have these promises, dear friends, let us purify ourselves from everything that contaminates body and spirit, perfecting holiness out of reverence for God."

Endnotes

1. Quoted by James DeForest Murch. *Christians Only*. (Cincinnati: Standard Publishing, 1962), p. 95.

2. B. W. Stone, "To the Public Teachers Who Are Called Christians." *Christian Messenger*. July, 1832, p. 200.

3. Alexander Campbell delivered "The Sermon on the Law" at the meeting of the Redstone Baptist Association on August 30, 1816. Essentially Campbell was attempting to show that Christians are under law to Christ and not to Moses. His message was met with stiff opposition by the Baptist leaders. From that point on relationship with the Baptists began to deteriorate. His delivery of the "Sermon on the Law" marked the beginning of a period in his career in which Campbell reacted to denominational traditions with severe criticism. It proved to be a watershed event in Restoration Movement history. For a full report on the events associated with the "Sermon on the Law," see James DeForest Murch. *Christians Only*, pp. 53-66.

4. W.T. Moore, *The Living Pulpit of the Christian Church*, reprinted by B.C. Goodpasture under the title, *Biographies and Sermons of Pioneer Preachers*. (Nashville, Tennessee: The Gospel Advocate Company, 1954).

5. Z.T. Sweeney, *New Testament Christianity*, Volumes I, II, and III. (Columbus, Indiana: New Testament Book Fund, Inc. 1923, 1926, and 1930).

6. G.E. Busenburg, "God Called Us To Holiness." (*Mission*, May, 1972), p. 6. Garth W. Black defines Campbell's view of the Holy Spirit as an understanding that ". . . the Holy Spirit exerts no influence upon man at any time or in any way except through the agency of the word." Garth W. Black. *The Holy Spirit*. (Abilene, Texas: Biblical Research Press, 1967), p. 76. This was essentially the premise that Campbell affirmed in his debate with N.L. Rice in 1843. However Black believes other records of Campbell's statements on the Holy Spirit may have allowed for a belief in the personal indwelling of the Holy Spirit (Ibid., pp. 76-77). That the philosopher, John Locke, influenced Campbell is well known. James DeForest Murch noted that Campbell and his intellectual colleagues took their philosophy from John Locke and thus denied that the Creator has any access to the human soul except by words and arguments. (Murch. *Christians Only*, p. 105). It should also be noted that the Restoration Movement is greatly indebted to Locke's philosophy. The notion that unity can occur when reasonable people apply themselves to the study of the Word with intellectual objectivity is solidly rooted in Locke. See Leonard Allen and Richard Hughes. *Discovering Our Roots: The Ancestry of the Churches of Christ.* (Abilene, Texas: ACU Press, 1989), pp. 78-80.

7. Vance Havner, *The Best of Vance Havner.* (Old Tappan, New Jersey: Fleming H. Revell Company, 1969), p. 112.

8. R.C. Sproul, *The Holiness of God.* (Wheaton, Illinois: Tyndale House Publishers, 1987), p. 207.

9. Cary N. Weisiger, III, *The Reformed Doctrine of Sanctification.* (Washington, D.C.: Christianity Today, n.d.).

10. A.W. Tozer, *The Knowledge of the Holy.* (San Francisco: Harper and Row Publishers, 1961), p. vii.

11. Donald G. Bloesch, *Essentials of Evangelical Theology, Volume 2.* (San Francisco: Harper and Row Publishers, 1978), p. 61.

12. James C. Fenhagen, *Invitation to Holiness.* (San Francisco: Harper and Row, 1985), p. 28.

13. Ibid.

2
The Biblical Mandate for Personal Holiness

Biblical admonitions to pursue holiness are repeated frequently in the scriptures. The Bible writers establish a tone of urgency when they discuss the concept of holy living. The thoughts expressed in this chapter will concentrate on the Bible's call to holiness.

THE OLD TESTAMENT CALL TO HOLINESS

Sproul contended that Genesis 1:26 presents the first concrete Old Testament evidence that God expects human beings to be holy.

We were created in the image of God. To be in God's image meant among other things, that we were made to mirror and reflect the character of God. We were created to shine forth to the world the holiness of God. This was the chief end of man, the very reason for his existence.[1]

25

Adam and Eve's lapse of holiness in the Garden of Eden led to their expulsion from that ideal environment. Sampling the forbidden fruit enabled our earliest parents to gain knowledge of good and evil, but they rendered themselves incapable of performing good. Therefore, God was left with no alternative but to expel them from paradise. "And the Lord God said, The man has now become like one of us knowing good and evil. He must not be allowed to reach out and take also from the tree of life and eat and live forever" (Gen. 3:23). Thus man's original quest for holiness ended in failure.

Recapturing the elusive goal of holiness has dominated the thoughts of spiritually minded people ever since. The spiritually sensitive pursuer of holiness recognizes the vastness of the great gulf between God and man. All human aspirations toward holiness fall short of satisfaction.

Although the holiness terms are never used with reference to the patriarchs, these ancient men of God understood the need to be holy. What led Cain and Abel to make an offering to God? Both men probably knew their lives had not measured up to God's standards. In some way they must have known their behavior was not totally acceptable to God. There can be no doubt that God's acceptance was important to them. When God refused to accept Cain's offering, Adam and Eve's first born son became so emotionally distraught that he projected the blame on his younger sibling and committed the world's first murder. He wouldn't have done that had he been totally lacking in spiritual sensitivity.

In a time when man's wickedness was so great that "every inclination of his heart was only evil all the time," Noah swam against the popular tide of public opinion in his time and pursued a life of holiness. The author of Genesis said, "Noah was a righteous man, blameless among the people of his time and he walked with God" (Gen. 6:9).

During Abram's 99th year, God spoke directly to him about the importance of holy living. "I am God Almighty; walk before me and be blameless" (Gen. 17:1). Jacob's strange experience at Jabbok may indicate something of his growth in holiness. After wrestling with the man who appeared out of nowhere, he was told, "Your name will no longer be Jacob, but Israel because you have struggled with God and with men and have overcome" (Gen. 32:28).

Qadash is the Hebrew word used most frequently by the Old Testament writers to convey the holiness concept. In our English Bibles the term, qadash, is usually translated "holy," "consecrate," "sanctify," or "hallow." Exodus 13:2 applies it to man. Following the passover God told Moses, "Consecrate (qadesh) to me every firstborn male. The first offspring of every womb among the Israelites belongs to me whether man or animal." Consequently, every firstborn Hebrew male knew that his life was to be set apart for God.

The Mosaic law specifically required holiness of the entire nation.

I am the Lord your God; Consecrate yourselves and be holy, because I am holy. Do not make yourselves unclean by any creature that moves on the ground. I am the God who brought you out of Egypt to be your God; therefore be holy because I am holy (Lev. 11:44- 45).

The covenant people expanded from a family, to a tribe, to a nation of slaves and then developed into a theocracy. There was never another nation like it on the face of the earth. They knew they were different. God required holiness of them as a means of making them aware of the special position. "The Israelites were to be a people 'separated out' of their environment."[2]

Unfortunately, the people of Israel frequently thought of their holiness only in ceremonial terms. To be sure the law did link holiness and ceremony together. When Moses poured oil on Aaron's head, "he anointed him to consecrate him" (Leviticus 8:12). Nevertheless the holiness concept went far beyond mere ceremony. In Leviticus 19:2, God said to Moses, "Speak to the entire assembly of Israel and say to them, 'Be holy because I the Lord your God am Holy.'" God then proceeded to define holiness in terms of morality and personal devotion.

Throughout most of Israel and Judah's history, the concern for holy ritual outweighed the concern for holy living in the minds of the people. That's why the prophets screamed so loudly! Micah asked, "With what shall I come before the Lord and bow down before the exalted God?" (Micah 6:6). With much sarcasm he then asked, "Shall I come before him with burnt offerings, with calves a year old?"

Micah's question was rhetorical. Everyone who followed his reasoning pattern knew the answer had to be "no." After asking more rhetorical questions, he dropped a straight answer on them in verse 8:

> He has showed you, O man
>   what is good.
> And what does the LORD
>   require of you?
> To act justly and to love
>   mercy
> And to walk humbly with
>   Your God.

THE CALL TO HOLINESS IN THE NEW TESTAMENT

The New Testament never depicts holiness as a channel through which we gain God's favor. Paradoxically, holiness is a response to God's grace and we cannot see him without it (Hebrews 12:14). As Peter presented it, we are able to reflect our status as creatures made in the image of God through our reception of his blessings.

> His divine power has given us everything we need for life and godliness through our knowledge of him who called us by his own glory and goodness. Through these he has given us very great and precious promises, so that through them you may participate in the divine nature and escape the corruption in the world caused by evil desires (II Peter 1:3-4).

As we shall see in subsequent chapters, Christians participate in three levels of holiness. There's a level of *positional holiness*. By positional holiness, we mean that a Christian is to be regarded as holy because he is a Christian. As members of the body, we are "a chosen people, a royal priesthood, a holy nation, a people belonging to God" (II Peter 2:9). *Progressive holiness* is the second level. Paul addresses the progressive level in II Corinthians 7:1, "Since we have these promises, dear friends, let us purify ourselves from everything that contaminates body and spirit, perfecting holiness out of reverence for God." To this may be added the level of *prospective holiness*. According to Ephesians 5:27, Christians belong to a holy bride which Christ will present to himself, ". . . without stain or wrinkle or any other blemish, but holy and blameless." These levels of holiness will be discussed in greater depth in chapter 19.

Donald G. Bloesch helps us to appreciate how these different levels integrate in God's total plan for human redemption. "The Scriptures do not teach self-sanctification, but they do depict man as active in realizing the fruits of his sanctification in Christ."[3]

On the night before his crucifixion, Jesus petitioned his Father, for "those you have given me" (John 17:9). Much has been said about his prayer for unity. Certainly the religious world has largely ignored what the Lord said about unity, but the prayer also includes a petition for holiness. He mentioned it twice. In verse 17, he said, "Sanctify them by the truth; Your word is truth." In verse 19, he said, "For them I sanctify myself that they too may be truly sanctified."

Throughout the writings of Paul heavy stress is placed on the importance of holiness. In Romans 12:2, Paul called for totally transformed lives as a response to God's mercy. That transformation included holiness. He wanted his readers to offer themselves as "living sacrifices, holy and pleasing to God."

The necessity of holy living is assumed in the New Testament when the writers speak of Christians as "saints." The term "saint" has lost its impact for many contemporary Christians. It's not uncommon to hear someone say, "I'm a Christian, but I'm certainly no saint." Why not? Paul even regarded the carnal Christians at Corinth brothers and sisters who were called to be saints (See I Corinthians 1:2 KJV).

"To be a saint means to be separated. . . . The saint is one who is in a vital process of sanctification."[4] If we had a greater sensitivity to our saintly position, perhaps we would be more saintly in our demeanor.

The Lord's atoning death on the cross also involved our holiness. As Paul presented it, the holiness of the church was in view at the crucifixion.

Husbands love your wives, just as Christ loved the church and gave himself up for her to make her holy cleansing her by the washing of water through the word and to present himself a radiant church without stain or wrinkle or any other blemish but holy and blameless (Eph. 5:25-27).

Holiness is never an option for the Christian. It's as vital to maintaining spiritual life as breathing is to maintaining physical life. Neither is holiness a peripheral doctrine. "The word *holy* in its various forms occurs more than 600 times in the Bible."[5]

The Bible writers assume that we understand our need for holiness. They do not set forth a rationale to convince us that we need to be holy. When they present a mandate for holiness, it's usually in the form of explaining why certain things are taking place. For example, in Hebrews 12:10, ". . . God disciplines us for our good, that we may share in his holiness." From the Hebrew writer's perspective, holiness is a desire felt in the heart of every true Christian. That's why he wrote in verse 14, "Make every effort to live in peace with all men and to be holy; without holiness no one will see the Lord."

HOLINESS, A RESPONSE TO GRACE

One does not achieve holiness in the same way that he climbs the ladder of success in American business. According to the American work ethic the person who gets up early, arrives at the work place before the work day begins, applies himself diligently to the tasks at hand, works through lunch, stays on an hour or so after it's time to go home and then takes work home with him is the person who is on the way to success. He is rewarded in direct proportion to the amount of time, energy and expertise he is willing to contribute to his job. We have a tendency to think that holiness comes in the same way, but holiness cannot be achieved through human effort.

In Titus 2:11-12, Paul wrote, "For the grace of God that brings salvation has appeared to all men. It teaches us to say, 'No' to ungodliness and worldly passions and to live self-controlled, upright and godly lives in this present age." The pursuit of progressive holiness grows out of an awareness that we have been made righteous through the blood of Christ.

According to Colossians 1:21-23,

Once you were alienated from God and were enemies in your minds because of your evil behavior. But now he has reconciled you by Christ's physical body through death to present you holy in his sight without blemish and free from accusation – if you continue in your faith, established and firm, not moved from the hope held out in the gospel.

Paul wanted to make sure that his readers understood that holiness is the result of reconciliation, not the cause of reconciliation.

Some church members believe too much talk about grace will give rise to permissive behavior. They are afraid people will view grace as a license to sin and take advantage of the grace of God to fulfill their fleshly lusts. They don't seem to think Paul's warning against such an abuse of the doctrine in Romans 6:1 is sufficient to deter such flagrant disregard for the standards of scripture. Such thinking is understandable because the unregenerated person behaves responsibly only when he is forced to do so or when it's to his immediate advantage to maintain a modicum of decency. Generally speaking, people don't observe speed limits in order to conserve fuel or save lives. They obey speed limits to avoid traffic tickets and escalating automobile insurance premiums.

When that kind of thinking dominates the secular environment that surrounds us, we are tempted to think the same kind of rationale governs the spiritual person's decision making process. Thus we conclude that the only way to keep people walking down the straight and narrow path is to keep telling them how hot Hell is and to keep warning them that even the slightest deviation from the straight and narrow path can result in the loss of God's blessings. A steady diet of that kind of emphasis convinces the most sensitive minded people that they are repulsive in God's sight and encourages a certain percentage of them to give up on the faith.

From the perspective of the church leader who thinks that frequent doses of Hell fire and brimstone are the only persuasive tools the Christian teacher can use, grace looks like a Satanic ploy to undermine his hard work. On the other hand, the grace-oriented instructor talks about receiving a free gift from God. He dares to suggest that

31

the sinner can do nothing to make himself acceptable to a holy God. Those who favor the grace program point out that "All our righteous acts are like filthy rags" (Isaiah 64:6). Consequently the only avenue to salvation is through the grace-faith program made possible through the blood of Christ.

That's very hard for some minds to accept. In the real world of Monday through Saturday, we're constantly being reminded that there is no free lunch. In the free enterprise system rewards go to those who give the greatest effort. Consequently, we have great difficulty comprehending the fact that salvation is a free gift of God and that holiness becomes possible only as a result of the gift.

To make matters worse, there are some people who would presume on the grace of God. Paul warned, "You, my brothers, were called to be free. But do not use your freedom to indulge the sinful nature, rather serve one another in love" (Gal. 5:13). Sometimes people suddenly discover grace and conclude that grace gives them carte blanche permission to fulfill the lusts of the flesh. Some years ago, a well known organized crime figure attended a Billy Graham Crusade and "professed faith in Christ." Later, he was offended when he discovered that the follow up counselors wanted him to cease his racketeering activities. He said, "Nobody told me I would have to give up my work to be a Christian."[6] He did not want to face the fact that being a Christian means turning away from a life of crime.

When Jimmy Carter was elected to the presidency in 1976, the news media reported that the new president professed to be a "born again" Christian. Shortly thereafter professing the new birth became something of a fad. Without impugning the motives of former President Carter or challenging his sincerity, we must recognize the fact that some of this new birth phenomenon does not produce any evidence of transformation. J. Edwin Orr noted,

A national poll has announced that 50 million Americans state they are "born again," but a national newspaper observes that this evangelical awakening (so called) seems to have little effect upon the morals of the country, as murder, robbery, rape, pornography, and other social evils abound.[7]

As Orr sees it, the problem lies in a misapplication of the gospel message, "Too many people are preaching a warped or truncated gospel and spiritual birth defects are the result."[8]

Like holiness, grace has not been widely proclaimed in Restoration Movement theology. That's beginning to change. People are discovering grace as a positive Biblical teaching. Unfortunately some discover grace and conclude that it releases them from the demands of responsible living. Grace becomes an excuse for self-centered, irresponsible behavior. In effect freedom in Christ means liberty to sin in the minds of some people. The Bible is no longer used as a measuring rod to gauge one's spiritual progress. Passages that make a person uncomfortable are explained away and rephrased to endorse one's behavior. This shoddy approach to Christian discipleship amounts to what Deitrich Bonhoeffer called "cheap grace."

Bonhoeffer, a German national, came to manhood during the terrible days of the Third Reich. He clearly saw that Hitler's government was an evil system. During the thirties many Lutherans accommodated themselves to the political order. They reasoned there was nothing they could do about Hitler, so they would go on with business as usual, while being careful to avoid saying anything negative about the Fuhrer. Bonhoeffer aligned himself with the "confessing" church, which meant that he would resist Nazism. He was arrested, imprisoned and hanged shortly before the end of World War II.

Bonhoeffer severely criticized those Lutherans who chose to ignore what was happening to Germany. He said, "Cheap grace is the deadly enemy of the church. We are fighting today for costly grace."[9] In today's world, we are still tempted to follow the path of least resistance. In an era when many of us are yearning for more exposure to God's loving nature, the idea of being called to a more disciplined approach to life sounds like a sinister plot to drag us back into the bondage of legalism. Bridges noted, ". . .the concept of discipline is suspect in our society today. It appears to counter our emphasis on freedom in Christ, and often smacks of legalism."[10]

Clearly God's grace frees us from the burden of trying to make it to heaven under our own power. Salvation can never be a self-help program. "For it is by grace you have been saved, through faith — and this is not from yourselves, it is the gift of God — not by works , so that no one can boast" (Eph. 2:8-9). That completely removed the salvation program from any consideration of human merit. Praise God that it is so!

Many people do not yet comprehend the truth that grace gives birth to transformation.

> Therefore, I urge you, brothers, in view of God's grace, to offer your bodies as living sacrifices, holy and pleasing to God — which is your spiritual worship. Do not conform any longer to the pattern of this world, but be transformed by the renewing of your mind. Then you will be able to test and approve what God's will is — his good, pleasing and perfect will (Rom. 12:1-2).

The transformed life is not an automatic response. Christians do not progress in holiness through some kind of mystical experience. It does not come as a result of infrequent periods of devoted living. It's a continuous, prolonged process. James Le Fan noted,

> It is not by a few rough spasmodic blows of the hammer that the graceful statue is brought out of the marble block, but by laboring continuously, and by many delicate touches of the sculptor's chisel. It is not with a rush and a spring that we are to reach God's holiness; but step by step, foot by foot, hand over hand, we are slowly and often painfully to mount the ladder that rests on earth and rises to heaven.[11]

God always respects the freedom of the human will. We have to decide if we're going to allow God to transform us. We live in a world that is being value programmed by humanistic thinking. Holy living doesn't figure into the priorities of the movers and shakers who influence public opinion. Consequently, we must constantly remind ourselves that Jesus bore our sins at Calvary and that his work on our behalf was done to get us ready for spending eternity in the presence of our heavenly Father. No one can claim to have perfected holiness in this life, but the grace of God demands that we pursue it. Notice the connection between holiness and grace in Hebrews 12. In verse 14, the writer makes the point that "without holiness, no one will see the Lord." In the very next verse, he says, "See to it that no one misses the grace of God."

SUMMARY AND CONCLUSION

From the moment God said, "Let us make man in our image," it has been the divine intent that men and women should be holy. Adam and Eve's expulsion from the Garden of Eden was the result of their lapse in holiness. Spiritually minded people have sought to recapture holiness ever since. Holiness is a major theme in both the Old and New Testaments. Although Israel was called to be a holy nation, many of Israel's leaders tended to view holiness almost exclusively as a ceremonial response. Little inward transformation took place.

The New Testament sharpens the focus on inward transformation. At least three levels of holiness are presented. Every Christian is holy by virtue of his status as a child of God. It can justly be said that every new Christian has attained a status of *positional* holiness. Growth in holiness can be described as *progressive* holiness. Ultimately, the child of God who enters heaven will enter into a final level of sanctification which may be described as *prospective* holiness.

Holiness cannot be achieved through human effort. Still we must desire it and pursue it if we are to make progress in it. Actual transformation takes place, however, because we have been given a new nature as the result of our identification with Christ (Gal. 2:20; Eph. 2:10).

Endnotes

1. R.C. Sproul, *The Holiness of God.* p.202.

2. Mike Houston, "How Can I Ever Be Holy?" *Firm Foundation.* April 13, 1976, p. 3. Houston pointed out, "The relationship between Yahweh and Israel was not like the typical relationship that existed between the Canaanite people and their gods. The pagan gods were essentially powers which had to be bribed by various sacrifices, prayers and acts of worship. Thus a god like Baal, for instance, could be bribed into giving the land and crops fertility through appropriate worship. The gods were essentially powers which could be controlled and used by proper ritualistic devices. Yahweh asserted from the beginning of his relationship with Israel that he was truly set apart from man and thus not merely a power to be used and coerced."

3. Donald G. Bloesch, *Essentials of Evangelical Theology, Vol. 2.* (San Francisco: Harper and Row, 1978), p. 32.

4. R.C. Sproul, *The Holiness of God,* p. 211.
5. Jerry Bridges, *The Pursuit of Holiness,* p. 19.
6. Edwin Orr, "Playing the Good News Melody Off Key." *Christianity Today.* January 1, 1982, p. 24.
7. Ibid.
8. Ibid.
9. Dietrich Bonhoeffer, *The Cost of Discipleship. (Macmillan, 1963),* p. 45.
10. Jerry Bridges, *The Pursuit of Holiness,* p. 99.
11. James Le Fan, "Be Ye Holy." *Abilene Christian College Lectures, 1963.* (Abilene, Texas: Abilene Christian College, 1963), p. 42.

3
Rationalizations Which Hinder the Pursuit of Holiness

Rationalizing and excuse making are common to the human experience. Most Christians are caught in the crunch of trying to make ends meet and struggling to survive in the material world. Consequently they devote only a fraction of their total energy to spiritual matters. The demands of holiness appear to be far removed from what we often call the real world. Actually it is the people who fixate on profits, popularity and power who have distorted reality, but you have to resist the powerful tide of public opinion to understand that.

To help us get our focus on the need to be holy, this chapter will deal with some of the common rationalizations which people employ to resist the challenge to grow in holiness.

THE FREEDOM RATIONALIZATION

Holiness involves personal discipline. The Hebrew writer said, "God disciplines us for our good that we may share in his holiness"

(Heb. 12:10). In our human weakness, we usually resist the demands of discipline. We think of discipline as some kind of painful drudgery. For some reason, we believe discipline will cramp our style and prevent us from enjoying life. One man rather candidly offered his reasons for not becoming a Christian. He said, "I want to enjoy life. I want to have a good time. Christianity gets in the way of that."

The call to holiness requires that we resist rebellious tendencies, reining in our thought patterns and setting some limits on our behavior. That's not what most people want to hear. The writers of the Bible realized that undisciplined behavior looks attractive to some people. "No discipline seems pleasant at the time, but painful. Later on, however it produces a harvest of righteousness and peace for those who have been trained by it" (Heb. 12:11). Romans 6:20, noted, "When you were slaves to sin, you were free from the control of righteousness." If you live for the short run, you can have what you want. If you can afford it and if somebody else doesn't want what you want, there is nothing to stop you from gratifying your most sensuous desires. Furthermore we are not accustomed to waiting for the fulfillment of our dreams. We live in an age of instant gratification. This morning, I turned on the shower nozzle in the bathroom and received instant hot water. We have instant coffee and instant tea in our cupboard. We can have instant oatmeal if we want it and we don't even have to wait for the television set to warm up anymore. This manuscript is being typed on a computer, but it's an outmoded one because we have to wait 25 seconds for the word processing program to load when we call it up. Computer buffs think that's archaic. We don't want to spend the time it takes to perk regular coffee and prepare the kind of breakfast a farmer would expect to eat before he embarks on a day of plowing, because we think we've got more important things to do with our time. When we're typing on the computer, we forget that it is several times faster than the electric typewriter we used just two years ago. We are geared to having our desires without waiting for them and without immediate cost.

The fans of instant everything will probably think it's bad news when they first learn that there is no instant holiness program. The person who is willing to accept the challenge to be holy is accepting a lifetime of struggle. The goal is an extremely lofty one. "Dear friends, now we are the children of God and what we will be has not yet been made known. But we know that when he appears, we shall be like him, for we shall see him as he is" (I John 3:2). We all have a very long way to go before we reach the plateau of truly being like him. Nevertheless, that's the goal.

It's understandable that we would try to find ways to avoid committing ourselves to such a lofty goal that will require us to engage all of our resources over the space of an entire lifetime. That is precisely what God has in mind. In Galatians 6:8-9 Paul reminded his readers, "The one who sows to please his sinful nature, from that nature will reap destruction; the one who sows to please the Spirit from the Spirit will reap eternal life. Let us not become weary in doing good, for at the proper time we will reap a harvest if we do not give up."

CULTIC FEARS

We Fear That An Emphasis on Holiness Will Be Equated With Cultism in the Minds of Others. A significant change took place in the American attitude toward cults when Jim Jones, leader of the People's Temple, carried out a threat to commit murder and suicide in defense of his twisted view of "the faith." The mass suicide/murder of 900 temple members at Jonestown, Guyana awoke the world to the stark realization that cultism must be viewed as a threat to the public good. Tolerance for cultic behavior ended when the American public learned the ghastly truth about the deaths at Jonestown.

Researchers have discovered that the dynamic leaders who head up cultic organizations often emphasize the concept of disciplined living. The required regimentation may include abstinence from alcohol, tobacco, and illicit sex. Sometimes cult members are expected to surrender material possessions when they enter the fellowship of the cult. One young lady reported that she was asked to give her car, stereo, guitar and bank account to the organization she joined.[1]

Cult leaders may also require members to spend long periods of time in study, meditation, prayer and other supervised activities.

Adherents and ex-members describe constant exhortation and

39

training to arrive at exalted spiritual states, altered consciousness and automatic submission to directives . . . and lengthy
repetitive lectures day and night.[2]

On the surface some of these actions sound very much like Biblical
requirements for holy living. We've already noted that Romans 12:2,
calls for transformed living. In II Corinthians 6:14, Paul exhorted his
readers, "Do not be yoked together with unbelievers. For what do
righteousness and wickedness have in common? Or what fellowship
can light have with darkness?" Transformation and separation are
part of the Biblical holiness rationale.

The Biblical requirements for holy living also call for self-denial, abstinence from immorality and submission to the Lord. Mutual submission to one another is even taught in the scriptures (Eph. 5:21).
However, it should be pointed out that human submission always
flows both ways in the scriptures. No person has the right to assume
dictatorial authority over another individual. Furthermore, if one person is expected to be accountable to another, then all persons are
equally accountable. When one leader demands that others report, account and submit to his authority and then does not report, account
and submit to any other person himself, that leader has assumed control privileges which lie outside the boundaries of Biblical permission.
His demands are not to be equated with the standards of holiness.
That kind of power play separates so called "Christian" cults from
non-manipulative religious bodies.

The general public doesn't always see this difference. They hear
cult leaders calling for holiness and they hear church leaders using the
same terminology. Many people never take time to investigate the
amount of mind control that's going on within these fellowships. The
demands of extremists sours them on the holiness idea altogether.
Most Americans and most Christians cherish the freedom to make decisions for themselves about what to believe and what not to believe.
When the plea for holiness begins to sound like coercion, they rebel
at the thought of responding to the appeal.

The difference between Biblical holiness and the cultic version of it
is similar to the difference between real money and counterfeit curren-
cy. Note the following contrasts.

1. Biblical holiness is always based on an appeal to the free will of man. Cultic holiness is grounded in loyalty to a cult leader.
2. Biblical holiness is a response to God's grace (Titus2:11). Cultic holiness is a response to the demands of human teachers.
3. Biblical holiness allows for latitude of expression with respect to taste, temperament, culture and custom. Cultic leaders demand uniform behavior of all their followers.
4. Biblical holiness is rooted in the holiness of God. Cultic holiness is rooted in the teachings of an exalted human leader.
5. Biblical holiness displays itself in character development. Cultic holiness exhibits itself in conformity to humanly prescribed levels of achievement.
6. Biblical holiness is activated by love. Cultic holiness is aroused by guilt and fear.

LOSS OF CREDIBILITY BY POPULAR RELIGIOUS PERSONALITIES

Many People Who Promote Holiness Lack Credibility. I had just settled back in my seat for a very long airplane flight. Soon I became aware of a conversation that was taking place about three rows behind me. One person was clearly dominating the conversation and his words seem to be aimed to everyone in earshot, not just the unfortunate person who sat next to him. He was discussing his theories concerning the second coming. The passengers around me did not seem to appreciate being forcibly exposed to a mini course on Biblical eschatology, but it is difficult to walk away from a conversation when you're 30,000 feet in the air.

Many people regard any attempt at sharing religious faith as an invasion of their privacy. To them faith is a personal matter, convictions to be shared only with the most intimate friends. They resent strangers who try to force them into religious discussions. Consequently, they view assertive expositions with great suspicion. Em Griffin noted that ". . . many people regard any effort at persuasion as an attempt to box them in."[3] A hard sell evangelistic pitch usually trips the non-Christian's set of defensive mechanisms. I remember one rather talkative seat mate who shut down his conversation entirely when he learned that I was a preacher. The non-Christian mind isn't wired like the Christian mind. If we want to gain a favorable hearing from a person steeped in secular values, we must make an effort to understand how that individual's head works. A huge red warning light goes on inside a non-Christian's head when someone tries to use a vulnerable circumstance as an occasion to share the gospel. He regards it as a crass attempt at parading religion. He also believes that such a pretension of holiness is not genuine. He reserves his strongest loathing for the person he views as trying to be "holier than thou."

We cannot expect people to desire holiness if they regard the people who profess to be holy as repugnant. The Christian must have credibility with the unbeliever if he expects to persuade him. It's significant to note that the overseers of the church must have "a good reputation with outsiders" (I Tim. 3:7). Rarely is such a reputation ever gained through forcing a person to talk about a spiritual subject when he does not care to. Such a reputation is never gained when a person's lifestyle is a blatant contradiction of what he professes.

Three hundred years before Christ, Aristotle said, "The character of the speaker is a cause of persuasion when the speech is so uttered as to make him worthy of belief."[4] The Roman rhetorician, Quintillian (c. 68 A.D.), saw the impact of character on communication when he said, "Rhetoric is a good man speaking well."[5]

Carl Rogers, the well known secular counselor, emphasizes communicating with integrity. Rogers claims that a counselor will be able to help his clients only when the counselor is in touch with his own feelings and is able to admit some of those feelings to a client.[6]

The public exposure of religious leaders mandates giving attention to communicating holiness through the personal integrity of the person who professes to be a Christian. Scandals involving media evangelists have made it more difficult for all Christians to maintain plausibility. When holiness can still be perceived by those who relate to the Christian in business dealings, in the privacy of the home, in recreation and in all of life's social contacts, it then becomes an admirable and desirable standard to emulate.

Of course, we must recognize that no one does it to absolute perfection. John wrote, "If we claim to be without sin, we deceive ourselves and the truth is not in us" (I John 1:8). But he also said, "If we confess our sins, he is faithful and just to forgive us our sins and purify us from all unrighteousness" (I John 1:9). The holy Christian is not a sinless Christian, but he is a Christian who does not pretend to be spotless and superior.

When holiness looks like a sham, everybody loses. The Christian loses because he's fallen into the hypocrisy trap. The unbeliever loses because he thinks Christianity causes people to behave in shameful ways. The church loses because it can't offer hope to the person who desperately needs its fellowship.

The following statement has been attributed to Abraham Lincoln. "You can fool some of the people all of the time and all of the people some of the time, but you cannot fool all of the people all of the time." Some years later, James Thurber quipped, "You can fool too many of the people too much of the time."[7]

SUMMARY AND CONCLUSION

If the Gallup organization undertook a survey of public attitudes on holiness, they would probably discover that holiness has a low priority among most contemporary Americans. The response would probably range from ignorance to indifference to indignation. While one would naturally expect holiness to have a higher priority among religious people, holiness doesn't rate nearly so high as "nickels, noise and numbers" in most church assemblies.

Serious minded Christians need to get holiness off the back burner. From the earliest history of God's dealing with the human race, God has expected His people to be holy. Throughout both the Old and New Testaments he was constantly prodding people toward higher levels of holy living.

It will not be easy to restore holiness in the twentieth century. The Christian community is bombarded by secular philosophy on the one side and by dismal failures among those who profess to be holy on the other side. Nevertheless, these disappointments must not deter us from our pursuit of holiness. God is holy and the quality of our relationship with him depends on our willingness to grow in this important attribute.

> Lord, lift me up and let me stand.
> By faith on heaven's tableland,
> A higher plane than I have found;
> Lord, plant my feet on higher ground.
> —Johnson Oatman

Endnotes

1. Reprinted from *Moody Magazine*. July/August, 1977 by *The Good News Herald*. November, 1983. p. 4.

2. Margaret Thale Sanger, "Coming Out of the Cults." *Psychology Today*. January, 1975. p. 75.

3. Em Griffin, *The Mindchangers*. (Wheaton, Illinois: Tyndale House, 1980) p. 51.

4. From *The Rhetoric* in *Essay on Rhetoric*. ed. Dudley Bailey. (New York: Oxford University Press, 1965) p. 60.

5. Quoted by Carley Dodd. "Position Paper on Ethics in Human Communication" at the Christian Scholars Conference. (Malibu, California: Pepperdine University, July 22, 1988) no page numbers given.

6. Carl Rogers, 9 Interpersonal Relationships, the Core of Guidance" in *Bridges Not Walls*. ed. John L. Stewart. (Reading, Massachusetts: Addison-Wesley Publishing Company, 1982) p. 299.

7. James Thurber in "The Owl Who Was God." Quoted in *The International Thesaurus of Quotations*. ed. Rhoda Thomas Tripp. (New York: Harper and Row Publications, 1970) p. 141.

4
Getting a Handle on
Vocabulary - Old Testament

Society has become so completely secularized that the term "holy"
has almost vanished from the language. When the term does appear
in the common vernacular, it often becomes a euphemism. Harry
Caray, the Chicago Cubs broadcaster observes a close play at second
base and screams "Holy Cow" into his microphone. A man feels
threatened by a co-worker's religiosity and nicknames his fellow employer, "Holy Joe." Charismatics and Pentecostals are often contemp-
tuously thought of as "Holy Rollers." That's about the extent of the
secular person's use of the term "holy." It gets reduced to the level of
caricature.

The modern Biblical student must develop a working knowledge of
the holiness vocabulary in order to grasp Biblical thought on that subject. The Old and New Testaments employ several different terms to
convey the idea of being set apart for God. All such terms have one
thing in common. They are used to describe people, places, events
and ideas which have special significance. God's people are being

45

asked to recognize superior values.

Such terms as "holiness," "sanctification," "dedication," "purity," "sacredness" and "perfection" have similar meanings. Sometimes the terms are used interchangeably. Quite often some of the English versions will translate a Greek or Hebrew word "holy" in one text and "sanctified" in another. A Bible student's comprehension of the holiness vocabulary can be greatly enhanced simply through comparing translations. It's a tedious job since the various cognates of the words related to holiness appear more than a thousand times in scripture. Even so a person who is willing to invest the time required to complete the task will be rewarded with a clearer understanding of the holiness idea.

THE ENGLISH TERMS

This chapter is being written with the English reader in mind. While readers might be challenged by a much more technical consideration of the holiness vocabulary in the languages of antiquity, it is assumed that most readers are either minimally trained in Hebrew and Greek or have no such training at all. The starting place for the English readers is developing a working knowledge of how holiness terminology is used in our native tongue. *Webster's Unabridged Dictionary* has been consulted as a basic source for getting a handle on the English terms.

Holy-holiness

The term "holy" first came into usage during the Middle English period. It was derived from *halig*, an ancient Anglo-Saxon term. In common English usage it means, "belonging to or coming from God; hallowed, consecrated or set apart for sacred use; having a sacred character or association."

Sacred

The word came into English from the French language and is of Latin derivation. The term "save" has the same Latin root. It means "consecrated to or belonging to a god or deity; dedicated, appropriated to religious use – made holy."

46

Sanctify, sanctification, saint, sanctuary, sanctity

This family of words is rooted in the Latin term *sanctus* and came into the English language from the French. As used in present day English, it means "to make holy; specifically (a) to make free from sin; to purify (b) to set apart as holy; to consecrate (c) to make a person holy."

Pure, purify, purification

It is derived from the Latin term, *purus*. It means "free from anything that adulterates, taints, impairs, etc.; unmixed, clear."

Perfect, perfection.

The root word is the Latin term, *perfectus*. It means "complete in all respects; without defect or omission; sacred, flawless."

Dedicate, dedication

The word stems from the Latin term, *dedicatus*. In its verb form it means "to set apart and consecrate to a deity or to a sacred purpose; to devote to a sacred use, by a solemn act or by religious ceremonies as to dedicate a temple or a church." In contemporary usage, the term does not always have religious implications. It may simply mean that one is devoted to some purpose or work.

Consecrate, consecration

The term is of Latin origin *(consecratus)*. It means "to make or declare to be sacred by certain ceremonies or rites; to appropriate to sacred uses; to set apart; to dedicate as holy."

Devote, devout

These terms came into usage through common Latin roots, via the Middle English. The term "devote" means "to appropriate by vow, to set apart or dedicate by a solemn act; to consecrate." "Devout," on the other hand, refers to a person who is pious or very religious.

Pious, piety

The words stem from the Latin term *pius* which means "devout, affectionate, good." There are several shades of meaning in contemporary usage. The definition most applicable to the current study is "sacred as distinguished from secular or profane."

All these words are used at one time or another to convey the idea of the holy. Contemporary Bible translations utilize these terms. It should be noted, however, that one might not find all of the words if study is confined to a single English translation.

While it is not deemed necessary to provide the reader with a definition of each antonym of the terms most commonly used in the holiness vocabulary, it should be noted that holiness antonyms are commonly used in contemporary English and that the Bible frequently makes use of such antonyms. Some of the holiness antonyms include "desecrate," "profane," "impurity," and "impious."

OLD TESTAMENT TERMINOLOGY

Most of the Old Testament allusions to holiness relate in one way or another to three Hebrew consonants - qds. Most scholars are cautious about committing themselves to hard and fast explanations of the etymology of qds. "Forms of the root qds occur some 830 times in the OT, about 350 of them in the Pentateuch."[1] The origin of the terms seems to be uncertain, although it is generally thought that the Canaanites used it first. This should not be viewed as a threat to our confidence in the scriptures as a book which reveals the mind of God. Many Biblical terms have a pagan counterpart. In educating the Hebrew people, God allowed the Bible writers to select terms which were already in common use, but those old terms took on new meanings when they were used by inspired writers. Words change in meaning over a long period of time and they come to express different ideas than they did at their point of origin. Although qds may have once been used to describe attitudes toward pagan religion, the Biblical writers used that terminology in reference to Yahweh. They never thought of it in idolatrous terms.

Scholars have not been able to discern the original Semitic meaning of the term with absolute certainty. It is probably safe to say that nearly all contemporary scholars agree that qds involved drawing a line of separation between sacred and secular matters. A. S. Wood concluded, "The root would then signify 'to cut off,' 'to withdraw,' 'to set apart.' The nuances of 'to deprive' and 'to elevate' have also been attached."[2]

The concept of purity and cleanness have also been associated with qds, but "most modern scholars incline to the view that the primary idea is that of cutting off or separation."[3] Even in pagan religion, people seem to recognize that a certain difference exists between common objects and those which attach themselves to deity.

In primitive Semitic usage, "holiness" seems to have expressed nothing more than spiritual separation of an object from common use which the modern study of savage religion has rendered familiar under the name *taboo*.[4]

The scholarly debate as to whether Old Testament holiness is properly confined to ceremonial separation from common things or if it also includes moral separateness generates much discussion among technical scholars. Such discussion is of little use to the Christian who struggles with his own fleshly nature and seeks a basis for fellowship with a holy God.

In the end God defines holiness. If God declares a certain thing to be holy that ends all contrary discussion about the matter regardless of how appropriate it may seem to modern sensibility. The same thing can be said of those things which God considers profane and a desecration of his holy standards. Perhaps Gerhard von Rad got close to a bottom line definition of holiness when he said, "If an object or a man is 'sanctified' this means only that it is separated, assigned to God for God is the source of all that is holy."[5]

Wood identifies the various Old Testament terms which are developed from qds.

The vocabulary stemming from the root qds with which we are concerned are as follows: *qodes*, noun, "holiness,""sacredness"; *qados*, adjective, "holy," "sacred"; *qadas*, verb "to be set apart," "consecrated" . . . *qodas* "to sanctify," "consecrate"; *miqdar*, noun, "a sacred place," "sanctuary."[6]

Contextual usage communicates more about the actual meaning of

49

these terms than etymological studies. It is helpful to take note of the way adjectives, nouns and verbs are used in various Old Testament contexts.

The noun forms

In the noun form most of our English Bibles translate *qodesh* as "holiness" or "sacredness." When Moses sang praises to God after the Israelites crossed the Red Sea, he declared that God is "majestic in holiness; awesome in glory" (Exod. 15:11). When the ark of the covenant was returned to Jerusalem, David extolled the virtue of God and urged the people to "worship the Lord in the splendor of his holiness" (I Chron. 16:29). As King Jehoshaphat prepared to place his armies in position against the Ammonites and Moabites he "appointed men to sing to the Lord and praise him for the splendor of his holiness (II Chron. 20:21). The expression "beauty" or "splendor of holiness" also occurs in Psalms 29:2 and 96:9. The author of Psalm 93 proclaimed, "holiness adorns your house" (Psa. 93:5). God has spoken in holiness (Psa. 108:7).

The prophets also echo the concept of God's holiness. When Isaiah anticipates the highway on which the coming King will make his presence felt, he calls it "the Way of Holiness" (Isa. 35:8). When the prophet Amos indicted the women of Bashan for basking in luxury and ignoring the poor, he said, "The Sovereign Lord *has sworn by his holiness:* 'The time will surely come when you will be taken away by fishhooks'" (Amos 4:2). Malachi indicted unfaithful Judah with the accusation that "Judah has profaned the holiness of the Lord" (Mal. 2:11 - KJV).

Most of the noun usages of holiness in the Old Testament relate to the character of God. The term describes his uniqueness. His nature, his standards and everything that is associated with him is elevated above the common attributes and experiences of man. The surrounding context in which these Old Testament nouns appear would also suggest that men and women who are spiritually inclined regard God's holiness as having an awesome and glorious quality.

The adjective form

When the adjective form of *qds* is used, the idea of separation is communicated. Any thing, place, person or being which is described as holy occupies a position on a higher level than common things, places and persons.

When Moses viewed the burning bush he soon learned that the dirt on which his feet rested was not to be regarded as common soil. God called it "holy ground" (Exod. 3:5). The inner chamber of the tabernacle which was to be visited only by the priests was designated "the holy place" and the room which housed the ark of the covenant was so special that it was called "the holy of holies" (Exod. 26:33). The sons of Aaron wore "sacred garments" (Exod. 28:2) and when they were consecrated the meat which they consumed was prepared in a "sacred place" (Exod. 29:31). The food was considered so sacred that anything left over was to be destroyed (Exod. 29:34).

The priests themselves were required to be holy (Lev. 21:6) and the animals they offered in sacrifice were also holy (Lev. 27:9). Provisions were made in the law for dedicating one's house as "something holy to the Lord" (Lev. 27:14). When a field was released in the year of Jubilee, it was said to be "holy" (Lev. 27:21).

God's place of abode is described as "a holy dwelling place" (Deut. 26:15). Throughout the Psalms and the prophets Zion is designated as the "holy hill." (Psa. 2:6. See also Ezek. 20:40; Dan. 9:16,20; Joel 2:1; Obad. 16; Zeph. 3:11; and Zech. 8:3).

The verb forms

The English translators chose from a wider variety of terms when they translated the verb *qadosh*. In Lev. 11:45 the nation of Israel is told, "Be holy because I am holy." The King James Version uses the word "sanctify" to translate the verb in Lev. 20:7. The NIV renders the phrase "consecrate yourselves," but the NEB chose, "hallow yourselves." According to Deut. 23:14, "the camp must be holy" (NIV, KJV), but the NEB suggests that it "must be kept holy."

In II Chronicles 35:3, the "Levites are holy unto the Lord" (KJV), "consecrated to the Lord" (NIV) or "dedicated to the Lord" (NEB). When the children of Israel celebrated the rebuilding of the wall in Nehemiah's time, the day was "holy unto the Lord" (KJV) or "sacred to the Lord" (NIV).

Semantic discussion of the holiness vocabulary in the Old Testa-

51

ment could go on endlessly. However it is sufficient for the serious student of the Bible to understand that God possesses a certain nature which separates him from mortal beings. His moral character and his glory are both embodied in the concept of holiness. While we stand in awe when confronted with such a magnificient display of holiness, we must never forget that God desires fellowship with us. As we turn to New Testament studies, we will be able to see clearly that man is able to achieve a position of holiness. Were it not possible to do so, God would never have said, "be holy for I am holy."

SUMMARY AND CONCLUSION

Because the thought of something being regarded as holy has been reduced to the level of caricature in contemporary thought and speech, the present day Bible student needs to understand how the holiness vocabulary is used in the Bible. The Old Testament serves as the entry point for ascertaining the mind of God on this important subject and is therefore the first source to be considered in developing a working knowledge of the holiness vocabulary.

Strange as it may seem when first considered, the root word on which the Old Testament vocabulary is built probably comes from Canaanite sources. The children of Israel didn't borrow the holiness *concept* from their pagan neighbors, but they did pick up their words. They simply appropriated the terminology that drifted into their culture. The *idea* of the holy was revealed by God, but the *terminology* developed in the passing of time in the same way that language has always evolved in the history of the human race.

While there is much technical discussion about the way the ancient people began to use the holiness terms, no one can doubt the message they sought to communicate with them. They understood that God and all things attached to God are set apart from the common things of life. It is only natural, therefore, that purity and moral uprightness should be connected with God's holiness. God can scarcely be regarded in any other way. "Good and upright is the Lord; therefore he instructs sinners in his ways" (Psa. 25:8).

Endnotes

1. W.A. Pratney, *The Nature and Character of God.* (Minneapolis: Bethany House Publishers, 1988) p. 227.

2. A.S. Wood, "Holiness" *Zondervan Pictorial Encyclopedia of the Bible.* (Grand Rapids, Michigan: Zondervan, 1975), Vol 3, p. 174. Wood also takes note of a somewhat lively controversy among Old Testament scholars regarding whether the root terms has moral implications in its usage in the Old Testament. Some scholars believe that the idea of separation or withdrawal is not always prominent.

3. W.L. Walker,. "Holiness." *International Standard Bible Encyclopedia.* (Grand Rapids, Michigan. Eerdmans, 1955), Volume 3. p. 1403.

4. Ibid.

5. Gerhard von Rad, *Old Testament Theology,* vol. 2. Trans. Dana Stalker. (New York: Harper and Row, 1962), 205.

6. Wood, "Holiness." p. 174.

5
Getting a Handle on Vocabulary - New Testament

The serious Biblical student soon realizes that his attempts to discern the will of God are seriously inhibited by the limits of language. That's especially true in the study of holiness. On the one hand, God is the ultimate Holy Being. He necessarily possesses attributes of "otherness" which no human language can adequately describe. On the other hand, language is the basic tool through which communication takes place. Because we work in the language medium, we are challenged to tackle the monumental task of researching the nuances of word meanings. Thus a study of the holiness terms and their cognates promises to expand our comprehension of the holiness idea.

Etymology is the study of word origins and sources. Language has evolved throughout human history. Some terms become obsolete and pass from the common vocabulary altogether. Other words change in meaning with the passing of time. An honest study of etymology will force us to recognize that some words, which are in common use today, first developed among people who worshipped pagan deities.

The Bible writers often appropriated these words to communicate their thoughts. During the course of the progressive revelation of God's will to people, God did not invent a new vocabulary to convey new truths. Instead, he used existing vocabulary as the means through which new and entirely different concepts were communicated.

This book is being composed on a computer. Computer programmers and operators have developed a language of their own. To some extent, every person who attempts to use a computer must learn to speak the "computer language." A computer novice will soon recognize that computer technicians have not actually invented a new language. They have simply lifted words from the world of common speech and expanded their meanings and applications. Take as an example the use of the term "housekeeping." It does not refer to mopping floors and washing windows in computerese. A computer operator takes care of housekeeping chores by removing unwanted data from the computer "memory" (another computer term, based on the memory of the human mind) and by organizing the data a person wants to keep. It is not difficult to see why "housekeeping" was chosen to describe this function, nor why "memory" is the term chosen to describe the retention of data.

Many Biblical words came into use in a similar way. The writers of scripture under the guidance of the Holy Spirit chose common terms and gave them new meanings in order to express fresh ideas. It is especially helpful to know how this was done with respect to the holiness vocabulary.

VOCABULARY BACKGROUND

Old Testament Background.

New Testament writers developed many of their ideas about holiness from concepts which had already been discussed in the Old Testament. When Peter (I Pet. 1:15) referred to the holiness of God, he recalled the language of Lev. 11:45, "Be holy because I am holy." References to the "Holy city" have Old Testament antecedents (cf. Matt. 27:53; Neh. 11:1). The church is described as a "holy temple" (Eph. 2:21, cf. Hab. 2:20).

In Hebrews 9:12, the author used the analogy of the "Most Holy Place" in the tabernacle to affirm the impact that Christ's sacrifice on the cross had on the world. John's vision of the throne room of God in Revelation 5 parallels a similar scene in the 6th chapter of Isaiah as it is said of the four living creatures, "Day and night they never stop saying Holy, Holy, Holy is the Lord Almighty who was, and is, and is to come."

Greek and Hellenistic Writings.

The New Testament holiness terms occur in the classical Greek language prior to the first century. In Homer *hagios* refers to such deities as Apollo and Zeus. Herodotus regarded Aphrodite as holy. In Hellenism, the term is connected with such oriental gods as Isis, Serapis and Baal.[1]

The Greeks used three word groups to denote the holy. *Hieros*, with its numerous derivatives denotes the essentially holy, the taboo, the divine power or what was consecrated to it., e.g. the sanctuary, sacrifice, priest. In contrast, *hagios* - the most frequent word group in the NT - contains an ethical element. The emphasis falls on duty to worship the holy. *Hosios* also points in this direction. On the one hand, it indicates divine commandment and providence; on the other human obligation and mortality.[2]

The holiness terms apparently do not occur with great frequency in secular Greek. In pre-New Testament Greek literature the Septuagint (often identified as LXX), the Greek translation of the Hebrew scriptures, contain more references to holiness terminology than any ancient Greek literature known to the contemporary world of scholarship.[3]

Rabbinic Tradition

The rabbinic tradition in Judaism was fully developed by the time of Christ. Although it is impossible to pinpoint the precise time of the beginning of the synagogue, it's usually agreed that the synagogue arrangement began during the period of the exile.

The synagogue was not controlled by the priests. It was an all male assembly which convened for worship. Study and Biblical interpretation dominated the life of the synagogue. The modern sermon emerged from the synagogue. Consequently, the synagogue became the primary focus of the rabbis – teachers of the law.

Jesus taught in the synagogue (Matt. 4:23) and so did Paul (Acts 9:20; 13:5; 17:17; 19:8). The first efforts at communicating the gospel were undertaken among audiences who were well versed in the traditions and vocabulary of the synagogue.

How did the synagogue understand the holiness words? In general the rabbinical scholars followed the lead of the Old Testament in their teaching about holiness. They did make an effort to advance the holiness concept beyond the Old Testament principles by systematizing and prioritizing the various things which were declared holy.[4]

In rabbinic thought the holy God is seen as a stern Judge and therefore thought of as "great, powerful and dreadful."

> Above all the name of God is holy. This explains why in later Judaism, the proper name of God was never pronounced except in temple worship. After the destruction of the temple it was not even known how to pronounce it.[5]

The rabbis taught that scripture is holy as the word of God, the Torah being more holy than the rest because it is more strictly God's word.[6] An ethical element can also be found in rabbinic Judaism. The person who is serious about obeying God and indicates a responsible approach to behavior and attitudes is said to be holy. One recognized standard of holiness involved ". . . dividing the day into three parts, one third for the Torah, one third for prayer, and one third for work."[7]

THE NEW TESTAMENT HOLINESS VOCABULARY

Adjectives

Adjectives will be considered first because they occur far more than any other terms in the holiness vocabulary.

1. *Hagios. Hagios* is found many more times in the New Testament than any other term in the holiness family of words. *Hagios*

"fundamentally signifies separated and hence in Scripture, its moral and spiritual significance, separated from sin and therefore consecrated to God."[8] "To translate this basic meaning into contemporary language would be to use the phrase 'a cut apart.' Perhaps even more accurate would be the phrase, 'a cut above something.'"[9]

"Holy," in the New Testament, is not often used as an adjective to describe God the Father. When it does appear, the passage in which it occurs is usually an Old Testament quotation (cf. Lk. 1:49; I Pet. 1:15). John connects the terms "holy" and "Father" more than any New Testament writer (cf. John 17:11; Rev. 4:8; 6:10). The sparse use of the adjective in relation to the first person of the Godhead should not be construed as a hesitancy to emphasize the holiness of God, because ". . . the holiness of God is everywhere presumed in the NT though seldom stated."[10]

"Christ is only once called holy in the same sense as God (Rev. 3:7; cf. I John 2:20)"[11] but other descriptions of Jesus as a holy personality do occur. The evil spirit in Capernaum described him as "the Holy one of God" (Mark 1:24). Peter used the same terminology in John 6:69. John spoke of receiving an "anointing from the Holy One in I John 2:20. The letter to the church at Philadelphia begins, "These are the words of him who is holy and true" (Rev. 3:7). Again the limited use of the adjective in no way diminishes from the holiness of Jesus. It is, however, an interesting New Testament phenomenon.

If the New Testament writers seem to avoid using *hagios* when describing the Father and the Son, they display no such reluctance in their references to the third personality in the Godhead. The Old Testament writers rarely referred to the Spirit of God as "the Holy Spirit," but their New Testament counterparts generously use the expression,"Holy Spirit" (Matt. 1:18; Acts 1:2; Rom. 5:5 and many others).

The adjective, *hagios*, often refers to people. Peter's speech at the temple contains a reference to "the holy prophets" (Acts 3:21). In I Corinthians 3:17 Paul recalls that God's temple is sacred, but he made it clear that he was not thinking about a building in Jerusalem. He said, ". . . you are that temple." He was thinking about the church in Ephesians 2:21 when he made another reference to the temple. The apostles were identified as "holy" in Ephesians 3:5. The Hebrew

59

writer addressed, "holy brothers" (Heb. 3:1) and Peter referred to the church as ". . . a holy nation" (I Pet. 2:9).

Hagios is also related to certain actions which are carried out by people in response to God. Christians greeted each other with a "holy kiss" (Rom. 16:16; I Cor. 16:20; 2 Cor. 13:12; I Thess. 5:26). The Christian life is a sacrifice offered the Lord and is regarded as holy (Rom. 12:1). In I Cor. 7:34, Paul presented the unmarried Christian woman with a goal statement. "Her aim is to be devoted (holy) to the Lord in both body and Spirit."

Christians were chosen before the creation of the world ". . . to be holy and blameless in his sight" (Eph. 1:4). Christ gave himself for the church ". . . to make her holy, cleansing her by the washing with water through the word and to present her to himself as a radiant church, without stain or wrinkle or any other blemish, but holy and blameless" (Eph. 5:25-26). According to Colossians 1:22 Christ died on the cross to reconcile those who were alienated from God ". . . to present you holy in his sight without blemish and free from accusation." The Christian has been called to a "holy life" (II Tim. 1:9). Peter admonished his readers to live "holy and godly lives." (II Pet 3:11).

Other usages of *hagios* in the New Testament include references to angels (Matt. 25:31), the law (Rom. 7:12), the children of a marriage between a believer and unbeliever (I Cor. 7:14), the Mount of Transfiguration (II Pet. 1:18), and the New Jerusalem (Rev. 21:2, 10).

Quite often *hagios* is translated "saint" in our English Bibles. Although "saint" is often translated as a noun in English, the Greek most often presents it in its adjective form. "Saint" occurs most frequently in the epistles and in Revelation. Paul addressed Romans "To all in Rome who are loved by God and called to be saints" (Rom. 1:7). He reported that he was on his way to Jerusalem ". . . in the service of the saints there" (15:26), and he was bringing along a contribution from Macedonia and Achaia ". . . for the poor among the saints in Jerusalem (15:27). He wanted Phoebe to be received in ". . . a way worthy of the saints" (16:2).

The Corinthians were also ". . . called to be saints" (I Cor. 1:2 KJV). Matters of disagreement were not to be taken to secular courts, but settled by the judgment of the saints (6:1- 2). In 16:15, Paul recommended the first converts in Asia, the household of Stephanas, noting ". . . they have devoted themselves to the service of the saints."

II Corinthians is also addressed to "the saints." The subject of the Jerusalem contribution surfaced again in the second letter when Paul commended the generosity of the Macedonians who ". . . urgently pleaded with us for the privilege of sharing in the service of the saints" (II Cor. 8:4; see also 9:1).

In Ephesians 1:15, Paul commended the church at Ephesus for their ". . . love for the saints." He also noted that God ". . . has called you into the riches of his glorious inheritance in the saints" (1:18), but he viewed himself as ". . .the least of all God's people (saints)" (3:8). In his prayer for spiritual growth among the members of the Ephesian church, he included a petition that they ". . . may have the power, together with the saints to grasp how wide and long and high and deep is the love of Christ (3:18). The leadership gifts were made available in the church ". . . to prepare God's people (saints) for works of service" (Eph. 4:12). Paul urged the Ephesians to ". . . always keep on praying for all the saints" (Eph. 6:18).

Similar usages abounded in the other writings of Paul. Among the applications, he mentioned the Second Coming and declared that Christ will come to be glorified in his holy people" (II Thess. 1:10). In I Timothy 5, Paul mentioned a special class of widows who were to receive favored treatment provided they conformed to certain requirements. Those requirements included ". . . washing the feet of the saints" (v. 10). Paul commended Philemon because he had ". . . refreshed the hearts of the saints" (Phile. 7).

The Hebrew writer uses *hagios* to mean saints on two occasions (Heb. 6:10 and 13:24). James and Peter did not use the expression at all, nor does it occur in the epistles of John. Jude used it twice. In verse 3 he took note of the fact that the faith was ". . . once for all entrusted to the saints." In verse 14 he wrote, "Enoch, the seventh from Adam, prophesied about these men: 'See the Lord is coming with thousands upon thousands of his holy ones (saints).' "

The expression appears frequently in Revelation. The golden bowls of incense are ". . . the prayers of the saints" (Rev. 5:8; 8:3,4). In their praise statement before the throne of God following the sounding of the seventh trumpet, the twenty-four elders said, "The time has come for the judging of the dead and for rewarding the prophets and your saints and those who reverence your name both small and great" (11:18). Throughout the book of Revelation, there's a conflict going on between the forces of Satan and the saints. The beast was given power ". . . to make war against the *saints*" (13:7), and the attack required ". . . patient endurance and faithfulness on the part of the saints" (13:10). The consequences of worshipping the beast also ". . . calls for patient endurance on the part of the saints . . ." (14:12). The woman who represented ". . .Mystery Babylon the Great . . . was drunk with the blood of the *saints*, the blood of those who bore testimony for Jesus" (17:6). When Babylon falls the *saints* will rejoice (18:20). "Fine linen stands for the righteous acts of the *saints*" (19:8). After Satan was loosed for a short time, he gathered his forces and ". . . surrounded the camp of God's people *(saints)*" (20:9).

It is unfortunate that the term "saint" has been corrupted in modern terminology. People either think of a "saint" as some exemplary person or they have in mind a person who has achieved a high level of moral and spiritual excellence beyond the grasp of normal people. Such usage never occurs in the New Testament.

> In the NT the apostolic designation for Christians is saint and it continued to be a designation at least up until the days of Irenaeus and Tertullian, though after that it degenerated in ecclesiastical usage into an honorific title. Though its primary significance was relationship, it was also descriptive of character, and more especially Christ like character.[12]

2. *Hosios. Hosios* refers to that which is ". . . religiously right as opposed to what is unrighteous."[13] It occurs only occasionally in the New Testament. Twice it refers to Jesus in the Acts of the Apostles (2:27; 13:35). Paul used the term to describe the posture of men in prayer – "I want men everywhere to lift up holy hands in prayer without anger or disputing" (I Tim. 2:8). The elders of the church are to be ". . . holy and disciplined" (Titus 1:8). Jesus as the perfect high priest is described as ". . . one who is holy, blameless, pure, set apart from sinners" (Heb. 7:26).

In the song of "Moses and the Lamb" those who gained victory over the beast sang "For you alone are holy" (Rev. 15:4). When God's bowl of wrath was poured out on the sea, the angel in charge of the waters said, "You were just in these judgments, you who are and who were, the Holy One . . ." (16:5).

3. *Hieros. Hieros* has reference to that which is ". . . sacred, outwardly associated with God."[14]   It appears only twice in the New Testament. When Paul discussed pay for ministers in I Corinthians 9, he drew an analogy between pay for ministers and support for the Israelite priests in the temple. He said, "Do you not know that they which minister about the holy things of the temple live of the things of the temple?" (v. 13 KJV). In II Tim. 3:15 Paul recalled that from infancy, Timothy ". . . had known the holy Scriptures."

Nouns

1. *Hagiasmos.* "It signifies separation to, the resultant state, the conduct befitting those so separated."[15] It ". . . is also used in the NT of the separation of the believer from evil things and evil ways."[16] Depending on the translation one reads, it may appear in English as "holiness," "sanctification," "consecration" or "sacredness." The noun usages are confined to the Pauline epistles except for one reference each in Hebrews and I Peter. In Romans 6:19 Paul compared Christian behavior to the slavery of ". . . righteousness which leads to holiness." The Christian's voluntary slavery to righteousness culminated in the favorable result of being led to holiness which is seen as a precursor to eternal life (Rom. 6:22). In I Corinthians 1:30 he equated ". . . righteousness, holiness and redemption with wisdom from God." To undergird the newly established Thessalonian church, Paul wrote, "It is God's will that you should be holy" (I Thess. 4:3). The holiness of which he speaks clearly has a practical application in terms of making moral choices. Each Christian must learn to ". . . control his own body in a way that is holy and honorable (4:4), because God has called us to ". . . live a holy life" (in holiness-KJV) (4:4).

The original language uses the noun form in II Thessalonians 2:13 when Paul expressed gratitude that ". . . God chose you from the beginning through the sanctifying work of the Spirit and through belief in the truth." In I Timothy 2:15 women are promised that they will ". . . be kept safe through childbirth, if they continue in faith, love and holiness with propriety."

The Hebrew writer exhorted his readers to ". . . make every effort to live in peace with all men and to be holy; without holiness, no one will see the Lord" (Heb. 12:14). Peter's lone use of *hagiasmos* appears in the salutation of his first letter. His readers ". . . have been chosen according to the foreknowledge of God through the sanctifying work of the Spirit, for obedience to Jesus Christ and sprinkling by his blood" (I Pet. 1:2).

2. *Hagiosune.* *Hagiosune* denotes the manifestation of holiness in personal conduct.[17] In the preface to the Roman letter Paul insisted that Jesus was declared to be the son of God ". . . through the Spirit of Holiness" (Rom. 1:4). Holiness is the objective of the person who seeks to be full grown in the Lord according to II Corinthians 7:1. It is attached to blamelessness in I Thessalonians 3:13.

3. *Hagiotes.* *Hagiotes* is used in two different ways in the New Testament. It means "sanctity, the abstract quality of holiness."[18] It refers to God in Heb. 12:10 and to the manner in which Paul conducted himself in II Corinthians 1:12.

4. *Hosiotes.* *Hosiotes* refers to ". . . the quality of holiness which is manifested in those who have regard equally to grace and truth."[19] In Luke 1:74-75 Zechariah praised the God of Israel and ascribed to him the capacity ". . . to enable us to serve him without fear in holiness and righteousness before him all our days." Paul urged the Ephesians to ". . . put on the new self, created to be like God in true righteousness and holiness" (Eph. 4:24).

Verb

The verb is *hagiazo,* which is usually translated "hallow" or "sanctify." It is perhaps most fully translated "let him be made holy." Most Christians are familiar with the term "hallow" as a result of the popular use of the Lord's Prayer in Matthew 6. In the prayer Jesus said, "Hallowed be thy name."

William Barclay suggested that the petition is probably the most difficult portion of the Lord's prayer to explain. The verb form of *hagios* clearly points the reader in the direction of holiness and suggests that God's name is to be treated differently from all other names, but that does not exhaust the meaning of the phrase. "In Hebrew the

64

name does not mean simply the name by which a person is called
. . . the name means the *nature*, the *character*, and the *personality*
of the person insofar as it is known or revealed to us."[20] Hallowing
the name of God involves our respect for all the attributes which
uniquely belong to God. "Therefore when we pray 'Hallowed be thy
name,' it means 'Enable us to give thee the unique place which thy
nature and character deserve and demand.' "[21]

Hagiazo may be translated "consecrate," "set apart," "sanctify,"
"make holy" or "make sacred." Jesus used the term in Matthew
23:17 when he said to the Pharisees, "Which is greater the gold, or
the temple which makes the gold sacred?" He used the same term in
comparison to the gift and the altar in verse 19. In John 10:36 he
claimed to be ". . . the one set apart." The intercessory prayer of Jesus on behalf of his disciples includes a request to "sanctify them"
(John 17:17). In verse 19 he said, "For them I sanctify myself that
they may be truly sanctified."

Twice the verb is used in the book of Acts. During the course of
his farewell remarks to the Ephesian elders, Paul said, "Now I commit
you to God and to the Word of his grace, which can build you up and
give you an inheritance among those who are sanctified" (Acts
20:32). As Paul explained his message to Agrippa in his trial at Caesarea, he said that God sent him to the Gentiles that they might receive ". . . a place among those who are sanctified by faith" (Acts
26:18)[22]

The Corinthians are said to be sanctified (I Cor. 1:2). Because the
behavior of the Corinthian people did not always match the demands
of holiness, some translators attempt to soften the introduction to I
Corinthians by having Paul say they were ". . . called to be sanctified." Manipulating Biblical phraseology to fit a certain preconceived
notion of who is holy and who is not can scarcely be justified, especially in view of the fact that 6:11 clearly marks the Corinthian church
as a sanctified group. In 7:14 Paul even spoke of a sense in which an
unbelieving husband is regarded as a sanctified person because his
Christian spouse has achieved a sanctified position.

According to Ephesians 5:26 Christ makes the church holy. Paul
asked God to sanctify the Thessalonian church ". . . through and
through" (I Thess. 5:23). Everything God created is ". . . consecrated

by the word of God and prayer" (I Tim. 4:5). The man who cleanses himself is ". . . made holy" (II Tim. 2:21.)

The Hebrew writer made use of *hagiazo* several different times. Christ makes men holy (Heb. 2:11). When the writer alluded to the animal sacrifice under the Mosaic covenant, he said, "The blood of goats and bulls and ashes of a heifer sprinkled on those who are ceremonially unclean sanctify them so that they are outwardly clean" (9:13). In 10:10 the child of God is made holy by the sacrifice of Christ. The same theme is enlarged upon in verse 14. The willful sinner is indicted for having ". . . treated as an unholy thing the blood of the covenant that sanctified him . . ." (10:29). In 13:12 the writer observed, "And so Jesus also suffered outside the city gate to make people holy through his own blood."

The rest of the New Testament includes the verb form only three times. In I Peter 3:15 the Christian is to "set apart" Christ in his heart as he prepares an answer for those who would question him about his hope. Jude 1 is addressed to ". . . them that are sanctified" (KJV). Revelation 22:11 includes an admonition – "Let him who is holy continue to be holy."

SUMMARY AND CONCLUSION

Perhaps the most difficult part of trying to get a handle on holiness is that of persuading people to look at the concept seriously. For today's trend setters holiness is but a quaint relic of past religious superstition. Its only legitimate use in the urbane mind is that of parody and satire. "Holy" is the "H" word, a term not suitable for use in commercial broadcasting. Obscenities and profane expressions never find their way to the cutting room floor of modern films, but if a character should seriously utter the "H" word, that portion of the dialogue will be summarily censored. It's considered too crass, too blunt, too offensive. It dares suggest that people ought to pursue a standard that is not natural to unregenerate hearts.

The person who discovers that living on a completely secular plane leaves one unfulfilled and empty will be driven to risk the stigma of a disapproving culture and will develop a burning desire to know more about being holy. To comprehend holiness in depth one needs to have a working knowledge of both the Old and New Testament holiness vocabulary.

Etymology - the study of the way words evolved is a tool which opens new windows of knowledge for the person who truly wants to know what it means to be holy. As one contemplates the New Testament usage of the term, it becomes apparent that the New Testament writers retain the Old Testament concepts. People, places, and things are still holy in the New Testament. Ceremonial holiness still exists, but there are new vistas to be explored and developed. The emphasis is more on what goes on within the heart than the external forms of religion. E. F. Harrison offered a credible summation when he observed,

> The most striking difference between the testaments is the virtual eclipse of the purely ceremonial aspect of holiness and the flooding of the sacred page with allusions to holiness as conformity to the nature of God.[23]

The discipline of studying the holiness vocabulary must be extended far beyond the small circle of people who think of themselves as "word freaks." The more one delves into the holiness vocabulary the more it becomes apparent that to aspire to be holy is to aspire to live on the level which brings peace between man and his Maker. "Holy" is not an "H" word that makes people uncomfortable, it is a vibrant approach to living.

Endnotes

1. H. Seebass, "Holy" *The New International Dictionary of New Testament Theology.* (Grand Rapids, Michigan: Zondervan Publishing House, 1976). Vol. 2 p. 223.

2. Ibid, Vol. 2 p. 223.

3. Otto Procksch, "Hagios." *Theological Dictionary of the New Testament.* (Grand Rapids, Michigan: Zondervan Publishing House, 1976) Vol. 1 p. 97.

4. Ibid, p. 97. Karl Kuhn offers a sample prioritized list. The following things were considered holy according to rank: 1. the city square where divine festivals might be held. 2. the synagogue. 3. the ark of the covenant with the Torah within it. 4. the veils of the holy scripture within this. 5. the scrolls of the Nebiim and Ketubim. 6. the scrolls of the Torah.

5. Ibid, p. 98.

6. Ibid, p. 100.

7. Ibid, p. 100.

8. W.E. Vine, *Expository Dictionary of New Testament Words.* (Old Tappan, New Jersey: Fleming H. Revell Co., r.p. 1966) Vol. 1 p. 155.

9. R. C. Sproul, *The Holiness of God.* (Wheaton, Il.: Tyndale House, 1987) p. 53.

10. TDNT, p. 101.

11. Seebass, p. 228.

12. R.A. Finlayson, "Holiness, Holy, Saints." *The Illustrated Bible Dictionary.* (Wheaton, IL: Tyndale House, 1980) Part two. pp. 656-657.

13. W.E. Vine, Vol. 2 p. 227.

14. Ibid, Vol. 2 p. 225.

15. Ibid.

16. Ibid, Vol. 3 p. 317.

17. Ibid, Vol. 2 p. 225.

18. Ibid, Vol. 2 p. 226.

19. Ibid.

20. William Barclay, *The Daily Study Bible – Gospel of Matthew.* (Edinburgh, Scotland: The Saint Andrew Press, 1956) Vol. 1 p. 205.

21. Ibid.

22. A similar expression occurs in Romans 15:16.

23. E.F. Harrison, sv "Holiness." *International Standard Bible Encyclopedia.* (Grand Rapids, Michigan; William B. Eerdmans Co., 1982) Vol. p. 727.

6
Holy Is the Way God Is

The scriptures mandate a holy way of living for the child of God. The Hebrew author expresses this requirement in the simplest kind of language. "Make every effort to live in peace with God and to be holy; Without holiness no one will see the Lord" (Heb. 12:14). You don't need a Greek scholar to explain it to you. You don't have to be a student of systematic theology to understand it. Holiness is essential to salvation.

The pursuit of holiness necessarily leads one to study the nature of God, because God is the epitome of holiness. "But just as he who called you is holy, so be holy in all you do; for it is written: 'Be holy, because I am holy'" (I Pet. 1:15-16). There is no way to overstate the urgency of attempting to understand the holiness of God. It is impossible to rationally contemplate any kind of human holiness, without first focusing on God, the model of holiness.

When the United States Congress authorizes funds to be allocated for a new fighter plane or a supersonic bomber, the defense contractor is expected to construct a prototype, a fully functional version of the aircraft to be mass produced. God is our prototype for holiness. He exposes his holy nature to us in scripture and even sent his Son to tangibly model his nature for us. A line from a favorite Christian hymn of praise suggests, "Only thou art holy, there is none beside thee."

We pursue holiness in response to his call and we learn its practice by coming to know him. Our entire relationship with him hinges on comprehending his holy nature. Our quest for the knowledge of holiness starts and ends with our perception of God's holy character. This chapter will concentrate on the practicality of that quest. To some this may sound like the introduction to a heavy duty theological discussion that can only generate excitement among intellectuals in a graduate level classroom. While there may be certain aspects of God's holy nature that would challenge the most complex mind, God's holy nature is so clearly exposed on the pages of scripture that even a person with minimal reading skills can quickly grasp the fact that we are being told to respond to a holy God who lives on a higher plane than we do. It is imperative that we understand the practical nature of our quest for holiness. It affects every Christian at every level of maturity.

PRACTICAL REASONS FOR CONDUCTING A STUDY OF GOD'S HOLINESS

1. The current culture shows little awareness of the existence of a holy God. A group of young Christians were sharing their faith door to door. A sleepy-eyed young man opened one door and listened only briefly to the callers. "I'm not into this God thing, man," he said, and quickly slammed the door. This young man was just bluntly stating a philosophy echoed by an increasing number of materialistically oriented people. Most of them would not express their hostility to holiness in such a blunt manner, but the truth is they have very little time for the things of God.

While it is true that most of the people who live in the United States say they believe in God, their perception of him is sometimes poorly defined. Monroe Hawley has observed,

The faith of the average person has little focus. He views his re-

70

ligion as a group of unrelated actions structured around a moral code more determined by the values of society than the teachings of the Bible. Somehow it involves the idea of getting right with God and a hazy expectation of life after death, and is like a parachute in time of distress – try it when all else fails.[1]

In 1985 Robert Bellah reported that 81 per cent of the American people believed in God at that point in time, but they also agreed that "an individual should arrive at his or her own religious belief independent of any church or synagogue."[2] While such a response might be construed to mean that people were saying they want to study the Bible for themselves, it more often points to a desire to have complete control of life's agenda. Most people would like to think God is there when they need him, but they are not interested in conforming to the requirements of a holy Deity.

Bellah reported the results of an interview with a woman named Sheilah. She said, "I believe in God. I can't remember the last time I went to church. But my faith has carried me a long way. It's 'Sheila-ism.' Just my own little voice."[3] Many people in today's world have their own version of Sheila-ism. Ken Durham offers an assessment of the current secular malaise.

. . . in the last 25 years, the American quest for greater personal freedom, self-fulfillment, and individual identity has been more intense than at any other time in our history. The pervasive influence of individualism – the view that my rights as an individual are the highest good, that what is right for *me* is the primary basis for my decisions and actions – can be heard in a host of popular cliches: "I did it my way." "Do your own thing," "Whatever turns you on," "Different strokes for different folks," "I gotta be me," and "I need to find myself."[4]

2. Many church members lack an appreciation of God's holiness. It might be interesting to conduct a survey in the membership of any given church concerning the members' perception of God. Undoubtedly their answers would vary. But how many would describe God in terms of his holiness? One has the uneasy feeling that there may just be a touch of "Sheila-ism" in the understanding of the people who regularly assemble with the church. Some sermons are little more than a rehash of popular psychological trends with a few scriptures thrown in to make it look respectable. Michael Weed contends that many churches have ". . . become 'relevant' at the cost of having anything to say to a world struggling with real moral and spiritual problems."[5]

It's even possible to be serious in considering Biblical content without ever getting around to God's holiness. R. C. Sproul recalled a time when he was anxious to study the scriptures, to grow in his understanding of the faith, to get involved in acts of Christian service. "But there was something missing in my early Christian life. I knew who Jesus was, but God the Father was shrouded in mystery. He was hidden, an enigma to my mind and a stranger to my soul."[6] Most of us have never really engaged in a serious study of the nature of God. We most certainly haven't given it the same level of attention that we've given to baptism, the Lord's Supper, elders in the church, the identifying characteristics of the New Testament church and numerous other popular Restoration themes. Weed claimed that we have developed ". . . a tendency to neglect or ignore important truths shared in common with others."[7] Such neglect cries for correction. If our view of God is flawed, it's of little consolation to be able to say that we clearly comprehend the Biblical purpose and form of baptism. We hear talk of emphasizing our uniqueness. If we truly want to be unique in a healthy way then we can decide to make the holiness of God a point of emphasis. It will establish our uniqueness in the religious community to a degree that we have never imagined.

3. *To know God is to be aware of his holiness.* The Bible repeatedly emphasizes the holiness of God. In Moses' sweet song of deliverance he asked, "Who among the gods is like you, O Lord? Who is like you in majestic holiness, awesome in glory, working wonders?" (Exod. 15:11). Psalm 99:9 declares ". . . for the Lord our God is holy." Ezekiel 39:7 identifies him as "the Holy one of Israel." According to Amos 4:2, "The Sovereign LORD has sworn by his holiness." Isaiah 52:10 speaks of his "holy arm." God's words are holy in Jeremiah 23:9. In Leviticus 20:3, Ezekiel 20:39 and Amos 2:7, God's name is holy. In Revelation 4:8, John describes the activities of the four living creatures in the throne room of God. "Day and night

they never stop saying: 'Holy, Holy, Holy is the Lord God Almighty, who was, and is and is to come.".

It is impossible to consider these passages and dozens of others which touch on the subject of God's holiness without realizing that we are dealing with extremely urgent material.

It would help us to grasp this important truth if we would stop thinking of holiness as one of God's attributes. Holiness is not some kind of sub-topic to be listed among the character traits of God. To treat holiness as a peculiar characteristic relegates it to a position of relatively small importanance. In truth all of God's various attributes are components of holiness. A. W. Tozer says simply, yet most profoundly, "Holy is the way God is."[8]

PRACTICAL BENEFITS WHICH RESULT FROM THE STUDY OF GOD'S HOLINESS

A German theologian, Rudolf Otto, undertook a major study of holiness early in this century. The English version of his study was published in 1923 under the title, *The Idea of the Holy*. Otto became so overwhelmed with divine holiness that he coined a phrase to describe the human response to a holy God. He called it "the *mysterium tremendum*" – the awful mystery.[9] As Otto saw it, the holiness of God causes a person to experience a feeling of dreadful fascination.

Only rarely do men and women find themselves placed in situations in which their sense of terror is equalled by their unquenchable fascination. I can recall one such event which occurred on April 28, 1950. I'll never forget the day. I was fifteen years of age. My father and I had gone to visit his twin brother. My uncle sometimes did my father's barber work, so we stayed long enough for my father to get a hair cut. When my father's hair was approximately half shorn of its unwanted volume, my aunt asked the two men to step to the back door. She had observed some ominous looking storm clouds and expressed her concern to them. I happened to be standing beside them as they scanned the skies just outside the back door. I tried to pretend that my aunt was only imagining a threat and said so. Hardly had those words fallen from my lips when a killer tornado dropped from one of those low lying clouds. It whirled dust and debris as it swept along a wide path, crushing houses like so many match stems and snuffing out the lives of those who were not adequately sheltered.

Nothing that I have experienced in life has equalled the fear I felt that afternoon. I could feel the hair rise on the back of my neck. A knot developed in the pit of my stomach. I lost control of certain bodily functions. I was afraid to look, but at the same time the scene was so spectacular I felt compelled to look, even after the adults told me not to. The two families gathered in a semi-sunken pump house near the family well to brace for the blow. As things turned out the tornado was moving the other way, but for a few dreadful moments, we wondered if we would survive. I was told to stay inside the pump house, but I kept finding excuses to peek outside and each time I did, I hurried back to my position because I couldn't stand to look at the destruction. It was such a profound experience that I still have occasional dreams about it forty years later.

Our response to a holy God can be something like that. The holiness of God should produce a sense of God's power within us. His glory ought to attract us the way a magnet attracts iron filings. His majesty can be so overpowering, however, that we feel tempted to withdraw from cultivating closeness to him out of a sense of sheer terror. With respect for the *mysterium tremendum* effect, let's turn our attention to the benefits of studying God's holiness.

1. The study of God's holiness increases our capacity to enjoy fellowship with God. At one level, we might say that God cannot be known. This aspect of his nature is spoken of in Romans 11:33, "Oh, the depth of the riches of the wisdom and knowledge of God! How unsearchable his judgments and his paths beyond tracing out." Still it is a fact that God has chosen to reveal something of himself to us and that he desires to establish fellowship with the human race. Consequently, the more we know of God, the more we can increase our capacity for intimate bonding with him. In the 119th Psalm, the author begs to be taught God's laws. His interest is not in being able to cite the location of all God's legal statutes by book, chapter and verse. He is not searching for a viable hermeneutic. The Psalmist clearly desires fellowship with God. The more he knows of God's holy desires, the

74

stronger his tie with God becomes. In verse 45 he says, "I will walk about in freedom for I have sought out your precepts."

When knowing the holy God becomes our priority, our fellowship with him becomes so important that some of our other worries and cares are reduced in importance. A. W. Tozer noted, "The man who comes to a right belief about God is relieved of ten thousand temporal problems."[10] But for that reduction to take place we must not overlook the fact that we are dealing with a *holy* God. A "gimme" God, who responds to our whims like the genie of the lamp, is not adequate to relieve the stresses that our materialistically centered culture has imposed upon us. The only truly satisfying fellowship with God occurs when we realize we have been offered the privilege of living in closeness with the architect, ruler and supreme role model of the universe. Only then can it be said that ". . . godliness has value for all things, holding promise for both the present life and the life to come" (I Timothy 4:8).

2. *An awareness of God's holiness is a deterrent to sin.* Even the most noble Christians are harassed by the temptations of the flesh. Our resistance level rises in direct proportion to our comprehension of God's nature. Tozer contended, "The history of mankind will probably show that no people has ever risen above its religion, and man's spiritual history will positively demonstrate that no religion is greater than its idea of God."[11] It can also be said that no Christian will rise above the individual's concept of the holiness of God. The person who has a lofty view of God's holiness will be more likely to live in conformity to God's commands than the person who has a low view. The Hebrew writer's challenge to the tired second generation Christians, who first read his letter, was based on a high view of God's holy purposes in the world. He noted that God had spoken (1:3), that the Son is "the radiance of God's glory" (3), that he has made everything subject to Jesus (1:13) and that those who have received the heavenly call are "holy brothers" (3:1). On the basis of such a holy relationship, the original readers of Hebrews were invited to enter God's rest (4:11) and reminded that "Nothing in all creation is hidden from God's sight. Everything is uncovered and laid bare before the eyes of him to whom we must give account" (4:13). The fact that every human act is being monitored by one who personifies holi-

ness reminds us to consider the nature of our behavior. Accountability works to our advantage.

   3.   *The study of God's holiness is comforting.* That almost sounds contradictory to the *mysterium tremendum* concept. How can you be comforted by someone whose glory is so awesome that even angelic beings must cover their eyes as they approach his throne? (Isa. 6:2). Perhaps the answer is seen in Isaiah's experience. He was so thoroughly devastated by his brief encounter with the glory of God in the throne room, that he could only be made conscious of his sinful condition. "'Woe to me!' I cried. 'I am ruined! For I am a man of unclean lips, and I live among a people of unclean lips, and my eyes have seen the King, the Lord Almighty'" (Isa. 6:5). We can never really comprehend the depth of the depression Isaiah felt when he saw his own life measured against the presence of a holy God.

   Nevertheless, it was out of this experience of personal disintegration that Isaiah found comfort. "Then one of the seraphs flew to me with a live coal in his hand, which he had taken with tongs from the altar. With it, he touched my mouth and said, 'See, this has touched your lips; your guilt is taken away and your sin atoned for'" (Isaiah 6:6-7). If it's impossible for us to imagine the burden of guilt that Isaiah felt when he saw the throne room, it is equally impossible for us to appreciate the relief that he felt when he realized that grace had rescued him.

   What does that mean to us? Simply this. Grace brings the greatest comfort to the people who understand that they once stood on the brink of spiritual annihilation. At one end of the pendulum, the holiness of God depresses us because we are overwhelmed when we are convicted of our complete moral and spiritual bankruptcy. No wonder Isaiah wrote, ". . . all our righteous acts are like filthy rags" (Isa. 64:6). But if God's holiness drives us to the brink of despair, it also lifts us up. How so? It's a relief to know that our guilt has been removed by the same God who indicts us.

   No one appreciates food like the person who is dying of hunger. Nobody treasures warmth like the person who is freezing to death and nobody values forgiveness like those people who have come to understand their hopeless condition. In Ephesians 2, Paul reminded his readers that at one time they were "dead in transgressions and sins" (1) and "objects of wrath" (3). Once an awareness of their desperate circumstances was fully understood, they were then in a position to appreciate what God had done. "But because of his great love for us, God who is rich in mercy, made us alive with Christ even when we were dead in transgressions – it is by grace you have been saved." Grace becomes real only when we realize that we have offended a holy God.

PRACTICAL PRINCIPLES IN CONDUCTING
A STUDY OF GOD'S HOLINESS

In seeking to gain knowledge of God's holiness, we must avoid the temptation to give up before we start. The divine mandate to know the Holy God surges to the forefront of our consciousness. It's true that his ways are unsearchable, but that should not deter us from delving into those matters which have been revealed. As we conduct our search, the following principles should guide us.

1. *The knowledge we seek to acquire includes more than information about God's holiness.* There is a difference between academic knowledge and experiential knowledge. Isaiah probably knew about God's holiness before he entered the throne room, but when he saw the throne and the seraphs; when he heard them calling to one another, "Holy, Holy, Holy is the Lord Almighty, the whole earth is full of this glory"; when he felt the doorposts and threshold shake and smelled the smoke that filled the temple, his knowledge of God's holiness was intensified and personalized. It became so personal that the thought of his own sinfulness consumed his mind.

J. I. Packer said that ". . . one can know a great deal about God without much knowledge of him."[12] Packer was not merely playing with prepositions. To know God is to be aware of his presence. That's what happened to Isaiah. No cynic would ever be able to convince Isaiah that God is not a real person. Isaiah's awareness of God's presence gave him strength to resist intense opposition from unbelievers.

The person who knows the holy God is well prepared for life's difficulties, but such knowledge must go beyond mere academic awareness of what the Bible teaches about God. Only the knowledge of the shared life will survive when the chips are down.

Packer tells of a friend who was under attack by certain church dignitaries. During the midst of the fight, the friend said, "But it doesn't matter. I've known God and they haven't."[13] It was the desire for more of this experienced knowledge which kept Paul going in prison. He said, "I consider everything a loss compared to the surpassing greatness of knowing Christ . . ." (Phil. 3:8).

Knowing God is a matter of personal involvement with God. In the 34th Psalm, the author says, "Taste and see that the Lord is good" (34:8). A few years ago, I heard someone talk about how beneficial a computer can be in the work of the church. For a long time I read about computers; I listened to people talk about computers; I even believed that computers can be a great blessing; but it wasn't until we got a computer that I began to know what a computer can do for the work of the church. You may know many things about God, but until you "taste and see that the Lord is good," you'll never really appreciate the blessings of God.

2. Knowledge of God's holiness can be acquired. We began our study by conceding that our knowledge is limited. He is God and we are people. We can never expect to rise to the divine level of knowledge. But God has taken it on himself to reveal something of his nature to us. In our Lord's last recorded prayer before facing the agony of the cross, he prayed, "Now this is eternal life that they may know you, the only true God and Jesus Christ whom you have sent" (John 17:3). On Mars Hill, Paul said, "From one man he made every nation of men, that they should inhabit the whole earth; and he determined the times set for them and the exact places where they should live. God did this so that men would seek him and find him, though he is not far from each one of us" (Acts 17:26-27). Not only did God choose to reveal himself to us, he also arranged the world in such a way as to encourage us to seek him.

3. God's attributes and God's holiness are the same thing. Tozer defined an attribute as ". . . whatever God has in any way revealed as being true of Himself."[14] Sometimes God is portrayed to us in connection with fire. He is described as a "consuming fire" in Heb. 12:26. That thought brings to mind God's statement to Moses when he was confronted by God at the burning bush. He was told, ". . . the place where you are standing is holy ground" (Exod. 3:5). God's requirement that people worship him to the exclusion of all other deities is described as a holy jealousy in Josh. 24:19, "He is a holy God; he is a jealous God." Even his wrath expresses his holiness. When Nadab and Abihu were unceremoniously cremated alive, God spoke through Moses, "Approach those who approach me. I will show myself holy; in the sight of all the people I will be honored" (Lev. 10:3). God's greatness, his purity, his grace, his love are all components of his holiness.

> To be holy He does not conform to a standard. He is that standard. He is absolutely holy with an infinite, incomprehensible fullness of purity that is incapable of becoming other than it. Because He is holy, His attributes are holy; whatever we think of as belonging to God must be thought of as holy.[15]

CONCLUSION

In a sense the study of God and the study of God's holiness are one and the same. The study of the Holy God needs a much greater share of our attention than it has been getting. If I were to ask you to make a list of the topics we need to be addressing in the teaching program of the church, what would you write down? If I were to conduct a survey and ask you to identify some of our instructional needs, I'm sure I'd probably get back a number of diverse answers. Some would say it's "evangelism." Some would say it's "the plan of salvation." Some might even say "it's Christ and him crucified." Some might say it's "Christian living" or identify some aspect of Christian living such as the problems of the Christian home. Others might think that we ought to concentrate more on answering false doctrine. All these have their place, but I wonder how many of us would even put "the Holiness of God" on our list?

To neglect holiness is to settle for shallowness which can never satisfy the demands of a hungry soul. It means practicing a surface level faith, never comprehending the joy of sharing in fellowship with a holy God. Johnson Oatman verbalized a desperate need of our time in the chorus of his familiar hymn, "Higher Ground."

Lord lift me up and let me stand,
By faith on heaven's table land,
A higher plane than I have found;
Lord plant my feet on higher ground.

Endnotes

1. Monroe Hawley, *The Focus of Our Faith.* (Nashville, Tennessee: The Twentieth Century Christian Foundation, 1985), p. 79.

2. Robert Bellah, *Habits of the Heart.* (Berkeley, California: University of California Press, 1985), p. 228.

3. Ibid, p. 221.

4. Ken Durham, "Challenging the Spirit of Individualism" in *Christ and Culture: The Problem of Secularism – Abilene Christian University Lectures.* (Abilene, Texas: ACU Press, 1989), p. 34.

5. Michael Weed, "Evangelism, Ethics, and Eschatological Existence" in *Christian Studies.* James W. Thompson (ed). (Austin, Texas: Institute for Christian Studies, 1989), p. 57. Weed argues his case by observing, "The fact that few Christians ever turn to the church for fundamental direction or moral guidance is indicative of the degree to which the church has lost its distinctive character. Thus unable to offer light or act as leaven, countless churches dissipate their energies in diversions and pathetic attempts to make themselves attractive to a buyers' market" (p. 57).

6. R.C. Sproul, *The Holiness of God.* (Wheaton, IL.: Tyndale House, 1987), pp. 14-15.

7. Weed, p. 54. Throughout Restoration history there has been an affinity for controversy. As noted in an earlier chapter, the index to the *Millennial Harbinger* lists only three entries on the subject of holiness during the 30 – year life span of the journal. In the issue for July, 1830, a writer named Philip (possibly a penname for Alexander Campbell) wrote on "True Holiness." The writer took his definition from another writer whom he identified only as a "great scripturean." The "scripturean" insisted that true holiness consists of "conformity to the nature, character and will of God whereby a saint is distinguished from the unrenewed world, and is not actuated by their principles and precepts, nor governed by their maxims and customs" (p. 326). Philip was willing to accept the position of another author, presumably outside the Restoration fellowship and leave the subject there. The *Harbinger* chose to address those issues that generated controversy. In May, 1836, Robert Richardson wrote an article entitled, "The Perfectionists." It was a rebuttal to a document which had been published under that title at New

Haven, Connecticut. Controversial ideas about holiness, such as the Wesleyan concept of "the second work of grace" have occasionally aroused the interest of Restoration Movement polemicists, but rarely has anyone ever undertaken a positive study of God's holy nature.

8. A.W. Tozer, *The Knowledge of the Holy.* (San Francisco: Harper and Row. 1961), p. 105.

9. Rudolf Otto, *The Idea of the Holy.* tr. by John W. Harvey. (London: Oxford University Press, 1923, 2nd ed. 1950, pb. 1958), pp. 12-30 Otto gives the following description of the *mysterium tremendum.* "The feeling of it may at times come sweeping like a gentle tide, pervading the mind with a tranquil mood of deepest worship. It may pass over into a more set and lasting attitude of the soul, continuing as it were, thrillingly vibrant and resonant, until at last it dies away and the soul resumes its 'profane', non-religius mood of everyday experience. It may burst in sudden eruption up from the depths of the soul with spasm and convulsions, or lead to the strangest excitement, to intoxicated frenzy to ecstasy. It has its wild and demonic forms and can sink into an almost grisly horror and shuddering. It has crude, barbaric antecedents and early manifestations, and again it may be developed into something beautiful pure and glorious. It may become the hushed, trembling, and speechless humility of the creature in the presence of – whom or what? In the presence of that which is a *mystery* inexpressible and above all creatures." (pp. 12-13).

10. Tozer, p. 2.

11. Ibid., p. 1

12. J.I. Packer, *Knowing God.* (Downers Grove, IL: Intervarsity Press, 1973), p. 21.

13. Ibid., p. 20.

14. Tozer, p. 12.

15. Ibid., pp. 106-107.

7

The Transcendence of God

I toyed with the idea of titling this chapter something like "The Greatness of God" or "How God Is Different." I harbor this irrational fear that some readers might see a seventy-five cent word like "transcendence" and go on to the next chapter. I decided I'd just have to run that risk. If you've stayed with me this far, please read my reasons for discussing transcendence before skipping the chapter.

Anyone who attempts to communicate the concept of God's greatness has to wrestle with a vocabulary problem. R. C. Sproul conceded the difficulty when he wrote,

> My editor gets nasty about big words. He exacted a promise from me that I would try to write this book without using any big words or scholarly language. . . . I'm stuck. I have to use a big word. Nuts to the editor. Get ready now for a big, abstract, theological word.[1]

His "big, abstract, theological term" was "transcendence."

When Allen, Hughes and Weed showed the pre-publication draft of *The Worldly Church* to friends and colleagues, they were warned that the concept of transcendence would not be understood by many members of the Churches of Christ. But they responded, "If these fears are justified, they point to the very problem we wish to address. For the loss of the transcendent is the very heart of the secular perspective."[2] Even A. W. Tozer, who was not given to using the technical terms of the theological world in print, conceded that a casual approach to the transcendence of God in our modern world has produced a "deep blindness of the heart."[3]

Worldly people dismiss transcendence as a subject of discussion. They prefer to leave all references to deity out of serious discussions concerning world affairs, societal trends and ethical standards. Secularism threatens to drown contemporary society in its polluted waters and no one can deny that the humanist sewage sloshes over into the church. Subconsciously, we allow the trends of the times to mold our values and ideals. These trends are not encouraging to those who believe that holiness ought to be a priority concern in life. Charles Colson's assessment of the current culture is extremely pessimistic.

Vestiges of Christian influence still remain, but those Christian absolutes that have so profoundly shaped Western culture through the centuries are being consciously rejected by the men and women who direct the flow of information and attitudes to the popular culture: communicators, educators, entertainers and lawyers.[4]

William Wordsworth graduated from Cambridge in 1791 and went to live in France for a year. He was there during part of the most turbulent years of the Revolution. He returned to England with his mind saturated in revolutionary rhetoric. Insofar as religion was concerned, he regarded himself as a radical.

Then Napoleon came to power in France. Wordsworth began to back down from his revolutionary stance. Slowly he began to retreat back toward religious orthodoxy, although no one is certain if he ever completely found his way back to orthodoxy as it was defined by the Church of England. In the midst of all this soul searching, he wrote

84

the following lines,

> The world is too much with us; late and soon
> Getting and spending, we lay waste our powers:
> Little we see in nature that is ours;
> We have given our hearts away, a sordid boon![5]

Wordsworth was not a prophet, but his indictment of the Western world in the early nineteenth century aptly describes conditions in our own time. So many of our values are secular. A person's worth is often measured by the dollar figure on his pay check, the number of square feet in his house and the number of cubic inches in his car's engine. These things that perish with the using consume most of our energy and interest.

Christians are not immune to the appeal of secular values. We have learned to compete on equal terms in the marketplace. Even as we gather among Christian brothers and sisters, our conversations tend to center around such matters as stock options, automobile performance, speculation about political conditions and the latest performances of popular sports figures. For some reason we are hesitant to talk about the values of the kingdom in casual conversation. Only in the Bible class and the pulpit is such talk encouraged. Have we forgotten that the Bible says, "Do not love the world or anything in the world. If anyone loves the world, the love of the Father is not in him" (I John 2:15)?

Perhaps there was a time when people of the Restoration Movement (at least certain segments of it) were culturally and geographically isolated from the mainstream of the world's ways of thinking, but that naive era has long since passed. We have adopted many of the world's values and have learned to compete on equal terms in the world's market place. Unfortunately, many of us fail to realize that "We live in and work in a world where the loss of transcendence is widely assumed."[6]

Some writers border on despair in their assessment of the spiritual condition of the church.

> I cannot see the slightest indication that most Christians of this age know God in personal experience. As a result we have a

85

God with whom we do not communicate, who cannot commune with us or have an impact on our lives and ministry. God is alive, but he might as well be dead.[7]

It can scarcely be denied that our churches have only a low level awareness of God's transcendence. It does not overstate the case to say that our survival as the people of God depends on our acceptance of God's transcendence. For that reason, I must address the subject and there is no substitute term that will serve us as well as the "big, abstract, theological word." Our spiritual survival depends on our confidence in a transcendent God.

WHAT IS TRANSCENDENCE?

The word "transcendence" does not appear in most of our English Bibles. It is derived from the Latin term *transcendere*. The primary definition is "exceeding usual limits." A secondary definition is, "extending or lying beyond the limits of ordinary experience."[8] To speak of God as being transcendent is to say that God cannot be limited to any kind of human category. That's why an expression like, "The greatness of God," seem inadequate. We commonly apply the term "great" to people, things, and ideas that simply aren't in the same class with God. William Jennings Bryan was known as "the great commoner." A member of the dog species is called a "great dane." There's also a "great horned owl." The Indians used to speak of our president as "the great white father." If someone asks you to describe your reaction to your vacation, you may give the one word response, "great!" Whatever people may want to call "great," God is greater. Transcendence may be the best available word to describe that concept.

1. The Distinctiveness of God.
To say that God is transcendent is to say that he is distinct from all things, people, angels – everything that has been created. Tozer noted, "We must not think of God as the highest in an ascending order of beings."[9] He goes on to point out that it is appropriate to compare

86

angels and caterpillars. An angel is one of God's created beings and so is a caterpillar. You can say that an angel is more important than a caterpillar, but you're still talking about something God made. God is in a category by himself, a perpetually existing being to whom all the earth must ultimately give account.

Eliezer Berkovitz, a Jewish scholar, draws on Isaiah's various descriptions of the "Lord of Hosts" (NIV "LORD Almighty" to construct his model of transcendence.

> The Lord of hosts alone is God; he is at the beginning of time and at the end of it; he alone and no one beside him. He is creator of heaven and earth; he is the sovereign power over all nature, as well as over all the kingdoms of men. Of this Sovereign Lord, it is maintained that he is "the Mighty One" who deals with his enemies, Jew or gentile, as he pleases. He acts, however as a judge, who "purges away the dross with lye." He brings low the haughty and the proud. He executes punishment, when punishment is required; and he does so, like a war lord he mustereth his armies. For Isaiah, the "Lord of Hosts" expressed the idea of divine transcendence, of elevation above everything created. The idea of transcendence is connected with divine might and power, which is exercised by the universal sovereign in his capacity as Supreme Judge and Ruler. Isaiah uses the phrase, the Lord of Hosts, consistently in this sense.[10]

Allen, Hughes and Weed write from a Christian perspective, yet their description of transcendence is remarkably close to that of Berkovitz.

> By this term, we point to the fact that God is infinitely greater than ourselves, that he is the majestic sovereign of the universe upon whom we must depend for life itself, that he works in mysterious ways which often defy our shallow understandings, that he is the very standard of holiness in whose light, our noblest efforts are very meager indeed and that we finally must acknowledge his will and not our own.[11]

To say that God is transcendent is to say that he is the creator of heaven and earth (Gen. 1:1). Because God is transcendent, even those who come close to him must maintain a certain distance. Moses, to whom God appeared in a burning bush at Horeb (Exod. 3:1-4:17) and on the summit of Sinai in the midst of thunder, cloud and smoke, was reminded of the distance which separated himself and his God in Exod. 33:19-20, "'I will proclaim my name, the LORD, in your presence. . . . But,' he said, 'you cannot see my face, for no one can see me and live.' " God's transcendence means that he maintains an aura of mysteriousness. He cannot be reduced to human formulas, analogies, syllogisms, ratios, rationalizations and explanations. He has been called "the great stranger in the human world."[12]

> For my thoughts are not your thoughts, neither are your ways my ways, declares the LORD. So are my ways higher than your ways and my thoughts than your thoughts (Isa. 55:8-9).

2. Designations of the Transcendent God.

In a later chapter attention will be given to the various names of God. At this point, it is essential to point out that some of the names of God call specific attention to his transcendence.

Isaiah referred to him as "The LORD of Hosts" ("God Almighty). In 37:16, "The LORD of Hosts is "enthroned between the cherubim." In 44:6, "the LORD of Hosts" declared "I am the first and am the last; apart from me there is no God." In 51:15 he is the "one who churns up the sea, so that its waves roar. . . ." In 1:24-25, he asserted, "Ah, I will get relief from my foes and avenge myself on my enemies. I will turn my hand against you, I will thoroughly purge away your dross and remove your impurities." Berkovitz noted,

> For Isaiah, the "Lord of Hosts" expressed the idea of divine transcendence, of elevation above everything created. The idea of transcendence is connected with divine might and power, which is exercised by the universal sovereign in his capacity as Supreme Judge and Ruler. Isaiah uses the phrase, "the Lord of Hosts" consistently in this sense."[13]

He is also said to be the "Most High God." In Genesis 14:18, Melchizedek is described as "priest of the God most high." And when giving his tithe to Melchizedek, Abram said in verse 22, "I have raised my hand to the Lord God Most High." The Psalmist declares, "I will sing praise to the name of the LORD Most High." (Psa. 7:17). In Isaiah 57:15, God himself said, "I live in a high and holy place." Even the pagan king, Nebuchadnezzar, called him the "Most High God" in Daniel 4:2. And in Luke 2, when the angels appeared to the shepherds to announce the birth of Jesus, in their utterance of praise to God, they said, "Glory to God in the highest."

Of course the term "high" means elevated. Actually expressions like "the Most High God" or "God over all" fall short of explaining God's transcendence. "High" and "Over" are space terms and God is not confined to space. We are forced to use such expressions because language is inadequate to completely express the nature of God. I've only given you a small percentage of the passages in which the word "High," "Most High" or "Highest" is associated with God. Every time you read it, you are dealing with the transcendence of God.

Isaiah refers to God as the "Holy One of Israel" 32 times in the Hebrew text. Berkovitz insisted that "the Holy One Of Israel" represents a totally different picture of God from the one expressed in the "LORD of Hosts" concept. He wrote,

> The Lord of hosts is transcendent, the Holy one is immanent. The Lord of hosts is far removed, he is above man and all creation; the Holy One of Israel is near. The Lord of hosts judges; the Holy one of Israel saves.[15]

The term "immanent" refers to God's closeness and is often contrasted with the concept of transcendence. Berkovitz was on target when he said that "the Holy One of Israel is Near." But he drew an unwarranted conclusion when he excluded the idea of transcendence from "the Holy One of Israel." He reacted negatively to Otto's portrayal of the Holy God as "the *mysterium tremendum*." He said, "Quite obviously the Holy One is not the *mysterium tremendum*."[16]

It would be more correct to say that Isaiah exposes a different dimension of the transcendent God when he speaks of "The Holy One of Israel." In 12:6, the prophet anticipates a time when the people will say, "Shout aloud and sing for joy, people of Zion, for great is the

Holy of Israel among you." It's true that God is bringing them an occasion of joy, but why do they have occasion to praise God? It's because God's power has reclaimed a remnant that's left of God's people. In 43:14-15, the prophet wrote,

> This what the LORD says - your redeemer, the Holy One of Israel; For your sake I will send to Babylon and bring down as fugitive all the Babylonians, in the ships in which they took pride. I am the LORD, your Holy One, Israel's Creator, your King.

You can't make a stronger statement of transcendence than that one. Then in 47:4, both the names come together in the same verse. "Our redeemer – the LORD Almighty (i.e the LORD of hosts) is his name - is the Holy One of Israel." God does not have a split personality! If indeed "the Holy One of Israel" is describing God's immanence, then it is also describing his transcendence at the same time.

SOME BIBLICAL DEMONSTRATIONS
OF TRANSCENDENCE

Throughout Biblical history the fact of God's transcendence has been impressed on the minds of people through God's intervention into the world. These occur with sufficient frequency to make us aware that God is to be treated with the deepest and most reverential amount of respect that his people can muster. The following Biblical events dramatically illustrate the kinds of things that take place when God's transcendence is fully realized.

1. Moses.

Following his abrupt and unceremonious transfer from Egypt to Midian, Moses settled down and started living the life of a gentleman farmer. He managed to find a congenial employer who just happened to have an eligible daughter. A wedding soon followed and on the heels of that happy event, came the birth of a little boy, whom they called Gershom. For most of forty years Moses' most serious problems consisted of trying to find suitable pasture for his sheep and staying ahead of the fluctuating wool market.

One day he led the flock to Horeb. Even then it was called "the mountain of God." Strange things are sometimes found in the desert, but whoever heard of a bush that would not burn up. "So Moses thought, 'I will go over and see this strange sight – why the bush does not burn up' " (Exod. 3:3). At that point he was nothing but a curiosity seeker, the kind of person who would pay to see the bearded woman at the circus. "When the Lord saw that he had gone over to look, God called to him from within the bush, 'Moses, Moses!'" (3:4).

Moses was about to experience the *mysterium tremendum*. The experience quickly went from one that he might have remembered to tell Zipporah to one that completely transformed his life. God was about to commission him to lead Israel, but before that could happen, Moses had to understand the transcendent nature of the God with whom he was dealing. "'Do not come any closer,' God said. 'Take off your sandals, for the place where you are standing is holy ground.'" Observe if you will how Moses was affected when he recognized that he had met the God of Abraham, Isaac and Jacob. "At this, Moses hid his face because he was afraid to look at God" (3:5).

2. Job.

Job was another man who experienced an encounter with God. Job had a strong faith long before he realized the vastness of God's transcendence. In Job 1:1 he is described as a man who "was blameless and upright; he feared God and shunned evil." You can be a righteous person. You can experience fellowship with God. You can live with integrity and still have a lot to learn about the transcendent nature of God. And that was the case with Job.

Tragedy exposed the shallowness of his understanding of God. It started with humiliating loss and when that came Job could say, "The Lord gave and the Lord has taken away. May the name of the Lord be praised" (21). Then there came sickness, the rejection of his wife and the unfair accusations of his friends. Again Job stood as solidly as the Rock of Gibraltar. "In all this Job did not sin in what he said" (2:10).

But then he had to deal with the one thing he could not stand, the silence of God. It's not that Job doubted the existence of God, but he did question whether God was giving him fair treatment. In 27:2, he said, "As surely as God lives, who has denied me justice, the Almighty, who has made me taste bitterness of soul." In 30:20, "I cry out to you, O God, but you do not answer; I stand up but you merely look at me." And then he did the unthinkable. He challenged God to answer him. Observe his brazen statement in 31:35, "Oh, that I had someone to hear me! I sign now my defense – let the Almighty answer me, let my accuser put his indictment in writing." Those are bold words. Their very boldness suggest that he did not comprehend God's transcendence.

There was a brief interlude after Job made this dramatic statement as Elihu contributed his thoughts, but then God answered out of a storm. Notice how God used the cataclysmic events of nature to demonstrate his transcendence. In the time of Noah it was the flood. With Moses it was the burning bush as well as the thunder, cloud and smoke on Sinai. Now with Job, God spoke out of the storm.

> Who is this that darkens my counsel with words without knowledge? Brace yourself like a man; I will question you, and you shall answer me (38:2-3).

God started by asking, "Where were you when I laid the earth's foundation. Tell me if you understand?" (38:4). That's an impossible question but God was just getting started. Relentlessly, he confronted Job with question after question that the beleaguered man could not answer. At the end of what had to be the most unanswerable kind of semester exam that's ever been given, God said, "Will the one who contends with the Almighty correct him? Let him who accuses God answer him!" Job didn't want to answer. It was time for the gag rule to go into effect, "I am unworthy – how can I reply to you? I put my hand over my mouth" (40:4). But God wasn't through with Job. If Job wanted a debate with God, he would have to take his turn at the rostrum. God said, "Would you discredit my justice? Would you condemn me to justify yourself?" At the end Job did the only thing God would accept. He confessed, "Surely I spoke of things I do not understand, things too wonderful for me to know" (42:3). Job finally realized how much distance there is between a transcendent God and

92

mortal man. Having seen the transcendent God, he said, "Therefore, I despise myself and repent in dust and ashes." (42:6).

3. John, the apostle.

Most people have a tendency to see John as an ideal disciple of Jesus. He's even been called the "Apostle of Love." No one can dispute the fact that some of the most penetrating thoughts about Jesus and the relationship that people can have with Jesus are expressed to us through the pen of John. "My little children, love one another," is a phrase inseparably linked with John.

But it was not always so. John started out his adult life in the fishing business, not exactly the most genteel profession in the world. He was high tempered and ambitious. He and his brother, James, were nicknamed "the Sons of Thunder" (Mark 3:17). When the people of a Samaritan village decided not to roll out the red carpet and offer their group the key to the city, the two sons of Zebedee devised a brilliant plan. They would call fire down from heaven and destroy them (Luke 9:54). John made an unwise decision to reprimand a man who had been exorcising demons and yet had not been among the followers of Jesus (Luke 9:49). Besides that John was so caught up with personal ambition that he, along with James, had the nerve to walk right up to Jesus and ask for first and second place in the kingdom (Mark 10:35). Sometimes we think of the apostles as spiritual supermen, but they were pretty ordinary people, with some pretty ordinary ideas. They respected Jesus but in the beginning they didn't really comprehend his true identity. That would all change for John when he understood transcendence.

If you turn the pages from the gospels to the book of Revelation, you will see a transformed John. Among the apostles, he was the only one living when he was sent to Patmos. Today Patmos is a nice resort community boasting a harbor that hosts the yachts of wealthy vacationers. But then it was a lonely island of rock and bare dirt, the Devil's Island of the Aegean Sea. The Romans sent their political prisoners there. It was there, in this forgotten place, that John had his most impressive encounter with the transcendent God. "On the Lord's Day, I was in the Spirit, and I heard behind me a loud voice like a trumpet" (1:10).

Today, many people read the book of Revelation in an attempt to figure out the future. They should read it to learn about the transcendent God. In God's throne room John saw four living creatures who never stop saying, "Holy, holy, holy is the Lord God Almighty, who was, and is, and is to come" (4:8).

He also observed twenty four elders as they fell down before the throne and said,

> You are worthy, our Lord and God, to receive glory and honor and power, for you created all things, and by your will they were created and have their being (4:11).

In the various visions that John recorded, he mentioned the unleashing of all the violent and threatening forces of nature. These forces were under God's control, indications of his power and majesty. At one point he reported seeing an angel of the Lord with a golden censer in his hand. The angel filled the censer with fire from the altar and heaved it to the earth, "and there came peals of thunder, rumblings, flashes of lightning and an earthquake" (8:5). A similar maelstrom of violence is described in 11:19, "Then God's temple in heaven was opened, and within his temple was seen the ark of his covenant. And there came flashes of lighting, rumblings, peals of thunder, an earthquake and a great hailstorm." In his description of the Lamb standing on Mount Zion, John said, "And I heard a sound from heaven like the sound of rushing waters and like the loud peal of thunder . . ." (14:2).

The people of John's day never heard the explosion of fireworks on the fourth of July. They never heard a cannon fire, the roar of a jet airplane, the blare of an automobile horn or, the rumble of a locomotive. A sonic boom would have terrified them. John drew on the most powerful and violent sight and sound exhibitions his readers had ever experienced to communicate the awesomeness of the environment in which the throne of God exists. He wanted his readers to realize that God lives in a habitat which cannot be pictured by the human imagination. When a person comes to such a profound realization, his first reaction will quite naturally be like John's initial response. "When I saw him, I fell at his feet as though dead" (1:17).

RESPONDING TO TRANSCENDENCE

The realization that we live in the presence of such an overpowering God can be so intimidating that we decide there is no point in trying to respond. He is God and we are people and the chasm between us is so great that it can never be bridged. But that's not the way God wants us to think. Peter provides a significant insight into God's program for the human race.

> His divine power has given us everything that we need for life and godliness through the knowledge of him who called us by his own glory and goodness. Through these he has given us very great and precious promises, so that through them you may participate in the divine nature and escape the corruptions in the world caused by evil desires (II Pet. 1:3-4).

It's God's transcendence (divine power) which makes it possible for us to participate in the divine nature. That's God's plan for the human race.

It's significant to notice that each time God revealed his transcendence in a supernatural way, he commissioned the person who saw the magnificent manifestations of his glory to execute an important mission for him. Moses was to free the children of Israel. Job was being used as a test case in the dispute between God and Satan. John was to write what he saw. While the transcendence of God exposes human sinfulness, at the same time, it assures us that the God of heaven has a limitless supply of resources that he's willing to place at our disposal if we'll just follow him.

We can only trust a transcendent God to forgive our sins. Let's suppose you owe the bank a million dollars. You took out the loan intending to make some investments that would return you a substantial profit, but the investments all went sour and you're facing economic ruin. You couldn't repay a hundred dollar loan, much less a million dollar debt.

Suppose you come to me and tell me your hard luck story. And suppose that I say, "Oh, don't worry about it. You're debt's been forgiven." You would question my sanity and wonder why you ever bothered to tell me your troubles. I don't have any power to forgive such a debt. I don't sit on the board of directors at the bank. I'm not a loan officer. I don't even own any stock.

But let's suppose you walk into the office of the bank's chairman of the board, who just happens to own 85 per cent of the stock. You're probably going to be shaking more than just a little bit when you begin telling him that you have a million dollar loan due today, and you can't even pay the interest. You wouldn't want to look a man like that in the eye. You would wish there might be some way for a hole to suddenly appear in the floor, so that the earth might swallow you up.

But let's suppose that our imaginary chairman of the board says, "I've just come from a meeting of the board of directors. We've unanimously voted to forgive you of your debt and besides that we want you to work at the bank for an annual salary of $100,000." You might have trouble believing it, but you could scarcely doubt his ability to forgive the loan if he chose to do so.

My illustration is flawed because nothing like that's ever going to happen at a bank. But that's exactly why I made it so preposterous, because something even more outlandish has happened in heaven. God, who has the power to destroy you completely, has offered to use that same power to remove all of your sin debt and to give you a place of honored service in his kingdom.

That's why we must understand his transcendence. We must not bring him down to our level. We must not make him a more powerful extension of ourselves. We see him as the one whose thoughts are not our thoughts and whose ways are not our ways, because only then can he bless us.

Endnotes

1. R.C. Sproul, *The Holiness of God.* (Wheaton, IL: Tyndale House Publisher, Inc. 1987), p. 54.

2. C. Leonard Allen, Richard T. Hughes and Michael R. Weed, *The Worldly Church.* (Abilene, Texas; ACU Press, 1988), p. 3.

3. A.W. Tozer, *The Knowledge of the Holy.* (San Francisco: Harper and Row, 1961), p. 72.

4. Charles Colson, *Against the Night.* (Ann Arbor, Michigan: Servant Books, 1989), p. 109. Colson quoted P.T. Forsythe who observed "Whole tracts of our religion are bare of spiritual passion, or spiritual depth. Christianity speaks the language of humane civilization; it does not speak the language of Christ" (p. 97).

5. William Wordsworth, "The World Is Too Much With Us" George B. Woods, Homer A. Watt and George K. Anderson (ed) *The Literature of England, an Anthology and a History.* (Chicago: Scott, Foresman and Company, 1948), Vol 2, p. 159.

6. Allen, Hughes, and Weed, *The Worldly Church.* p. 6. The authors of *The Worldly Church* clearly believe that secularism has severely eroded our belief in a transcendent God. "American members of Churches of Christ have spiraled upward to a much higher socio-economic plane. Now we are educated and often affluent. Many of us wield power in our communities. By virtue of our training and our work we are often skilled in the art of management, manipulation and technique. These very skills subtly promote the loss of a sense of transcendence among us."

7. Edwin F. White, *A Sense of Presence.* (Nashville: Gospel Advocate Company, 1989), p. 3.

8. *Webster's New Collegiate Dictionary.* Springfield, Massachusetts: G. and C. Merriam Co., 1977), p. 1239.

9. A. W. Tozer, *The Knowledge of the Holy.* p. 70.

10. Eliezer Berkovitz, *Man and God. Studies in Biblical Theology.* (Detroit: Wayne State University press, 1969), p. 142. Some of the Isaiah passages which include references to the "Lord of Hosts" are 37:16, 44:6; 51:15; 1:24-25; 2:12; 3:1; 13:4; 13:3.

11. Allen, *et al.,* *The Worldly Church.* p. 3.

12. Gerhard von Rad, *Old Testament Theology.* tr. Dana Stalker. Vol. I. (New York: Harper and Row, 1962), p. 205.

13. Berkovitz, *Man and God – Studies in Biblical Theology.* p. 142.

14. Edward Mack, "God, Names of" *International Standard Bible Encyclopedia.* (Grand Rapids, Michigan: William B. Eerdmans Company, 1929, r.p. 1955), Vol. 2, p. 1266.

15. Berkovitz, *Man and God – Studies in Biblical Theology,* p. 144.

16. Ibid.

8
The God of Pure Eyes

The prophet Habakkuk lived during a time of moral and spiritual decline in Judah. Violence and injustice saturated the nation's social structure. In righteous indignation the prophet boldly complained to God, "Why do you make me look at injustice? Why do you tolerate wrong?" (Hab. 1:3). If Hezekiah was upset over God's failure to deal with Judah's lack of moral discernment, the prophet was aghast when he heard God's answer. "I am raising up the Babylonians, that ruthless and impetuous people who sweep across the whole earth to seize dwelling places not their own" (1:6). Habakkuk protested, "Your eyes are too pure to look on evil; you cannot tolerate wrong" (1:13).

Habakkuk demanded that God punish Judah because moral integrity had vanished, but it appeared to him that God's solution was equally evil since the Babylonians were worse than the people being punished. He viewed God's announcement of his plan as an affront to justice. How could God use pagan barbarians to chastise people whom God himself had chosen? Habakkuk had carefully constructed his own set of theological beliefs. He assumed that he possessed correct understanding of the things that God will and will not do. He was baffled because his list didn't agree with God's. Habakkuk knew that God's eyes are pure. He would have staked his life on that premise, but when he tried to match his beliefs with God's revelation he kept coming up with question marks.

Habakkuk's allusion to God's "pure eyes" suggests an important aspect of the Almighty's holy nature. God is not merely the transcendent God of glory and power. His holiness has a moral and ethical dimension. "The holiness of God denotes his moral perfection, his absolute freedom from blemish of any kind."[1]

In this chapter attention will be focused on identifying some of the moral attributes of God's character.

GOD IS GOOD

Sometimes the most profound theological concepts are best communicated in simple terms. When our children were just learning to string sentences together, we taught them to pray by repeating short, simple prayers. The following prayer is one that we used in their formative years.

> God is great.
> God is good.
> Let us thank him for our food.

That's great theology for a three year old, but we soon expect a child to progress beyond such elementary petitions. Little did we realize that we were making a profound theological statement when we taught the children to repeat that simple prayer. In those brief sentences the child repeats three important theological concepts. 1) God is transcendent - "God is great." 2) God is ethically pure – "God is good." and 3) God is involved with human life – "Let us thank him for our food." While it's good theology for three year olds, many thirty year olds have never grasped it.

The prayer is particularly appropriate because it focuses attention on the goodness of God at a time when a child's mind is open to receiving it. Edwin White describes a child's sensitivity to the goodness of God by relating an incident which took place during Helen Keller's childhood.

> She found a bright and bustling world through the vocabulary of touch. Phillips Brooks allowed Helen to place her fingers on his lips as he talked in simple language about God and the disclosure of himself in the person of his son Jesus Christ. While listening with her fingers, Helen grew fidgety. Abruptly, she cried out, "I knew him! I knew him! I didn't know his name, but I knew him!"[2]

The conscientious parent can find no better starting point in a child's spiritual education than exposing them to the concept of God's goodness, a principle which the Bible consistently declares. The Psalmist wrote, "Good and upright is the LORD," (Psa. 25:8). In the 34th Psalm, the reader is invited to "taste and see that the LORD is good" (v. 8). God's goodness benefits the human race. Nahum, the prophet said, "The LORD is good, a refuge in times of trouble" (Nah. 1:7). When the rich young ruler inquired about the "good thing" that he needed to do in order to obtain eternal life, Jesus responded, "There is only One who is good" (Matt. 19:17).

In the years before leaving childhood innocence, the human mind is especially open to the concept that a good and loving Father watches over all the earth. As people grow older they ask more complex questions, but the concept of the goodness of God still has credibility even after we have been exposed to life's cruel side. What do the Bible writers mean when they say that God is good?

> Goodness, in God as in man, means something admirable, attractive and praiseworthy. When the biblical writers call God "good," they are thinking in general of all those moral qualities which prompt his people to call him "perfect," and in particular of the generosity which moves them to call him "merciful" and "gracious" and to speak of His "love."[3]

The goodness of God is sometimes equated with his complete

101

moral perfection. In Exodus 33:19, God told Moses, "I will cause all my goodness to pass in front of you." When the goodness of God was actually revealed to Moses, these specific characteristics were identified. God said, "The LORD, the LORD, the compassionate and gracious God, slow to anger, abounding in love and faithfulness, maintaining love to thousands, and forgiving wickedness, rebellion and sin" (Exod. 34:6-7a). There's a flip side to God's goodness. His abhorrence of sin is mandated by the purity of his being. In this very same context, God said, "Yet he does not leave the guilty unpunished; he punishes the children and their children for the sins of their fathers to the third and fourth generation" (Exod. 34:7b).

THE LOVING SIDE OF GOD'S NATURE

It may beg the question to separate the quality of goodness from the quality of love, but there are some slight differences. Goodness emphasizes the perfection of God's character, while love stresses his benevolent nature. John said it so elegantly, yet so simply - "God is love" (I John 4:8). Profound as it is, that short declaration of God's loving nature can be misleading, especially if we view it as a comprehensive definition of God. A. W. Tozer observed,

> We must escape the slavery of words and give loyal adherence to meanings instead. Words should express ideas not originate them. . . . The words "God is love" mean that love is an essential attribute of God, but it is not God. It expresses the way God is in his unitary being, as do the words holiness, justice, faithfulness and truth.[4]

What truth is communicated in the phrase, "God is love?" It implies that God completely assimilates love into his divine character. We can also be assured that God's love is directed toward the entire world. "For God so loved the world that he gave his one and only Son, that whoever believes in him shall not perish but have eternal life" (John 3:16). Without God's love the human race lives in a "perishing" condition. God's love for people caused him to set in motion a chain of events that would "rescue the perishing." Christ's atoning

102

sacrifice on the cross is the specific act which makes possible the gift of salvation. "But God demonstrated his own love for us in this: While we were still sinners, Christ died for us" (Rom. 5:8).

The far reaching effects of God's saving work are understood when we realize that justification is not contingent on the nobility of human character. Jesus reported that he is even ". . . kind to the ungrateful and the wicked" (Luke 6:35). The sinner can never perform any deed, offer any gift, or make any sacrifice that would qualify him to claim God's blessing of salvation. The offer of grace is so extensive that it extends even to the worst of sinners (I Tim. 1:15). Packer noted "The Greek and Roman world of New Testament times had never dreamed of such love; its gods were credited with lusting after women, but never loving sinners. . . ."[5]

Many people think God's love for the sinner is a New Testament concept. They have a mental picture of a harsh God in the Old Testament, an ill-tempered, vindicative God who takes special delight in punishing disobedience. They miss the Old Testament portrait of a compassionate God. According to Exod. 34:7, he maintains "love to thousands" and forgives "wickedness, rebellion and sin." The author of the 103rd Psalm said.

> For as high as the heavens are above the earth,
> So great is his love for those who fear him;
> As far as the east is from the west,
> So far he has removed our transgressions from us.
> As a father has compassion on his children,
> So the LORD has compassion on those who fear him
> (Psa. 103:11-13).

Those who draw a contradictory picture between the God of the Old Testament and the God of the New Testament must ignore numerous passages which praise God for his loving response to people.

We should banish from our minds forever the common but erroneous notion that justice and judgment characterize the God of Israel, while mercy and grace belong to the Lord of the Church. Actually, there is in principle no difference between the Old Testament and the New. In the New Testament Scriptures

103

there is a fuller development of redemptive truth, but one God speaks in both dispensations, and what he speaks agrees with what he is.[6]

THE RIGHTEOUSNESS OF GOD

"Righteousness" is almost a synonym for "holiness." Righteousness and sin are opposites. In II Corinthians 6:14, Paul asked, "For what do righteousness and wickedness have in common?" This is not the kind of question that one raises in an effort to gain information. It's a rhetorical question in which the answer is suggested by the question itself. The force of Paul's argument is, "righteousness and wickedness have nothing in common." It has been said that "God's holiness denotes not merely his separation from sin in the perfection of his being, but his abhorrence and hostility to it."[7]

In Deuteronomy 32:4, a part of Moses' song extolled the righteousness of God.

> He is the Rock, his works are perfect,
> And all his ways are just.
> A faithful God who does not wrong,
> Upright and just is he.

The same sentiment is expressed in various ways throughout the Bible. "Clouds and thick darkness surround him; righteousness and justice are the foundation of this throne" (Psa. 97:2). In Psalm 119 the writer verbalized repeated expressions of praise for the law of the Lord. At one point he wrote, "Righteous are you O LORD, and your laws are right" (Psa. 119:137). John wrote, "If you know that he is righteous, you know that everyone who does what is right is born of him" (I John 2:29).

To say that God is righteous is to say that nothing about his nature or his actions in the world can be called into question. "God is morally spotless in character and action, upright, pure and untainted with evil desires, motives, thoughts, words or acts."[8]

If that is the case then how do we account for Habakkuk's challenge to God? This challenge reveals an incomplete understanding of

104

God's nature. He didn't understand all the ramifications of God's having "pure eyes."

It's not really a wise thing to do battle with God. Jacob tried it and limped the rest of his life as a result (Gen. 32:22-32). Job challenged God to debate (Job 30:20-23), but ended up completely broken in spirit and forced to confess his ignorance (Job 40:3-5; 42:2-6). As a result of his impetuous challenge of God, he finally said, "I despise myself and repent in dust and ashes." Jeremiah thought God had deceived him, but recognized that his word was in "his heart like a burning fire shut up in my bones" (Jer. 20:9). Habakkuk thought he saw an inconsistency in God's behavior and said so, but in the end he conceded,

> I heard and my heart pounded,
> My lips quivered at the sound; decay crept into my bones,
> And my legs trembled (Hab. 3:16).

The person who wants to challenge God needs to think carefully about it before doing so. R. C. Sproul observed,

> Jacob, Job and Habakkuk all declared war on God. They stormed the battlements of heaven. They were all defeated, yet they came away with uplifted souls. They paid a price in pain. God allowed the debate, but the battle was fierce before the peace was established.[9]

Every Christian will face disappointment sooner or later. Some may choose to challenge God. Such challenges do not necessarily suggest unbelief. More often it exposes a limited understanding of divine things. If a person decides to file a complaint with the Almighty, that same person ought to realize that the appeal of an umpire's close call at first base has a much better chance of being changed. God knows what we do not know. Those who attack God from the posture of faith may well grow as a result of the encounter, but it must be understood that pain is the price of such growth. The experience of Jacob, Job, Habakkuk and others suggest that acceptance of the light that God has already given us is normally the better part of valor.

THE JUSTICE OF GOD

There's not a whole lot of difference between the righteousness of God and the justice of God. In this study, our consideration of God's justice will concentrate on the issue of whether God is fair. Tozer said,

Justice embodies the idea of moral equity, and iniquity is the opposite, it is inequity, the absence of equity from human thoughts and acts. Judgment is the application of equity to moral situations and may be favorable or unfavorable according to whether the one under consideration has been equitable or inequitable in conduct.[10]

God's righteousness requires him to punish evil. That premise is frequently stated in scripture. As Joshua prepared to relinquish his leadership of Israel, he talked about the nation's options.

You are not able to serve the LORD. He is a holy God; he is a jealous God. He will not forgive your rebellion and your sins. If you forsake the LORD and serve foreign gods, he will turn and bring disaster on you and make an end of you, after he has been good to you (Josh. 24:19-20).

God "cannot take pleasure in evil" (Psa. 5:4). On occasion people have attempted to balance their sinful behavior against their fidelity to God in ceremonial matters (Isa. 1:10-17). Such injustice precipitates divine indignation. Note his words of rejection. "I have no pleasure in the blood of bulls and lambs and goats" (11). "Your incense is detestable to me" (13). "I cannot bear your evil assemblies" (13). "Your New Moon festivals and appointed feasts my soul hates" (14).

Failure to respect God's standards results in divine punishment both in the lives of individuals and in the affairs of nations. In the days of Amos recriminations were announced against Damascus (1:3-5), Gaza (1:6-8), against Tyre (1:9-10), against Edom (1:11-12), against Ammon (1:13—15), against Moab (2:1-3), against Judah (2:4-5) and against Israel (2:6-16). His reasons might well be summed up in his statement to Judah. "I will not turn back my wrath because they have rejected the law of the Lord and have not kept his decrees" (2:4). God

106

judges individuals in eternity (Heb. 9:27), but nations are judged in time.

The prophet Nahum said "The LORD is slow to anger and great in power; the LORD will not leave the guilty unpunished" (Nah. 1:3). There are those who are greatly offended because God's sense of justice includes the necessity of divine punishment. But our sense of justice is not the same as that of God. Our sense of justice is influenced by our experiences, by our relationships with others, and by our exposure to the ideas of others. God is not so influenced. God is not held accountable to anyone but himself.

Plato asked the question, "Is God good because he wills it or does God will it because he is good?"[11] But there's not universal principle hanging over God's head, called "justice" to which he must conform. Justice ". . . is an outflow of God's nature."[12] His justice is even handed. Peter said that "God does not show favoritism" (Acts 10:34-35), but his impartiality is tempered by his grace which is also offered to everyone. "Whoever is thirsty, let him come; and whoever wishes, let him take the free gift of the water of life" (Rev. 22:17).

The sense of justice that people have in our day and time is not always based on the understanding that God is the ultimate and just judge. Justice and morality are often determined by relative standards. Those who don't want to abandon the idea of God entirely often rationalize these relative standards by insisting on the right to form their own picture of God's nature. Their methodology is exposed when they make such statements as "My God just wouldn't do that" or "A just God would never do thus and so." Such people have made up their mind about what is right to start with and have required God to conform to their own standards. It never occurs to them that God's nature is not subject to such manipulation. God's nature has been revealed on the pages of scripture. There is no provision for a recall election if you don't like the God who presides over the divine court. We're back to the issue of transcendence. If God is God and we are people, then we have no right to call his justice into question.

CONCLUSION

Even so there are some difficult questions to answer. The Old Testament in particular and even the New Testament, to some extent, record acts of God which appear harsh and brutal to our sensitive minds. God commanded Saul to destroy the Amalekite men, women and children with no leniency to be given. He struck down Uzzah just for touching the ark of the covenant. He caused two bears to come out of the woods and attack 42 youths who ridiculed Elisha's bald head (II Kings 2:23-25). In the New Testament, Ananias and Sapphira were put to death when they lied about their contribution and Elymas was struck blind when he resisted the preaching of Paul. We may not know the final answers, but to some degree we must deal with the seeming brutality of God and that will be the subject of the next chapter.

In summation, it can be said in the words of Gerhard von Rad, "The concept of the holy cannot be deduced from other human standards of value."[13] God is not a powerful bully. It was not just God's power that caused Isaiah's confidence to disintegrate when he entered God's throne room. It was his awareness of God's ethical purity. That's why he said, "Woe to me! I am ruined! For I am a man of unclean lips, and I live among a people of unclean lips, and my eyes have seen the king, the LORD Almighty" (Isa 6:5).

Endnotes

1. E. F. Harrison, "Holiness." *International Standard Bible Encyclopedia.* (Grand Rapids, Michigan: William B. Eerdman's Company, 1982), Vol. I, p. 725.

2. Edwin F. White, *A Sense of Presence.* (Nashville, Tennessee: Gospel Advocate Company, 1989), p. 19.

3. J.I. Packer, *Knowing God.* (Downers Grove, IL: Intervarsity Press. 1973), p. 145.

4. A.W. Tozer, *The Knowledge of the Holy.* (San Francisco: Harper and Row. 1961), p. 98.

5. Packer, *Knowing God*, p. 112.

6. Tozer, *The Knowledge of the Holy,* p. 91.

7. S. Barabas, "Holiness" *Zondervan Pictorial Encyclopedia of the Bible,* (Grand Rapids, Michigan: Zondervan Publishing House, 1975), Vol. 3, p. 455.

8. G.R. Lewis, "God, Attributes of." *Evangelical Dictionary of Theology.* (ed) Walter A. Elwell. (Grand Rapids, Michigan: Baker Book House,

1984), p. 455.

9. R.C. Sproul, *The Holiness of God.* (Wheaton, IL: Tyndale House Publishers, 1987), p. 184.

10. Tozer, *The Knowledge of the Holy,* p. 87.

11. Lewis, "God, Attributes of." p. 455-456.

12. Ibid., p. 456. "He wills the good because he is good and because God is good, he consistently hates sin and is repulsed by all evil without respect of persons" (p. 456). The author also suggests, "God is devoid of caprice, injustice, or emotions out of control" (456).

13. Gerhard von Rad, *Old Testament Theology,* tr. H. Dana Stalker. (New York: Harper and Row, 1962) p. 205.

9
Is God Fair?

Having survived the experience of functioning in the role of father as four strong-willed children struggled through their turbulent adolescent years, I know what it's like to have my sense of fairness challenged. In all candor I'll have to admit that my parental decisions were not fair on every occasion. Like every other human father, my parental performance was flawed. Inadequate information, mood swings and pure bias got in the way of truly objective judgment.

My children were usually sharp enough to know when my judgment lacked wisdom and they weren't afraid to tell me so. If I had put a quarter in an interest-bearing savings account every time they protested, "But Dad, it's not fair," I would probably be one of the bank's major depositors by now. They were also not afraid to challenge me when they thought I was wrong.

By the time children reach adulthood they come to understand that Dads aren't perfect. They forgive Dad for the time he unjustly took car privileges away for a week, but there's no way to forgive God.

111

God is responsible for defining right and wrong. We can't appeal his decisions to a higher court.

While we expect judgment to be flawed even in the best of people, we conclude that God's judgment is completely equitable. If God must express himself in punitive terms, He does so only because his sense of fairness requires it. J. I. Packer noted,

> God's wrath in the Bible is never the capricious, self-indulgent, irritable, morally ignoble thing that human anger so often is. It is instead a right and necessary reaction to objective moral evil.[1]

When Abraham bargained with God on behalf of Sodom he asked, "Will not the Judge of all the earth do right?" (Gen. 18:25). Jephthah, judge in Israel, was quite willing to put matters in the hands of God when a dispute arose with Sihon, king of the Ammonites. He said, "I have not wronged you, but you are doing wrong by waging war against me. Let the LORD, the Judge, decide the dispute this day between the Israelites and the Ammonites" (Judges 11:27). The Psalmist was certain that God would judge the world evenhandedly. "He will judge the world in righteousness and the peoples in his truth" (Psa. 96:13). Although the prophet Zephaniah pronounced woe upon the city of Jerusalem, he confidently announced, "The LORD within her is righteous; he does no wrong. Morning by morning he dispenses his justice . . ." (Zeph. 3:5).

WHY IT'S IMPORTANT FOR GOD TO BE FAIR

The validity of the Christian faith hinges on the morality of God. In Dostoyevsky's novel, *The Brothers Karamazov,* one of the characters concludes, "If there is no God then anything is permissible."[2] Anthony Campolo commented on this observation, "If there were no God, man would be left to make his own laws and establish his own principles of living."[3] If, however, we grant the premise that God does not exist and that we are permitted to make up whatever laws we choose, we virtually have no rationale for morality at all.

Thomas Hobbes believed that society itself decrees moral stan-

112

dards. It does so because it has an interest in self-preservation. Moral standards are simply an alternative to anarchy. But why would men choose one form of morality over another if there is no divine presence? Indeed, how could one contend that free world morality is superior to Marxist morality or that Christian morality is superior to secular morality? Philosophers like Hobbes may theoretically argue that any standard of morality which a society chooses to adopt is equal in value to the morality chosen by another society, but the practical fact is that everyone believes certain standards of morality to be superior to other standards. C. S. Lewis noted,

> If no set of moral ideas were truer or better than any other, there would be no sense in preferring civilised morality to savage morality, or Christian morality to Nazi morality. In fact, of course we all do believe that some moralities are better than others. We do believe that some of the people who tried to change the moral ideas of their own age were what we would call Reformers or Pioneers – people who understood morality better than their neighbors did. Very well then. The moment that you say one set of moral ideas can be better than another, you are, in fact measuring them both by a standard, saying that one of them conforms to the standard more nearly than the other. But the standard that measures two things is somewhat different from either. You are, in fact, comparing them both with some Real Morality, admitting that there is such a thing as real Right, independent of what people think, and that some people's ideas get nearer to the real Right than others.[5]

From the Biblical perspective the source of this "Real Morality" (note that Lewis identified it with capital letters) is the transcendent God. It is God who issued the Torah from the summit of Sinai. The continuity of God's authority to establish right and wrong was established by Jesus when he said,

> "Love the LORD your God with all your heart and with all your soul and with all your mind." This is the first and great commandment. And the second is like it: "Love your neighbor as yourself." All the Law and the Prophets hang on these two commandments (Matt. 22:37- 40).

THE ISSUE OF JUSTICE

The skeptic is faced with a dilemma in trying to explain why people universally recognize that some standards of morality are superior to others if there is no God to set those standards. The Christian is faced with the difficulty of defending the actions of God against the charge of injustice. R. C. Sproul noted "Whoever reads the Old Testament must struggle with the apparent brutality of God's judgment found there."[6] He might have also added some of the New Testament examples of seeming brutality which include the death of Ananias and Sapphira and the blinding of Elymas.

We cannot afford to skirt the issue. If we try to avoid the issue, the unbeliever will assume that our case for God's justice is flawed. If we just say, "we believe because we believe" then our faith is of the "leap-in-the-dark" variety. We criticize the existentialists when they reason that way. We cannot evade the issue by simply announcing, "I believe because I believe." We have to meet the issue head on. We may not have the final answers, but we can at least suggest some possible explanations. I have chosen to select several examples of alleged brutality and deal with them on a case by case basis.

NADAB AND ABIHU

Leviticus 10 records the story of God's destruction of Nadab and Abihu, sons of Aaron. Those who oppose instrumental music in worship are fond of using the case of Nadab and Abihu as an example of the seriousness of assuming that anything not specifically commanded in Scripture is inappropriate in worship. Those who use the instrument counter by pointing out that non-instrumentalists actually use many aids not expressly commanded in scripture, pitch pipes, hymn books, overhead projectors, sound systems, etc. In the heat of the battle both camps may have overlooked the real issue.

Nadab and Abihu were not destroyed just because they didn't get every detail of their worship exactly right. They were not the only persons who offered sacrifice in this story. Aaron had two other sons,

Eleazar and Ithamar. In Leviticus 10:13 Moses gave a specific command to Aaron and his sons (the two remaining sons, Eleazar and Ithamar). They were to consume a certain portion of meat which was offered in sacrifice. Moses said, "Eat it in a holy place, because it is your share and your son's share of the offerings made to the Lord by fire, for so I have been commanded."

The sacrifices were offered, but nobody ate the goat meat. When Moses found out about it, he was angry. "Why didn't you eat the sin offering in the sanctuary area? It is most holy. It was given to you to take away the guilt of the community by making atonement for them before the Lord. Since the blood was not taken into the Holy Place, you should have eaten the goat in the sanctuary as I have commanded" (Lev. 10:17,18).

If the theory holds that Nadab and Abihu were destroyed for being negligent about a single detail, then one would have expected fire from heaven to consume the other two brothers, but it didn't happen! Aaron began to explain himself. I'm not fully sure what he meant. It seems to be something like this, "Look, Moses. This has been a tough day for me. Two of my boys are already dead. We're so overcome by our grief and our own sense of sinfulness that we don't even feel like eating. Would it really be right to eat?" You may want to argue that Aaron's speech sounds like situation ethics, but the fact is that Moses bought it and God held off sending down the fire from heaven.

How do we explain the destruction of Nadab and Abihu? Nadab and Abihu were privileged men. According to Exod. 24:1, they were selected to ascend to a certain point on Mount Sinai where they offered worship to God. They ". . . saw the God of Israel" (Exod. 24:10).

They had been allowed into the presence of God and they should have come away with an overwhelming sense of reverence and awe. Instead they came away feeling their own importance and invincibility. Nobody could stop them. After all, they had been in the presence of God.

And so when it came time for Nadab and Abihu to prepare the sacrifice, they ". . . took their censers, put fire on them and added incense and they offered unauthorized fire before the Lord contrary to his command" (Lev. 10:1). There is no way of actually knowing what the "alien fire" might have been, but one thing is clear. God had made it plain how he wanted this sacrificial offering to be carried out. They had understood the instruction and they had pledged themselves to obey God (Exod. 24:7). But instead of doing that, they took matters into their own hands. They presumed on the grace of God. They thought they were above reproach in doing whatever they wanted to do.

In effect, God said to these two brothers, "You cannot presume upon my grace without consequences." Consequently, it is reported, "So fire came out from the presence of the Lord and consumed them and they died before the Lord" (Lev. 10:2).

That still sounds harsh to our sensitive ears. We can understand that they did wrong, but did the punishment fit the crime? To answer that question, it's essential to understand the context in which they lived. We must carefully consider Moses' comment in Lev. 10:3. "This is what the Lord spoke of when he said, Among those who approach me I will show myself holy; in the sight of all the people will I be honored."

Nadab and Abihu insulted the holiness of God! But why was their sin an affront to the holiness of God, while the sin of Eleazar and Ithamar was not? The Old Testament makes a difference between the sins of presumption and the sins of human weakness. According to Numbers 15:30, ". . . anyone who sins defiantly . . . must be cut off from his people." "But a prophet who presumes to speak in my name anything I have not commanded him to say, or a prophet who speaks in the names of other gods must be put to death." (Deut. 18:20).

That may still sound too harsh to us, but we've been conditioned by a different culture. The people who lived in the culture of the time would have agreed that the punishment fit the crime.

Whatever might be said about the propriety of using instrumental music, the practice is not parallel to the sin of Nadab and Abihu. Theirs was a sin of wilful, blatant rebellion against God. They thought they could get away with it and God taught them and the nation of Israel a lesson about tampering with holy things. If instrumental music be a sin, it's more likely that it falls in the category of the sin committed by Eleazar and Ithamar.

116

THE AMALEKITES

The issue of God's justice becomes increasingly more difficult when we ponder the implication of God's command to destroy the nation of Amalek. Through the prophet Samuel, God told King Saul, "I will punish the Amalekites for what they did to Israel when they waylaid them as they came up out of Egypt. Now go attack the Amalekites and totally destroy everything that belongs to them. Do not spare them; put to death men and women, children and infants, cattle and sheep, camels and donkeys" (I Sam. 15:2-3).

If you don't have any questions about God's justice in his dealing with the Amalekites, it's not likely that you'll ever have any. Its sounds as if God were ordering Saul to commit genocide.

Some of our sense of outrage stems from our tendency to view ancient history in the light of our present social structure. In our society we are so sensitized to the life issues that many people think the lives of a certain owl species in the Pacific Northwest are more important than the jobs and livelihood of lumber industry workers and their families. When a serial killer is legally executed in our county, an immediate outcry of cruel and unusual punishment goes up from certain bleeding heart elements, who amazingly enough display absolutely no compassion for the families who suffered the loss of loved ones as a result of the killer's rampage. We seem to be selective in our compassion, but nevertheless a mindset exists in which the thought of exterminating a nation seems morally reprehensible, even if God is the one who orders it.

Our sense of outrage also fails to take into consideration the history of the Amalekites. Their history goes back beyond the time of Abraham (Gen. 14:7). After Moses led the children of Israel into the wilderness, the Amalekites were the first group of people to launch an unprovoked attack on the people of God (Exod. 17:8-15). Throughout the period of the Judges, they were a constant thorn in the side of Israel. It must be remembered that God had promised to bless all nations under the earth through Israel. The hope of human salvation was directly connected with the future of Israel. Amalek had set out to exterminate God's chosen people, thus to thwart God's holy purpose. Their sin was a sustained and impenitent challenge to God.

117

The Amalekites were not a peace-loving people who minded their own business. They were a barbaric and irreverent nation. Many years before Samuel issued the ominous order to destroy Amalek, Moses had said to Joshua,

> Remember what the Amalekites did to you along the way when you came out of Egypt. When you were weary and worn out, they met you on your journey and cut off all who were lagging behind; they had no fear of God. When the Lord your God gives rest from all the enemies around you in the land he is giving you to possess as an inheritance, you shall blot out the memory of Amalek under heaven. Do not forget! (Deut. 25:17-19).

Samuel's statement to Amalek's King Agag indicated the extent of their violence. "As your sword has made women childless, so will your mother be childless among women" (I Sam. 15:33). Amalek had dared to challenge the transcendent God. God will not indefinitely tolerate such rebellion among nations. He judges the nations in time.

Still we haven't dealt with the problem of the children and infants. Most of us probably picture some sweet little Amalekite children who are just learning how to walk and to speak their first few words in the Amalekite language. We visualize the Amalekite warrior coming into his own tent and beaming with a broad smile as his wife says, "Our little boy took his first step today."

I'm sure those things happened, but you must also understand that Amalekite education was training in violence and guerilla warfare. A child growing up in an Amalekite home learned to despise God and to hate Israel, God's chosen nation. To be born Amalekite was to be born into a culture that would resist God. God could only put a stop to it by "blotting out the memory of Amalek." Saul failed to do that and Amalek went on being a resistance force against Israel. Certainly the children at that stage of life were innocent, but God was not declaring eternal judgment against them in their innocence. He was preventing them from growing up in an environment that would most certainly cause them to be lost. Willard Winter asks the question, "Was God cruel in ordering the slaughter of all?" He answers,

118

To allow even the women to continue in such a life would not be mercy. Infants growing up in such a society would have no hope beyond that of a reprobate. God was attempting to work an act of mercy through the sword of Saul.[7]

UZZAH

A friend of mine had gone to Israel to research a book he was writing about the life of David. His guide, a Jewish Christian, drove to the site where it is believed that Uzzah was struck dead for reaching out his hand to steady the ark of the covenant (II Sam. 6:1-11; I Chron. 13:7-11). My friend asked, "How do the Jews explain why God killed Uzzah?" His guide said, "From a Jewish perspective that's not even a proper question. You ask that question because you have assumed that you can tell God what is fair and what is not fair. The appropriate question is not 'Why was Uzzah killed?', but why weren't the rest of us killed too?"

The guide's answer to my friend demonstrates the human tendency to arbitrarily define the limits of justice. Sproul observed, "The basic assumption of Israel is that God's judgments are always according to righteousness."[8] Our basic assumption is that our own basic instincts about justice are correct.

Why did God take the life of Uzzah? Bible scholars offer two plausible explanations. These interpretations hinge on the tribal ancestry of Uzzah. R. C. Sproul represents one school of thought. He assumes that Uzzah was a Levite and observes that among the Levites, the descendants of Kohath, were specifically assigned to care for the holy things in the tabernacle (Num. 4:14). The Kohathites were also given the responsibility of moving the objects which were kept in the tent of meeting. They were specifically forbidden to touch any of the holy things and they were duly warned that death would be the penalty for violation of this directive (Num. 4:15-20). Sproul assumes that Uzzah was a Kohathite. If so, Uzzah knew the precise penalty for his indiscretion. The entire project ignored God's law. The ark was being transported on an ox cart when it should have been carried on the shoulders of four men. Presumably, it was not covered as it should

119

have been to prevent the Kohathites from looking at it. If all this took place, then Uzzah's sin was not the sin of an innocent man. Sproul contended,

It was an act of arrogance, a sin of presumption. Uzzah assumed that his hand was less polluted than the earth. But it wasn't the ground or the mud that would desecrate the ark; it was the touch of man.[9]

Other expositors start with the assumption that Uzzah was not a Kohathite. If so he would have known that only Kohathites were permitted to carry the ark. Willard W. Winter, a proponent of this theory observes,

Uzzah was the son of Abinadab, the man in whose home the ark had been kept. He became overly familiar with sacred things. God had ordained that the Ark should be cared for only by the Kohathites, out of the tribe of Levi. . . . Only the sons of Kohath were to carry these sacred articles of the tabernacle furniture. These directions were not followed by David at all. Had the Ark been carried by Levites, it would not have been sitting on the oxcart in the first place.[10]

It is not necessary to decide between the two alternatives to assert the justice of God. Both point to the fact that Uzzah's sin was high handed and presumptive. Perhaps Sproul has the last word on the matter. "There was no caprice about this act of judgment. There was nothing arbitrary or whimsical about what God did in that moment. But there was something unusual about it."[11]

THE YOUTHS WHO MOCKED ELISHA

In II Kings 2:23-25, the following incident is recorded.

From there Elisha went up to Bethel. As he walked along the road, some youths came out of the town and jeered at him. "Go on up, you baldhead!" they said. "Go on up you baldhead!" He turned around, looked at them and called a curse on them in the name of the LORD. Then two bears came out of the woods and mauled forty-two of the youths. And he went on to Mount Carmel and from there returned to Samaria.

I still recall the time my father told me this story in an attempt to encourage me to show respect for balding men. I suspect that he was motivated by the fact that his own hairline was beginning to recede. He made his point quite effectively; to this day I'm not very comfortable with jokes about baldness.

Still the incident sounds brutal and my father managed to embellish it with sufficient prose to make it sound like God is pretty ill tempered. I think he may have left an erroneous impression on my young mind because he related the story from the King James Version, which reads "children." In my mind I could visualize a kindergarten class out on a picnic. They got a little carried away with silliness as children will do and just about that time they encountered an ill tempered, bald-headed man. One little urchin made a derogatory comment about his bald head and before long, the whole class picked up the chant. Children don't always have a sense of propriety in such situations. While I could concede that they should have been corrected, I couldn't understand why God would bring a couple of bears out of the woods to injure these children.

My mental picture was flawed. They were not cherub-faced kindergarten children who eat milk and cookies, take naps in the afternoon and carry peanut butter and jelly sandwiches to the school picnic. The NIV calls them "youths." The Hebrew literally means "young men."[12] They probably resembled a street gang in Los Angeles more than the afternoon kindergarten class at Sunnyvale School.

The text does not say they were killed; they were "mauled." How badly they were hurt, we have no way of knowing.

Their mistake was that of ridiculing a Man of God. God was not making a special statement of respect for bald-headed men, although such put down humor indeed reveals poor taste. Elisha's baldness just happened to be the focal point of their ridicule. As the anointed prophet of God, he was entitled to a special measure of respect. Those who took God's anointing seriously observed extreme caution when dealing with anyone who had been anointed. David had refused to lay a hand on Saul because he was the Lord's anointed (I Sam. 26:9). In Elisha's case, the Spirit of the Lord has just been given to him when Elijah was taken up into heaven (II Kings 2:11-15). On the heels of that momentous occasion, these reckless young men took the sacred things of God so lightly that they dared to make fun of an anointed prophet. They had shown disrespect against things that are holy.

Throughout the Biblical record there is a consistency in the way God treats desecration of holy things. Smith noted, "This frightening example of God's wrath was no doubt intended to serve as an unforgettable lesson to the new generation which was growing up in contempt of God and true religion."[13]

ANANIAS AND SAPPHIRA

The accounts of instant justice are by no means limited to the Old Testament. As Luke provides the reader with a fast paced, action portrait of a rapidly expanding church, he devotes the first few chapters to chronicling the success of the early Christians. He reports the baptism of 3,000 people on the day of Pentecost, and the spiritual growth of the church as believers were sharing their property and goods with each other. He records external opposition, yet he also notes that God was using persecution as a means of extending the influence of the infant church.

Internally, the church appears to be in good shape as the reader moves into Acts 5. Then, from out of nowhere Luke drops a bomb on us without warning. People are selling their property and laying the money at the apostle's feet. Ananias and Sapphira get all caught up in the drama of these exciting times and sell their property, contributing to the treasury, but holding back some of it for themselves. They inform the apostles that their gift represents the total purchase price of their property. Instant death strikes them both as "Great fear seized the whole church and all who heard about these events" (Acts 5:11).

Throughout this chapter I have insisted that God is not capricious

122

and that he administers his justice evenhandedly. On the surface it appears that the treatment Ananias and Sapphira received was inequitable. Many people have lied about their contribution and have not been punished with immediate death as a result of their false report.

In the first place, it should be pointed out that neither saint nor sinner is guaranteed a certain number of years to be alive on the earth. All of us are just a heartbeat away from eternity and it is only by the mercy of God that we are allowed a continued existence. God was free to terminate their earthly lives at any point in time just as he is free to do the same thing with us.

Another factor to be considered is the way their deaths affected the infant church. God made it clear that we're walking into the severest kind of hazard when we engage in hypocritical behavior. William LaSor has observed,

> They were the first (but not the last) hypocrites in the Church, and God intended it to serve as warning against coming generations. Often in the Scripture, the first event or the first person in a new situation assumes a representative character. To the person who has no certain conviction of Divine Providence, this is often dismissed as some kind of typological fantasy. But some of us believe we see God's purpose: "These things happened to them as a warning, but they were written down for our instruction" (I Cor. 10:11).[14]

CONCLUSION

It is beyond the ability of any human teacher to resolve all the questions concerning the justice of God. We are accountable to God. It is not the other way around. There are mysteries which we cannot resolve with our present understanding. I have endeavored to show through a look at several Biblical events involving God and violence that some degree of plausibility can be discerned even with our limited degree of knowledge.

When my friend visited the alleged spot of Uzzah's demise he learned that he posed the wrong question when he asked, "Why did God kill Uzzah?" He should have been asking why God has been so patient with us in view of the many times we have denied him, rebelled against him and resisted him.

After considering many different facets of God's punitive actions, R. C. Sproul concluded that he could do no better than guess as to why God may have acted so suddenly and violently. He noted that people have a tendency to take grace for granted. Consequently God has occasionally intervened in history to demonstrate his power and justice. He said it seems like God is saying, "Be careful while you enjoy the benefits of my grace. Don't forget my justice. Don't forget the gravity of sin. Remember that I am holy."[15]

Endnotes

1. J.I. Packer, *Knowing God.* (Downers Grove, IL: Intervarsity Press, 1973), p. 136.
2. Paraphrased by Anthony Campolo, *A Reasonable Faith.* (Waco, Texas: Word Books, 1983), p. 136.
3. Ibid.
4. Ibid., Campolo devoted an entire chapter to a discussion of Hobbes and the theory of moral relativity in the light of contemporary social issues. pp. 136-152.
5. C.S. Lewis, *Mere Christianity.* (London: Fontana Books, 1955), pp. 23-24.
6. R.C. Sproul, *The Holiness of God.* (Wheaton, IL: Tyndale House Publishers, 1987), p. 129.
7. Willard W. Winter, *Bible Textbook Series: Studies in Samuel.* (Joplin, Missouri: College Press, 1967, rp 1987), p. 180.
8. Sproul, *The Holiness of God.* p. 135.
9. Ibid., p. 141. Sproul adds, "The earth is an obedient creature. It does what God tells it to do. It brings forth its yield in its season. It obeys the laws of nature that God has established. When the temperature falls to a certain point, the ground freezes. When water is added to the dust, it becomes mud, just as God designed it. The ground does not commit cosmic treason.
10. Winter, *Bible Study Textbook: Studies in Samuel.* p. 419.
11. Sproul, *The Holiness of God.* pp. 141-142.
12. James E. Smith, *Bible Study Textbook: I and II Kings.* (Joplin, Missouri: College Press, 1975, rp 1986), p. 466.
13. Ibid.
14. William Sanford LaSor, *Church Alive.* (Glendale, California: Regal Books, 1972), p. 76.
15. Sproul, *The Holiness of God,* p. 168.

10
Hallowed Be Thy Name

In the sermon on the mount Jesus said, "This is how you should pray: Our Father in heaven, hallowed be your name" (Matt. 6:9). William Barclay suggested, ". . . it is probably true that of all the petitions in the Lord's Prayer, this is the one the meaning of which we would find it most difficult to express."[1] What does it mean to "hallow" the name of God? Why must God's name be hallowed? These questions will occupy our attention in this chapter.

THE MEANING OF NAMES

Names provide identification.

We give people names in order to distinguish them from other people. A name helps to establish a person's uniqueness; it expresses individuality.

A person without a name is without identity. A person's name is closely linked to one's self-image. When I was a high school student, I won first place in the mile run at a district track meet. We didn't subscribe to the local newspaper at home, so I got to school early and eagerly sought the copy which was delivered to my home room every day. I turned to the sports section and learned that somebody named "Dales" won the mile run. My ego was deflated. Didn't the reporter know the difference between a "D" and a "B?" My name had never appeared in the paper more than two or three times in my whole life. To have my name misspelled was disappointing to say the least. That experience helped me to realize that knowing another person's name, spelling and pronouncing it correctly is very important.

If human names mean so much to us, think how much more God's name must mean to him. Jesus said it is to be "hallowed," which means to regard it as holy. Some people in today's world never give a second thought to the name of God. Take the subject of creation. In the name of broad-minded tolerance it has been suggested that we should not be so adamant about insisting on divine creation. Some would try to smooth over the creation/evolution debate by simply saying, "Some call it evolution; others call it God." In the name of tolerance spontaneous generation becomes a substitute for God.

Others would take their tolerance another step farther. They would say "There are many different names that people give to the same God. The Christian and the Jew call him Jehovah. The Moslem calls him Allah. Buddhists recognize him as Buddha." The idea seems to be that all religions have the same source and it really doesn't matter what name you call God.

Perhaps the renaming of God has been taken to its ultimate extreme by some of the militant feminists. They reason that the names we give God are nothing more than mere language symbols. We've assigned various names to God because they communicate our ideals. On that basis, it has been proposed that we change the names of God. They are concerned about the way we address deity. We are urged to reflect the social realities of the contemporary age. One church group has recommended that its members drop the use of masculine based language when describing God. What are these masculine based names? They include, "Father," "Son," "Lord," "King" and "Master." A lectionary put out by the National Council of

Churches in 1983 even calls upon those who use it to address God as "Father and Mother."[2]

In a conference at the Montview Presbyterian Church in Denver, Jean Bolen suggested advancing the gender change to heretofore unthinkable levels. She ". . . encouraged her hearers to offer prayers to such goddesses as Athena, Demeter, Artemis and Aphrodite."[3]

It's true that God does have many names, but they are not just symbols arbitrarily chosen at random by those who worship him. It does matter to God what he is called. The names for God have not been selected by men. They are the product of revelation. His names demand the most profound respect. The Lord guided Moses to "Tell Aaron and his son to treat with respect the sacred offering the Israelites consecrate to me, so they will not profane my holy name" (Lev. 22:2). The nation of Israel was warned, "If you do not carefully follow all the words of this law, which are written in this book, and do not revere this glorious and awesome name – the LORD your God – the LORD will send fearful plagues on you and your descendants, harsh and prolonged disasters, and severe and lengthening illnesses" (Deut. 28:58-59). Through the lips of the prophet Isaiah God instructed the house of Jacob "to keep my name holy" (Isa. 29:23). "He has many names to be sure, but there are some names to which he will not respond. His name is not Baal. He does not answer to Dagon. His attention is not given to the name Buddha."[4]

My given name is Norman. I didn't choose it and I'm not sure I would have chosen it if I had been the one to make the selection. But I've got it and I'm proud of it. My name is so important to me that I'm offended when somebody makes light of it or puts it down. A few years ago I read a set of writers' guidelines from a fiction publisher. He advised aspiring writers not to name any characters Norman. I wanted to know why not. Norman is a noble and respected name. Had the publisher forgotten that it was the Norman conquest which brought us the English language? He wouldn't even have a business had it not been for the Normans in the world. I want my name treated with respect. I barely tolerate "Norm" and there's no way I'm going to put up with "Normie."

If I sound like I'm willing to go to war over my name, that's not quite the way it is. I don't like it when people treat my name as if it were a disease, but I get over it when they do. I even forgave the preacher who said the church must rid itself of "Negative Normans."

If people are sensitive about the misuse of *their* names, think how much more *God* must resent the mistreating of *his holy and exalted name*. One of the ten commandments explicitly said, "You shall not misuse the name of the Lord your God, for the Lord will not hold anyone guiltless who misuses his name" (Exod. 20:7). R. C. Sproul said of God's name,

> His name is sacred, is protected by weighty sanctions and is to be honored. The law requires that His name not be taken in vain. God's names reveal something of his person. His names are important.[5]

Names Indicate Character.

In contemporary society many people accumulate additional names throughout life. A person's appearance, character, personality or occupation may be reflected in these acquired names. We call them nicknames. The practice is so widely accepted that some people are better known for their nicknames than their real names. George Herman Ruth was "Babe;" Paul Bryant answered to "Bear;" and John Wayne was often called "Duke." Sometimes a descriptive title is added to a person's name. Abraham Lincoln was called "The Railsplitter" at one point in his life and later on was thought of as "The Great Emancipator." More recently Ronald Reagan was called "The Great Communicator."

Like most people I've picked up a few nicknames here and there. One of the great advantages of moving to a new city is the privilege of leaving old nicknames behind. Most of them I won't tell you about, but I can remember being called, "Slim" at one point in my life. There are some obvious reasons why that nickname no longer fits. At another period I was called, "Smiley" because I tend to show a lot of teeth when I'm around people. These names expressed something of my nature.

Biblical names express the nature of people even more than names do today. Sometimes people even had their names changed to reflect their character or purpose. The name, "Abram," means

128

exalted father, but Genesis 17:5 describes the time it was changed to "Abraham." "No longer will you be called Abram; your name will be Abraham, for I have made you a father of many nations." "Abraham" means father of many nations.

When Jacob wrestled with the angel he was told, "Your name will no longer be Jacob, but Israel, because you have struggled with God and with men and have overcome" (Gen. 32:28). "Jacob" means supplanter, but "Israel" means "he who struggles with God."

W. L. Walker noted, "Besides designating persons, the name also stands for force, renown, reputation, character gained or expressed."[6] God's character is often indicated by both his personal and descriptive names. Edward Mack said,

> Since the Scriptures of the OT and the NT are essentially for the purposes of revelation and since the Hebrews laid such store by names, we should confidently expect them to make the Divine name a medium of importance. People accustomed by long usage to significant character indication by their own name would regard the names of deity as expressive of his nature.[7]

THE NAMES OF GOD

The scriptures indicate that God has many names. Some of them are proper names – names which can appropriately be used to address God. Others describe him. Both kinds of names reveal to us something of his holy character.

Old Testament Names – Proper Names.
   1. ELOHIM. *Elohim* is the first Biblical name for God (Gen. 1:1). It is also the name which occurs most frequently in the Old Testament. It is used 35 times between Genesis 1:1 and 2:4. It's Greek equivalent, *Theos,* appears about 200 times in the New Testament. W. A. Pratney suggested, "The name's early link with creation gives it a primary meaning as Creator."[8]

Some confusion exists about the name, *Elohim,* because it is plural in its grammatical construction. It can even be translated "gods." In fact the Bible does precisely that when *Elohim* is used to describe

129

pagan deities (See Psa. 96:5; 97:7).

How are we to explain the plural usage of God? Those who subscribe to the evolutionary hypothesis – the view that a monotheistic concept of God slowly evolved in the thinking of the Hebrew people – see *Elohim* as evidence which confirms their theory.

For Biblical believers the evolutionary hypothesis is totally unacceptable. Sproul pointed out,

> There is much at stake here. If it can be shown that the Jewish people were polytheistic like other nations, then the conclusion follows that the early chapters of the Bible reflect human mythology, not divine revelation. If the Bible is ultimately based on mythology, it has no authority to bind us. It becomes an interesting source of primitive religion, but it loses its power to proclaim.[9]

If the evolutionary hypothesis is true, the Bible errs because it claims to be a revelation from God. If the concept of only one God just slowly developed throughout the process of Biblical history, then we do not have revealed religion. Instead we have a humanly developed religion. Again the comments of Sproul are worthy of consideration.

> That the God of Israel is one and that he is the Creator of the whole world is interwoven in the fabric of the Old Testament, so thoroughly that only a vandal with a pair of scissors could crudely rip it out.[10]

To say that plural usage does not indicate polytheism is one thing, to explain what it does mean is something else again. Traditionally, the Christian community has said that *Elohim* encompasses the Trinity. While it may sound convincing to many of us, many Bible scholars, some conservative ones included, aren't buying it. While it is conceded that the plural usage of the name for God allows for the Trinitarian concept of God, many students believe that is unlikely that it would have been the purpose of the Bible writers to vaguely introduce the concept in the early part of Genesis and then never offer any kind of explanation until many centuries had passed.

130

Several scholars have suggested that the plural usage of the term indicates strength.[11] It has been called a "plurality of majesty." Apparently the rules which govern plural usages in Hebrew don't precisely line up with English rules. It is clear that the Old Testament uses *Elohim* when it is intended to apply to a singular Deity. It is used that way in Deut. 6:4, "Hear O Israel the Lord our God is one God." That ought to end any speculation about polytheism.

2. EL. Many of the names for God are derived from *El. Elohim,* in fact, is one of those. Many times *El* is combined with some other word as a compound name for God. In Gen. 35:7, *El Bethel* is the name given to a place, but it means "God of Peace." In the city of Shechem, Jacob set up an altar and called it, *El Elohe Israel,* which means "God of Israel."

El is a word for God that finds common expression in many languages. It's from *El* that Moslems get the term "Allah." The root meaning of the word apparently is "power." One writer describes it as the "numinous divine power that fills men with awe and dread."[12] It is often used in poetic passages and occurs more frequently in Job and Psalms than anywhere else.

3. ADONAI. *Adonai* suggests God's sovereignty. It is frequently translated "Lord." Quite often it is used in connection with "Jehovah" or "Yahweh." *Kyrios* is the Greek equivalent. When it is used in connection with Yahweh in the Old Testament, it ". . . describes God in general as the sovereign of the universe and in particular as the master of mankind, and as the One who has the right to exercise such authority."[13]

4. YAHWEH (Jehovah). "*Yahweh* is the most distinctive name of God."[14] No one knows for sure that it was actually pronounced, *Yahweh.* The word is based on four Hebrew consonants, YHWH (sometimes said to be JHWH or JHVH – hence Jehovah). It was regarded as such a sacred name that some Jews at one point in their history refused to pronounce the name out of regard for its sacredness, which is probably why we don't know how to pronounce it today.

Elohim was a generic name. *Yahweh* was a proper name. The old American Standard Version makes it very easy to determine when this name for God appears. It uses the term "Jehovah" rather consistently. The New International Version employs a different technique,

131

which is explained in the preface,

> In regard to the divine name YHWH, commonly referred to as the *Tetragrammaton*, the translators added the device used in most English versions of rendering that name as "LORD" in capital letters to distinguish it from *Adonai*, another Hebrew word rendered, "Lord," for which small letters are used. Whenever the two names stand together in the Old Testament as a compound name of God, they are rendered, "Sovereign Lord."[15]

A most significant usage of *Yahweh* is recorded in the burning bush incident in Exodus 3.

> Moses said to God, "Suppose I go to the Israelites and say to them, 'The God of your fathers has sent me to you,' and they ask me, 'What is his name?' Then what shall I tell them? God said to Moses, " I am who I am. This is what you are to say to the Israelites: 'I AM has sent me to you.'" God also said to Moses, "Say to the Israelites, 'The LORD, the God of your fathers – the God of Abraham, the God of Isaac, and the God of Jacob – has sent me to you.' This is my name forever, the name by which I am to be remembered from generation to generation" (Exod. 3:13-15).

The name *Yahweh* emphasizes God's self-existence and his eternal nature.

5. CUR. The term means "rock" and occurs most frequently in Old Testament poetry. One such usage is in Psalm 18:46, "The Lord lives! Praise be to the rock! Exalted be God my Savior." Rock is included among the proper names of God because direct praise is offered to the *Rock*. The concept communicated here is that of shelter and protection. Other terms which are used in a similar way include, "fortress," "shield," "light," and "bread."

6. KADOSH YISRAEL. This is one of the compound names of God. It is translated, "Holy One of Israel." The expression appears in Isaiah more than anywhere else. On the one hand it emphasizes God's transcendence, but it also concentrates on the caring relationship that he offers to his people. Berkovitz noted,

The "Holy One of Israel" is the cause of joy and happiness. He is the friend of the poor and the needy; he protects them when they are in trouble. He is the Savior. He is "with thee;" he is "in the midst of thee." He is the One on whom man should rely.[16]

When Sennacherib threatened the city of Jerusalem, God sent a message to Hezekiah, the king of Judah, through Isaiah the prophet. The message declared that Sennacherib had insulted, blasphemed and lifted up his eyes in pride "against the Holy One of Israel" (Isa. 37:23). His insult was repaid when the angel of the Lord put to death 185,000 men in the Assyrian camp.

7. SHADDAI. The name refers to the power of God. The combination form *El Shaddai* occurs 35 times in the Old Testament, 29 in Job. It is translated *Almighty*. "Shaddai . . . does not refer to his creative power, but to his power to supply all His people's needs."[17] *El Shaddai* is the name God used when he established the covenant of circumcision.

When Abraham was ninety-nine years old, the Lord appeared to him and said, 'I am God Almighty, walk before me and be blameless. I will confirm my covenant between me and you and will greatly increase your numbers (Gen. 17:1-2).

Old Testament – Descriptive Names.
One has to be somewhat arbitrary in separating descriptive names from personal names. They are somewhat overlapping. Listed below are some of the more prominent descriptions of God in the Old Testament. Edward Mack's excellent essay on the names of God in the original version of the *International Standard Bible Encyclopedia,* will serve as an outline for this section.

1. ABHIR. The term means "Mighty One." It is always used in connection with Jacob or Israel. Jacob used the term when he blessed his sons (Gen. 49:24). Isaiah uses it to assure the oppressed that God will give them relief (Isa. 1:24).

2. ELYON. This term is translated "Most High." "It is used of persons or things to indicate their elevation of exaltation."[18] It is used in Balaam's prophecy (Num. 24:16), in Moses' song, (Deut 32:8-9) and in David's prayers (Psa. 7:17; 9:2; 21:7).

133

3. GIBBOR. The word means "Mighty." A form of this word is used to describe David's "mighty men." "In like manner the Hebrew thought of his God as fighting for him and easily then this title was applied to God. . . . "[19] David described the King of glory as "The LORD Almighty" (Psa. 24:8).

4. EL ROI. When God spoke to Hagar in the wilderness, the text says, "She gave this name to the Lord who spoke to her: 'You are the God who sees for me, for she said I have now seen the One who sees me" (Gen. 16:13). It literally means the God of vision. It suggests God's omniscience.

5. CADDIK. The term means righteous. Pharaoh used it in connection with *Yahweh* in Exod. 9:27 as he spoke of him as the "Righteous Yahweh." It is also used in Jeremiah 23:6.

6 SABAOTH. The expression means "Lord of Hosts." Isaiah makes frequent use of the expression, "Lord of Hosts." "Hosts" can either refer to heavenly bodies (Gen. 2:1), the armies of Israel (2 Sam. 8:16) or heavenly beings (Psa. 103:21). "It is probable that the title is intended to include all created agencies and beings of which Jeh. is maker and leader."[20] Berkovitz noted, "For Isaiah the 'Lord of hosts' expresses the idea of divine transcendence of elevation above everything that is created."[21]

New Testament Names

The New Testament greatly reduces the number of names by which God is called. Basically there are two names which appear with great frequency in the New Testament. The first is (1) *Theos*, which is usually translated, "God." It is from this term that we get our English word "theology." (2) *Kyrios* is the Greek equivalent of *Adonai*, and most often translated, "Lord."

1. THEOS

All of the terms which involve *El* in the Old Testament are contemplated in the New Testament term, *Theos*. It has been suggested that "In general, NT usage of the name *Theos* takes for granted some familiarity with OT conceptions of the divine Being, whose existence is usually assumed."[22] That's why it's so very important to read the Old Testament. There was no need for the New Testament writers to re-invent the wheel. The nature of the Holy God had been clearly explained in the Old Testament and the rich repository of information about God's character, disclosed through his various names, is still valid for the New Testament reader.

It is important to note that *Theos* is applied to Christ in the New Testament. When Thomas confessed Jesus after his brief period of doubt, he addressed him with both terms of deity. He exclaimed, "My Lord *(Kyrios)* and my God *(Theos)*" (John 20:28). In Romans 9:5, Paul said, "Theirs are the patriarchs and from them is traced the human ancestry of Christ, who is God *(Theos)* over all, forever praised."

Theiotes is a New Testament word closely connected with *Theos.* It is translated various ways. The King James Version translates it "Godhead" in Romans 1:20 and Colossians 2:9. The Revised Standard Version renders it "deity" in both passages. In the American Standard Version it becomes "divinity" in Romans 1:20 and "Godhead" in Colossians 2:9. The New International Version prefers "divine nature" at Romans 1:20 and "deity" at Colossians 2:9. W. E. Vine suggested that *Theiotes* indicates, ". . . the attributes of God, his divine nature and properties."[23] New Testament writers clearly use the term to establish the divinity of Christ. Vine commented on Colossians 2:9, "He was, and is, absolute and perfect God."[24]

2. KYRIOS

In the New Testament *Kyrios* expresses God's control of the creation, but it also becomes the supreme title given to Jesus.

> By referring to Jesus as Lord, the Early Church declared Him as standing above the human level, an object of prayer (Acts 7:59, 60; I Cor. 12:8; 16:22) and trust (Acts 5:14; 9:42; 11:24: cf. also the fourth gospel), sharing with God in his sovereign rule (Acts 2:34), and ultimately sharing with God in his nature. For being conscious that the OT regularly used *kyrios* to designate YHWH, early Christians, even Jewish Christians, nevertheless chose that title as the supreme title to convey their understanding of Jesus. By it therefore, they intended to identify him with the God of the OT.[25]

The concept of "Lordship" suggests authority, sovereignty and mastery. However, for the early Christians, the idea of Lord did not depict an arrogant tyrant. It was their ability to draw near to God through Christ the Lord, which gave the Christians their reason for hope. Paul said, "For I am convinced that neither death nor life, neither angels nor demons, neither present nor the future nor many powers, neither height nor depth nor anything else in all creation, will be able to separate us from the love of God that is in Christ Jesus our *Lord*" (Rom. 8:38-39).

WHY THE NAMES ARE IMPORTANT

It seems like the Bible student is required to wade through a great deal of technical data to study the names of God. Is it worth the effort? Certainly so. The various names of God have revealed much to us about the holy character of God. Although this chapter has not discussed every descriptive and proper name for God in detail, certain truths about God have emerged from this study.

The writer of Hebrews said, "Nothing in all creation is hidden from God's sight. Everything is uncovered and laid bare before the eyes of him to whom we must give account" (Heb. 4:13). From the study of his names, we know a great deal about the nature of the God to whom we must give account.

He is creator of the universe, of every animate and inanimate thing that's in the universe. He's transcendent over all, surpassing every other category of beings in the universe. He's sovereign, master, the one with authority. But he's not just an authoritative deity. He's a compassionate, caring God who uses his unlimited power for the benefit of the people who call on his name. He's authoritative, assertive, approachable and assuring. All of that is suggested by the names that are given to him on the pages of the Bible.

CONCLUSION

In the model prayer Jesus taught the disciples to pray "Hallowed is your name." How do we hallow the name of God? Barclay suggested, it means, "Let God's name be treated differently from all other names; let God's name be given a position which is absolutely unique."[26]

To "hallow" God's name is to treat his name with reverence and respect. That's why it shouldn't be taken in vain. Many people whose speech includes invoking the name of God in profanity, excuse themselves by saying they really don't mean anything by it. That's exactly what's wrong with it. The name of God should never be invoked except for serious purposes.

But there are people who would never think of using profane or vulgar speech, yet they fail to "hallow" the name of God. They simply don't take God seriously in the way they live. They run their lives totally on human energy and employ only human solutions to their problem. When they are facing problems, they don't put their trust in God. Is that not also a serious breech of the command not to take the Lord's name in vain? Which is more serious, using the Lord's name in light and flippant conversation, or failing to take his name with us through our times of deepest trial and heartaches?

> If the name of the Savior is precious to you.
> If his care has been constant and tender and true,
> If the light of his presence has brightened your way,
> O will you not tell of your gladness today.
>
> —Jessie Brown Pounds

Endnotes

1. William Barclay, *The Daily Study Bible: Gospel of Matthew.* Vol. 1. (Edinburgh, Scotland: The Saint Andrew Press, 1956, r.p. 1963), p. 205.

2. Donald G. Bloesch, *The Battle for the Trinity.* (Ann Arbor, Michigan: Vine Books, 1985), p. 3. The author adds, "While discounting these as literal or anthropomorphic deities, she nonetheless accepts them as powerful symbols of creative powers within us all."

3. Ibid. The report was based on a news story which appeared in the *Denver Post* on April 12, 1984.

4. R.C. Sproul, *One Holy Passion.* (Nashville: Thomas Publishers, 1987), p. 171.

5. Ibid., p. 176.

6. W.L. Walker, "Name." *International Standard Bible Encyclopedia,* Vol. II. (Grand Rapids, Michigan: William B. Eerdmans Company, 1929 r.p. 1955), p. 2112.

7. Edward Mack, "God, Names of." *International Standard Bible Encyclopedia.* Vol. II (Grand Rapids, Michigan: William B. Eerdmans Company, 1929; r.p. 1955), p. 1265.

8. W.A. Pratney, *The Nature and Character of God.* (Minneapolis: Bethany House Publishers, 1988), p. 433. Pratney added, "*Elohim* is possessor and ruler of heaven and earth. He who brings light out of darkness, cosmos out of chaos, habitation out of desolation, and life in his image" (p. 434).

9. Sproul, *One Holy Passion.* pp. 177-178.

10. Ibid., p. 178.

11. G.W. Bromiley, "Names of God." *International Standard Bible Encyclopedia.* Vol. II (Grand Rapids, Michigan: William B. Eerdmans Company, 1982), p. 497. Sproul. *One Holy Passion.* p. 178. Mack. s.v. "God, Names of." p. 1265. Mack observed, "It is characteristic that extension, magnitude and dignity as well as actual multiplicity are expressed by the pl."

12. Pratney, *The Nature and Character of God.* p. 435.

13. G.F. Hawthorne, "Lord." *Zondervan Pictorial Bible Encyclopedia.* Vol 3. (Grand Rapids, Michigan: Zondervan Publishing House, 1975, r. p. 1978), p. 959.

14. Mack, "God, Names of," *International Standard Bible Encyclopedia.* Vol. II p. 1266.

15. "Preface" *The New International Version of the Holy Bible.* (Grand Rapids, Michigan: Zondervan Bible Publications, 1978), p. ix.

16. Eliezer Berkovitz, *Man and God. Studies in Biblical Theology.* (Detroit: Wayne State University press, 1969), p. 143.

17. Pratney, *The Nature and Character of God.* p. 436.

18. Mack, "God, Names of." *International Standard Bible Encyclopedia.* Vol. II, p. 1267.

19. Ibid.

20. Ibid, p. 1267.

21. Berkovitz, *Man and God. Studies in Basic Theology.* p. 142.

22. H.B. Kuhn, "God, Names of." *Zondervan Pictorial Bible Encyclopedia.* Vol. II. (Grand Rapids, Michigan: Zondervan Publishing House, 1975. r.p. 1978), p. 764.

23. W.E. Vine, *Expository Dictionary of New Testament Words.* Vol. I. (Old Tappan, New Jersey: Fleming H. Revell Company, 1940, r.p. 1966), p. 329.

24. Ibid.

25. G.F. Hawthorne, "Lord" *Zondervan Pictorial Bible Dictionary.* Vol. III. p. 959.

26. Barclay, *Daily Study Bible. Gospel of Matthew.* Vol. I. p. 205.

11

The Fatherhood of God

A Sunday School teacher observed a young student working feverishly to complete a drawing. Her curiosity was aroused so she asked, "What are you drawing?" He said, "I'm drawing a picture of God." The teacher informed the student, "But Johnny, nobody knows what God looks like." Johnny replied, "They will when I get through."

Most of us have probably wished we could have a picture of God, maybe even a television transmission from heaven with God making himself available for an interview. At times we may be frustrated by our awareness that our picture of God can only be drawn from the inspired pages of the Bible. We see the results of his handiwork in nature, but we can only know of his character and his nature from the revelation of scripture.

Perhaps there are times when we would like the privilege of engaging in a two way, audible conversation with God. You might want to say something like, "Lord, do you really mind if I stay home from church this Sunday? I'm sure you've seen how tall the grass is in the yard; the drain pipe in the bathroom's stopped up and the house is a mess. You know how hard I worked this week. I'm sure you've noticed that I put in fifteen hours of overtime and my in-laws are coming next week to spend two weeks with us. I was just wondering if it might be all right to skip church this one Sunday and take care of my ox-in-the-ditch kind of problems."

You can ask the Lord a question like that, but you cannot expect him to come back with a voice from heaven that says something like, "I've been giving due thought to your request and even though many of your problems stem from poor stewardship of your time, I'm going to relent this one time and let you stay at home. Just don't make a habit of it."

We cannot deal with God on that basis. What we know about God and his will for us is on the pages of the Bible. While it's not possible to sketch a two dimensional picture of God or converse with him on the telephone, we do have some word pictures in the Bible.

The Bible writers used various techniques to enable us to develop powerful mental images of the kind of being that God is. In describing himself God draws from our own experiences. He uses words, names and descriptions which are familiar ones to tell us about himself. Perhaps the most graphic word description in the entire Bible occurs when God reveals himself to us as "Father."[1] The term encompasses God's authority, his protective care and his desire for closeness with people who have been created in his image.

Previous chapters have been devoted to concepts of transcendence. The transcendence concept tends to emphasize the distance between us and God. God is also immanent. Immanence refers to the presence of God in creation. It is through God's immanence that he deals compassionately with the human condition.

A God transcendent, like some consummate painter, adorns with his brush the lilies of the field; but a God who is immanent breathes into the lilies and they become the expression of himself. A God transcendent, like some master-craftsman, fashions the fowls of the air for flight; but God who is immanent lives in every bird, and breaks the eternal silence in their song. A God transcendent, like some mighty sculptor models with his deft hand the human form; but a God who is immanent looks

140

through human eyes, and thinks in the thinking of the human brain.[2]

It is necessary to establish the transcendence of God in order to properly appreciate his holiness, but then if transcendence is not balanced with a sense of immanence, we run the risk of leaving the impression that God is so distant we can never hope to establish a meaningful relationship with him. To dispel that mistaken notion, we now consider him as our Heavenly Father. The Bible does not describe him as the CEO, the Manager, the General, the Commandant. He's our Father. We can believe that we actually are capable of having a family relationship with the Creator of the universe.

THE USE OF FATHER IN RELIGION

Addressing deity as Father is not unique to the Judeo-Christian tradition. It shows up in pagan religions. The Greek god, Zeus, was called the "father of men and gods." The Greek philosophers who came under the influence of Plato spoke of the "fatherhood of God."[3] The Bible writers did not borrow the concept of God's Fatherhood from the pagans, but the concept was not alien to pagan experience.

THE FATHERHOOD OF GOD IN THE OLD TESTAMENT

The Christian use of the Father image is actually derived from the Old Testament. It is a mistake to claim that the Fatherhood of God does not occur in the Old Testament. In fact it has been suggested that "Nowhere is the personhood of God more evident than in his Biblical description as Father." That motif is clearly presented in the Old Testament. Isaiah wrote a significant statement of praise in Isaiah 63:16.

But you are our Father, though Abraham does not know us; or Israel acknowledge us; you, O LORD, are our Father, our Redeemer from of old is your name.

141

In a later portion of the same praise section he wrote, "Yet, O LORD, you are our Father. We are the clay, you are the potter; we are all the work of your hand" (Isa. 64:8). One of the great grace passages appears in the 103rd Psalm.

> As a father has compassion on his children,
> So the Lord has compassion on those who fear him;
> For he knows how we are formed;
> He remembers that we are dust (Psa. 103:14-15).

Even though many references to God as Father are included in the text, the portrait of God, as an intimate and personal parent, is generally missing from the Old Testament literature. God is a Father, but in terms of his personal relationship with individuals, there's still a certain distance.

He is portrayed as Father of the Hebrew nation. God instructed Moses to go before Pharaoh and say, "This is what the LORD says: Israel is my firstborn son" (Exod. 4:22). Through the prophet Hosea, God recalled, "When Israel was a child, I loved him. Out of Egypt I called my son" (Hos. 11:1). God maintained a special father relationship to the kings of Israel. Nathan's message to David included the following assurance. "I will be his father and he will be my son. When he does wrong I will punish him with the rod of men, with floggings inflicted by men" (II Sam. 7:14).

How Israel Benefitted from the Fatherhood of God.
1. Protection. God's relationship with Israel as a Father meant that he would protect Israel. "The LORD your God, who is going before you, will fight for you, as he did for you in Egypt before your very eyes, and in the desert. There you saw how the LORD God carried you, as a father carries his son, all the way you went until you reached this place" (Deut. 1:30-31).
2. Discipline. God's role as a father also involved the discipline of Israel. "Know then in your heart that as a man disciplines his son, so the LORD your God disciplines you" (Deut 8:5).

Israel's Responsibilities.
Although God regarded the nation as his children, he made it clear

that they would experience the blessing of being in his family only if they responded as obedient children. Being the children of God placed Israel under an obligation to be a holy people.

> You are the children of the LORD your God. Do not cut yourselves nor shave the fronts of your head for the dead, for you are a people holy to the LORD your God. Out of all the peoples on the face of the earth, the LORD has chosen you to be his treasured possession (Deut. 14:1-2).

If everything had gone according to plan, the history of Israel would have been a story of unbroken prosperity and happiness, but it didn't happen that way. Israel often forgot the responsibilities that go with being God's children. Isaiah's first message to Israel from God lamented the rebellion of God's children.

> Hear O heavens! Listen, O earth! For the Lord has spoken: I reared children and brought them up, but they have rebelled against me (Isaiah 1:2)

Through the prophet Malachi, God said, "'A son honors his father, and a servant his master. If I am a father, where is the honor due me?' says the LORD Almighty" (Mal. 1:6). Christian parents, whose children have disappointed them, ought to consider the implication of these verses. Even though God himself was a father to Israel, he could not keep the nation entirely faithful to him. Once he granted them the privilege of free moral agency, they were then free to rebel and some of them did. It wasn't that God did anything wrong. Israel failed to behave responsibly. The nation was responsible for its own behavior. Some Christians seem to think that Proverbs 22:6 is an ironclad guarantee that every properly trained child will remain faithful to God from the cradle to the grave. If that were so, then the free moral agency of the child would be circumvented. Do we believe the individual has a free will or not? If God could not control Israel throughout its history, what makes us think we can control our children for an entire lifetime? It's true that many of us make mistakes with our children and sometimes those mistakes do affect the spiritual direction a child takes. But there also comes a time when children are responsible for their own behavior. If God cannot be held responsible for the disobedience of his children then why should Christians be forced to bear some kind of stigma of guilt when their children walk down the wrong path?

God's Continual Love for His Children

Even though God was sorely disappointed with his children, he kept coming back and showing his love to them again and again. In Jeremiah 31:20, God said,

> Is not Ephraim my dear son, the child in whom I delight? Though I often speak against him, I still remember him. Therefore my heart yearns for him; I have great compassion for him.

Hosea's home was a picture of God's compassion for Israel. Hosea had taken a wife who was not faithful to him. She left his home and brought shame to the family. Years later Hosea bought her on the slave market and returned her to his home. Hosea is the champion lover of the Old Testament. But the story of Hosea is more than a tragic tale of Hebrew family life. God's love for Israel was mirrored in Hosea's love for Gomer. God described his love for Israel in Hosea 11:8-9,

> How can I give you up Ephraim? How can I hand you over, Israel? How can I treat you like Admah? How can I make you like Zeboiim? My heart is changed within me; all my compassion is aroused. I will not carry out my fierce anger, nor devastate Ephraim again. For I am God, and not man – The Holy One among you. I will not come in wrath.

Have you ever known a father with a rebellious child? I mean the kind of child that's in constant trouble, maybe even in trouble with the law. And the father keeps going down and bailing the child out of jail, keeps trying to help, keeps showing kindness and gets no appreciation in return. From your position on the outside you can just see that father setting himself up to get hurt. You shake your head and say, "Why does he keep doing it?" You don't understand because you're not the father. Why did God keep blessing Israel even after they rebelled many times? Because he was Israel's Father. According to Isaiah 49:15, his love for his children even exceeded that of a mother's love for her baby. We need to be cautious in criticizing what appears to us to be an over generous expression of parental love for their children, lest we also find ourselves in the unenviable position of criticizing the love of God.

THE FATHERHOOD OF GOD IN THE NEW TESTAMENT

While there is no difference between the God of the Old Testament and the God of the New Testament, there is a difference in emphasis. The holiness of God is emphasized throughout the Old Testament. J. I. Packer observed,

> The whole spirit of Old Testament religion was determined by God's holiness. The constant emphasis was that man, because of his weakness as a creature and his defilement as a sinful creature, must learn to humble himself and be reverent before God. Religion was the "fear of the Lord" – a matter of knowing your own littleness, of confessing your faults and abasing yourself in God's presence, of sheltering thankfully under His promises of mercy and of taking care above all things to avoid presumptuous sins. Again and again it was stressed that man must keep his place, and his distance in the presence of a holy God. This emphasis overshadowed everything else.[5]

There's a shift of emphasis in the New Testament and with this shift in emphasis, more attention is given to the fatherhood of God. Matthew's gospel describes God as Father 44 times. In the writings of John, the fatherhood of God is referred to more than 100 times. Paul makes liberal use of the term. If the holiness of God demands a posture of distance in the Old Testament, the fatherhood of God invites closeness in the New Testament. Paul wrote in Romans 8:15, "For you did not receive a spirit that makes you a slave again to fear, but you received the Spirit of sonship. And by him we cry 'Abba' Father."

A new factor has come in. New Testament believers deal with God as their Father. "Father" is the name by which they call

145

Him. "Father" has now become His covenant name – for the covenant which binds Him to His people now stands revealed as a family covenant. Christians are His children, His own sons and heirs. And the stress of the New Testament is not on the difficulty and danger of drawing near to the holy God, but on the boldness and confidence with which believers may approach Him: a boldness that springs directly from faith in Christ, and from the knowledge of his saving work.[6]

Jesus, the Unique Son

The New Testament reader is made aware of the fact that God has a unique Father relationship with Jesus Christ as his son. Jesus was virgin born, conceived by a special act of the Holy Spirit (Luke 1:35). At his baptism, the Father opened the channels of audible communication and declared, "This is my Son, whom I love, with him I am well pleased" (Matt. 3:17). A similar procedure took place on the mount of transfiguration (Matt. 17:5). Throughout his personal ministry Jesus expressed a consciousness of his unity with the Father. In John 5:19 he said, "I tell you the truth, the Son can do nothing by himself; he can only do what he sees his Father doing, because whatever the Father does the Son also does." When Philip asked Jesus to show them the Father, he responded, "Anyone who has seen me has seen the Father" (John 14:9). In the prayer of John 17 he affirmed his oneness with the Father. He prayed that his disciples might be ". . . one, Father, just as you are in me and I in you . . ." (John 17:21).

Jesus did not come to this earth for the purpose of asserting his unique identification with the Father. There was no need to. From the beginning he enjoyed the position of glorified sonship. In the John 17 prayer he asked, "And now Father glorify me in your presence with the glory I had with you before the world began" (John. 17:5). In order to make his appearance on the earth, Jesus voluntarily relinquished his heavenly privileges. Paul said that even though he was God in his very nature, he "made himself nothing, taking the very nature of a servant, being made in human likeness" (Phil. 2:7).

Christians – God's Children

In the prologue of John's gospel, the writer emphasized the capacity of people to enter into God's family.

146

Yet to all who received him, to those who believed in his name, he gave the right to become the children of God – children born not of natural descent, nor human decision or a husband's will, but born of God (John 1:12-13).

Christ's earthly ministry was begun for the purpose of enabling the people of the earth to enjoy a child – Father relationship with the God of heaven. There is a sense in which every person on the earth can claim God as Father. In the sermon on Mars Hill, Paul said, "For in him we live and move and have our very being. As some of your own poets have said, 'We are his offspring" (Acts 17:28). However, it cannot be said that every person in the world is a child of God in the spiritual sense. Pratney observed,

God does sustain a fatherly relationship to all men because of his creatorship. "He maketh his sun to rise on the evil and on the good and sendeth rain on the just and the unjust" (Matt. 5:45). But to sin is to abandon our true Father's house and to lose ourselves in a foreign land. What we lose in relationship with our Creator can only be restored in redemption by the Savior. Jesus said of the Pharisees, "You are of your father the devil" (John 8:44) and that no man could come to the Father but by him (John 14:6).[7]

The New Testament uses two important metaphors to describe the beginning of our family relationship with God. In one sense of the term we are born into God's family. In John 3:5, Jesus said to Nicodemus, "I tell you the truth, unless a man is born of the water and the Spirit, he cannot enter the kingdom of God."

In Paul's letter to Titus, he employed the birth metaphor. "He saved us through the washing of rebirth and by renewal of the Holy Spirit" (Tit. 3:5). Peter wrote, "For you have been born again, not of perishable seed, but of imperishable, through the living and enduring word of God" (I Pet. 1:23).

The new birth experience takes place when the penitent believer is baptized into Christ. Paul identified it as the beginning point of the new life when he wrote, "Or don't you know that all of us who were baptized into Christ Jesus were baptized into his death? We were therefore buried with him through baptism into death in order that, just as Christ was raised from the dead through the glory of the Father, we too may live a new life" (Rom. 6:3-4).

The other figure of speech is the adoption metaphor. In Ephesians 1:5, Paul wrote, ". . . he predestined us to be adopted as his sons through Christ Jesus in accordance with his pleasure and will." As God's adopted children, we are entitled to the same kind of inheritance that natural children receive. Paul claimed that we have the "full rights of sons" (Gal. 4:5).

WHAT IT MEANS TO HAVE GOD AS FATHER

1. Closeness. Some people have difficulty identifying with God as father because they have negative memories of their earthly Father. Many fathers fail to perform as they should. Some are violent and abusive. Others mistreat their families as the result of chemical dependency. Some fathers are too wrapped up in their careers to provide any kind of meaningful role model for their children. In today's society many fathers are on the road a great deal of the time and serve as father in absentia. It's understandable that people who have grown up with those kinds of negative role models might have difficulty understanding what God has communicated to us by telling us that he is our Father.

On the other hand, even the best father has feet of clay. Perhaps it would help to clarify the picture if we could develop a mental picture of what our fathers might have been like had they been the kind of men they should have been. Actually God is not telling us that he is like any earthly father. He is the ideal Father.[8]

To be able to relate to God as Father means that we are privileged to enjoy closeness with him. The Hebrew writer captured the essence of this blessing when he wrote, "Let us then approach the throne of grace with confidence, so that we may receive mercy and find grace to help us in time of need" (Heb. 4:16). The Aramaic name "Abba" also suggests closeness. In Gal. 4:6, Paul wrote, "Because you are sons, God sent the Spirit of his Son into our hearts, the Spirit who calls out 'Abba' Father." The proof that we are sons comes from the instinctive cry of the heart. In his deepest need, man looks up and cries, "Abba! Father!"

At one time all four of my children lived a great distance from me, but all of them knew that if they had a serious problem they could pick up the phone and call me. In fact it's not even necessary to have a serious problem. Sometimes they call just to share good news. They also know that if they had a real need that required my presence, I would find a way to be on a plane within twenty-four hours to respond to their need. That's the kind of closeness a father has with children. God is willing to respond to us in the same way. He's always right there to hear our prayers and to give us what we need. God may not always give us what we ask. My children have sometimes asked for things I didn't grant, because I thought what they asked wasn't good for them. God does the same thing. He never withholds what we truly need.

To be adopted in the family of God means that we are given the privileges of childhood status without consideration of any merit on our part. We have an adopted son. He has all the same rights and privileges as our natural children. In fact there have been times that the bond has been so close that we had to stop and think about it when somebody asked which one is adopted. We knew that we were going to get Jim before he was born. There are always questions that come up. Some people asked us, "What are you going to do if this child is born with a physical deformity? What are you going to do if he's born with Down's Syndrome?" Our answer was always the same. "We're going to do what we would do if one of our natural children had been born that way." We've made a commitment to that child. He did not have to qualify himself for entrance into the family. As a matter of fact I remember a time when one of our children became angry with Jim over some little disagreement and he said, "You're not really part of our family." My wife, Ann, said, "Oh, yes he is. In fact, he was chosen to be a member of our family. We had to take what we got when you were born." That was the last time we heard that complaint.

The Bible says that "God so loved the world that he gave his one and only Son that whoever believes in him shall not perish but have eternal life." The passage doesn't say that God loved the beautiful people in the world. It doesn't say that God loved the talented people in the world or those with great potential. God loved the world without qualification. He loved us so much that he was willing to adopt us into his family regardless of our background, regardless of the sinfulness of our past and regardless of our abilities and skills.

Let me tell you about a friend, whom I shall call Clarence. Clarence was born with certain mental deficiencies. He has never been able to comprehend an in depth Bible discussion and I would suspect that most sermons probably go right over his head. But Clarence loves the Lord. Many years ago, he surrendered to Jesus, confessed his faith and was baptized for the remission of sins. His devotion to the Lord is apparent to all. I can recall a time when the person who unlocked the church building was always the second person to arrive. Clarence got there first. If Clarence didn't get there first, you could be absolutely certain that something was wrong. Clarence always read his Sunday School lesson, read the Bible every day and led simple prayers. Many times he has passed the Lord's Supper to me. Clarence is getting old and is now spending out his last years in a public care institution. The people who care for his needs just see a mentally deficient old man, but God sees a child whom he adopted into his family and soon He will bring Clarence home to enjoy his fellowship. And the good part is the fact that Clarence will no longer feel disadvantaged by his intellectual shortcomings.

The Father relationship means that God continues to love us even when we've disappointed him as children. Remember what he said to Israel in Hosea 11. "My heart is changed within me. All my compassion is aroused" (8). The compassion that God has for his wayward children is communicated to us most graphically in the parable of the prodigal son in Luke 15. Think of the extremity of love that's displayed in this passionate story. The boy does everything but throw mud in his father's face. He's self-centered, demanding and immoral. He has treated the values of his home with disrespect. But the father never loses his love for the son. He's just waiting for the day when he can see that familiar figure top the horizon. And when the day comes, he doesn't say, "Son, go take a shower and we'll talk." He doesn't say "You're not going to live under my roof unless you meet my conditions." He really didn't need to. The son had already imposed far more severe conditions upon himself than the father would ever impose. The father said, "Get the barbecue pit ready. We're going to have a party."

Our picture of the fatherhood of God is not complete until we recognize that a father has to discipline his children. Remember that God is holy and so are his children. These children are not true to their holy nature unless they are living in holiness. Because we all live in the flesh, discipline is necessary. The Hebrew writer said,

My son, do not make light of the Lord's discipline, And do not lose heart when he rebukes you, because the Lord disciplines those he loves, and he punishes everyone he accepts as a son (Hebrews 12:5)

Discipline is one of the toughest jobs that a parent has to perform. It's difficult to know when you're holding the reins too lightly and when you're cutting a child too much slack, but every responsible child knows that discipline is essential. When my oldest son was two years old, we were living in Houston, Texas. One day he walked to the edge of North Shepherd Drive, one of the busiest streets in that city. When I caught up with him he was not a foot from the cars that were speeding down the street. My disciplinary action was swift and painful. I didn't dust his britches because I had some kind of violent desire to vent my anger on my child. I spanked him so he would associate pain with the experience of walking into traffic. My love for my son dictated disciplinary action. He doesn't hate his father because I gave him a spanking. Now he has children of his own and on occasion he has to assume the same role I did out on North Shepherd Drive that day. God has not abandoned us when he disciplines us through circumstances, through firm people, or perhaps even through our enemies. He's shaping us and making us more responsible members of his family.

CONCLUSION

We still don't know what God looks like. I can't send you to the

151

chalkboard and say, "Now, draw a picture of God." But we do know a great deal more about what our Holy Father is like. He's not just the God who is out there beyond all the boundaries of human experience. As our heavenly father, God is always available to us. Paul said on Mars Hill we can "reach out and find him, though he is not far from each one of us" (Acts 17:27).

Endnotes

1. Many of the names of God are in the form of metaphor and analogy. A metaphor is a figure of speech, which suggests likeness. When the Bible describes God as a "Rock," a metaphor is being used. A metaphor is different from the object to which it is being compared. An analogy, on the other hand bears similarity. Thomas Aquinas once suggested that the nearest we can come to comprehending God is through analogy. Analogy is in the realm of similarity. There is a partial resemblance between the objects being compared. "Father" is an analogy. For an excellent discussion of the use of metaphors, analogies, and symbols in describing God, see Donald G. Bloesch. *The Battle for the Trinity*. Ann Arbor, Michigan: Servant Publication, 1985. Of special interest is his chapter, "The Enigma of God-Language" pp. 13-27. Bloesch responds to the efforts of extreme feminists to change the names by which we recognize God. He contends that metaphors may be changed, but not analogies. He points out, "It is important to understand that it is not we who name God, but it is God who names himself by showing us who he is" (p. 25).

2. George Morrison, "Transcendence and Immanence of God." *Pulpit Helps*. February, 1990, pp. 1, 4.

3. Arthur Wainwright, *The Trinity in the New Testament*. (London: SPCK, 1961), p. 43. quoted by W.A. Pratney, *The Nature and Character of God*. (Minneapolis: Bethany House Publisher, 1988).

3. R.L. Saucy, "God, Doctrine of." *Evangelical Dictionary of Theology*. (Grand Rapids, Michigan: Baker Book House, 1984), p. 461.

5. J.I. Packer, *Knowing God*. (Downers Grove, Illinois: Intervarsity Press, 1973), p. 183.

6. Ibid., pp. 183-184.

7. Pratney, *The Nature and Character of God*. pp. 332-333.

8. William Barclay, *The Daily Study Bible. The Letters to the Galatians and Ephesians*. (Edinburgh: The Saint Andrew Press, 1954, rp. 1965) p. 38.

12
The Glory of God

During the years that I was involved in Christian camp work I used to hear our young people sing the following lyrics:

Rise and Shine
And give God the Glory
Children of the Lord.

The song has simple lyrics which are easily understood. They assume that it is desirable to recognize God's glory. If you've heard the song, you know that it has an upbeat melody and the people who sing it clap their hands at one point in the song. You might be tempted to explain its appeal on the ground that it identifies with a contemporary musical style. However, I'm convinced that there's another reason for the song's popularity among young Christians. Many of them have developed a hunger to know more of God's nature and with that has come a heightened appreciation for the concept of glory.

One of the weaknesses of the Restoration Movement has been its failure to offer extensive instruction concerning the nature of God. Most of our emphasis has been in the direction of the human response to God. Consequently, we know a great deal about God's commands. When we talk about the plan of salvation, the focus is almost entirely on what people do in response to the cross of Christ, but almost never on the saving work of Christ on the cross. When we talk about worship, we concentrate on the appropriate forms for worship, but we give little attention to the God who is the object of that worship.

Such neglect is not ours alone. In the preface to his book, *Your God Is Too Small*, J. B. Phillips said, "Many men and women today are living, often with inner dissatisfaction without any faith in God at all."[1] J. I. Packer complained of a woeful lack of emphasis on the greatness of God among evangelicals.

> We are poles apart from our evangelical forefathers at this point, even when we confess our faith in their words. When you start reading Luther, or Edwards, or Whitefield, though your doctrine may be theirs, you soon find yourself wondering whether you have any acquaintance at all with the mighty God whom they knew so intimately.[2]

For the sake of those of a younger generation, who now show evidence of hungering for knowledge which a previous generation has not seriously desired, we need to peruse the subject of God's glory. The devoted Christian, who is serious about being Biblically correct and is formulating spiritual concepts, needs to know more about the glory of the God who is behind the written message.

WHAT IS GLORY ?

What is "glory?" In the common language of our time, the term "glory" sometimes has a negative connotation. A basketball player who will not pass the ball to another player who is open, so that he might make more baskets himself, may be described as a *glory* hog. Most fans are repelled by such conspicuous attempts to gain notoriety.

154

In every area of life, those who blatantly solicit attention are resented. Dizzy Dean could get away with saying, "If you can do it, it ain't bragging," but most people dislike blowhards. The term "glory" has a negative connotation in that kind of context. Here we're thinking of glory in a way that is far different from the way the word is used in the Bible. Some of the synonyms for our secular use of the term *glory* include, "praise, adulation, prestige and fame."

There are about fifty Hebrew and Greek word forms which are either translated, "glory," "glorify" or "glorious" in the Bible. However, there are two terms, one Hebrew and the other Greek, which are used more than any others.

Kabod

Kabod (pronounced kaw-bode) and other forms of the Hebrew root word *kabed* are used 376 times in the Old Testament.[3] Contextual usage of the term suggests three different aspects of God's character.

1. Sometimes it means "heavy" or "weighty." It's not heavy in the same sense that a ton of lead is heavy. It has more to do with a sense of importance and substance.[4] When the head of a government is forced to make decisions concerning the future welfare of his country, one might say that he has "heavy" responsibilities. It's in that sense that the Hebrew term translated "glory" has the meaning of heavy.

It's often associated with the glory of men. In Genesis 45:13, Joseph said to his brothers, "You must tell my father about all the honor (glory) accorded to me in Egypt and about everything you have seen."

The concept of glory as weight or heaviness is also indicated when describing a person's wealth or substance. The term which is translated glory in other places, is rendered "wealth" in Esther 5:11 as a reference to the status of Haman. The Psalmist warns "Do not be overawed when a man grows rich, when the splendor (glory) of his house increases" (Psa. 49:16). The splendor or glory of Moab is mentioned in Isaiah 16:14.

The Hebrew language used the concept of glory to describe the temple (I Chron. 22:5), the garments of Aaron (Exod. 28:2), the dress and demeanor of a king's daughter (Psa. 45:13) and a regal crown (Job 19:9). Michal used the term in derision when she was offended by David's dancing in II Samuel 6:20.

2. It means military strength and the power of governments. In Isaiah 8:7 the term is used with reference to the armies of Assyria. The author of Proverbs wrote, "A large population is a king's glory" (Prov. 16:28). Isaiah 60:13 speaks of the "glory of Lebanon."

3. It sometimes means brilliance. In Ezekiel's vision of the glory of God, he saw "radiance around him" (Ezek. 1:28). According to Exodus 24:17, "To the Israelites the glory of God looked like a consuming fire on top of the mountain."

Doxa

Doxa is the New Testament term used to communicate the concept of glory. It is also the term the Septuagint translators used to express the meaning of *kabod*. "This word group affords one of the clearest examples of a change in the meaning of a Greek word when it came under the influence of the Bible."[5] In secular Greek, the term meant an opinion. It could range from an opinion that a person was willing to defend, to the way one person evaluated another.

In New Testament usage, the term was stretched out of its original mold. The Septuagint translators chose the word to describe God's revelation of himself.[6] The New Testament continues in the Septuagint tradition.

W. E. Vine suggests that *doxa* is used in four different ways in the New Testament. *1. "DOXA primarily signifies an opinion, estimate and hence the honour resulting from a good opinion."*[7] When the term is used in that context it sometimes describes what God does and how he acts (eg. John. 17:5; Heb. 1:3). *2. It indicates "the character and ways of God as exhibited through Christ to and through believers."* In II Corinthians 3:18, Paul wrote, "And we, who with unveiled faces all reflect the Lord's glory, are all being transformed into his likeness with ever-increasing glory, which comes from the Lord, who is the Spirit." *3. It describes "the state of blessedness into which believers are to enter hereafter through being brought into the likeness of Christ."* In Romans 8:18, Paul said, "I consider that our present sufferings are not worth comparing with the glory that will be revealed in us." Paul even suggested that Christ will "transform our lowly bodies so that they will be like his glorious body" (Phil. 3:21). 4. *It also suggests the idea of brightness.*[8]

WHAT MAKES GOD GLORIOUS

The focus of our current study is on the glory of God. There are two aspects of God's glory that we want to emphasize.

The Visible Expressions of God's Glory.
In coming to grips with the definition of the term *glory,* the concept of visible brilliance keeps occurring. The association with glory and light is frequently presented in scripture. God's glory cannot be adequately considered without studying it.

> God's glory can be a tangible, physically manifested demonstration of light and terrible power, a place where He reveals himself in a divine 'radiation zone' that literally affects and transforms the created objects of matter and energy.[9]

Light has the capacity to reveal, illuminate and expose. It is also a symbol of truth and wisdom. In the Old Testament, the glory of God was frequently displayed in what we today might call a "light show." The Hebrew name for it was the "Shekinah." It's the Shekinah that's referred to when Moses and the children of Israel stood poised on the banks of the Red Sea as they were pursed by the Egyptian armies. After declaring that the children of Israel would see the deliverance of the Lord, the text notes,

> Then the angel of God, who had been traveling in front of Israel's army, withdrew and went behind them. The pillar of cloud also moved in front and stood behind them, coming between the armies of Egypt and Israel. Throughout the night the cloud brought darkness to the one side and light to the other side; so neither went near the other all night long (Exod. 14:19-20).

In Exodus 16:10-11, the cloud is associated with the glory of God.

157

When Moses went up on Sinai, "the glory of the Lord looked like a consuming fire on top of the mountain" (Exod. 24:17). In Exodus 33:18 Moses asked to see a visible demonstration of God's glory. In verses 21 and 22, God told Moses how he would answer the request.

> There is a place near me where you may stand on a rock. When my glory passes by, I will put you in the cleft of the rock and cover you with my hand until I have passed by. Then I will remove my hand and you will see my back, but my face must not be seen.

The text does not describe the precise nature of this exhibition of God's glory. It is safe to assume that it was such a visible, dazzling display of glory that Moses had to be protected from its effects.

The *Shekinah* was present wherever the tabernacle went. "Then the cloud covered the Tent of Meeting, and the glory of the Lord filled the tabernacle. Moses could not enter the Tent of Meeting because the cloud had settled upon it and the glory of the Lord filled the tabernacle" (Exod. 40:34-35). The *Shekinah* was visible in two forms - a cloud by day and a pillar of fire by night (Exod. 40:36-38).

Occasional references to these visible expressions of God's glory appear at various points in the Old Testament. When Solomon built the temple and the ark of the covenant was positioned in the Most Holy Place, this same visible manifestation of God's glory took place. I Kings 8:10-11 provides an account of what happened.

> When the priests withdrew from the Holy Place, the cloud filled the temple of the LORD. And priests could not perform their service because of the cloud, for the glory of the Lord filled his temple.

In II Chronicles7:1 we are given a report of the visible occurrence of God's glory in association with Solomon's prayer at the dedication of the temple. "When Solomon finished praying, fire came down from heaven and consumed the burnt offerings and the sacrifices and the glory of the Lord filled the temple."

Later there came a time when God would discipline his own people through the cruelty of a foreign leader. His name was Nebuchadnezzar, leader of the Babylonians. Habakkuk 1:6 describes them as a "ruthless and impetuous people." They cared nothing for the glory of God. When the Chaldean soldiers came to the temple, they smashed the wall and set fire to everything that would burn. The king "carried to Babylon all the articles from the temple of God, both large and small, and the treasures of the LORD'S temple and the treasures of the king and his officials" (II Chron. 36:18). There was one thing Nebuchadnezzar could not take to Babylon - the Shekinah, the visible presence of the glory of God.

In a prophetic flashback portrait, Ezekiel the prophet, in exile, explained what happened in Ezek. 9 and 10. He saw a man clothed in linen, who apparently was the messenger of destruction. At the end of his gruesome mission he entered the temple where the glory of God was present.

> Then the cherubim were standing on the south side of the temple when the man went in and a cloud filled the inner court. Then the glory of the LORD rose from above the cherubim and moved to the threshold of the temple. The cloud filled the temple, and the court was filled with the radiance of the glory of the LORD (verses 3-4). . . . Then the glory of the LORD departed from over the threshold of the temple and stopped above the cherubim (verse 18).

When the Babylonians dismantled the temple, the visible presence of God's glory was no longer to be seen.

In the New Testament, it appeared again. When the angel of the Lord appeared to the shepherds during their nightwatch "the glory of the Lord shone round them" (Luke 2:9). Light was present at the transfiguration. "His clothes shone like the sun, and his clothes became white as light" (Matt. 17:3). Significantly, the Lord's encounter with Saul of Tarsus on the road to Damascus involved a display of blinding light (Acts 9:3; 22:11).

However in the New Testament the connection between the display of light and the glory of God is not confined to a sight and sound show. The emphasis is on the spiritual concept of Christ as the true light. John described Jesus as "The true light that gives light to every man. . . (John 1:9). John described Jesus with two figures of speech.

159

He is both Word and light at the same time. Because the "Word be-came flesh and lived for awhile among us," John could have said "we have seen light." He actually said, "we have seen his glory." (John 1:14). Peter said something similar in II Peter 1:16-17,

> We did not follow cleverly invented stories when we told you about the power and coming of our Lord Jesus Christ, but we were eye witnesses of his majesty. For he received honor and glory from God the Father when the voice came to him in Ma-jestic Glory, saying, "This is my Son, whom I love; with him I am well pleased."

The Moral Character of God

"The second aspect of God's glory is his worth as an infinite love-ly, pure, and holy person."[10] Although it is true that people are made in God's image (Gen. 1:26) and that we are capable of participating in the divine nature (II Pet. 1:4), there is a measure of God's glory that he does not share with the human race. Paul reminded us that "all have sinned and fall short of the glory of God" (Rom. 3:23).

Isaiah's experience in the throne room of God brought him to an awareness of God's moral excellence (Isa. 6:1-7). He came to the painful realization that "I am a man of unclean lips and I live among a people of unclean lips." Isaiah's feeling of unworthiness was not real-ized at the hands of a manipulative preacher attempting to build a reputation by scaring sinners into coming down the aisle. His feeling of moral inferiority was based on his heightened awareness of God's moral purity. He said, ". . . my eyes have seen the king, the LORD Almighty." It's here that the concept of God's holiness and God's glo-ry merge into one.

Because of his perfect holiness, God cannot allow mere mortals to fully share his glory. In Isaiah 42:8, he said, "I am the LORD; that is my name! I will not give my glory to another or my praise to idols."

In a later chapter, we will deal with the Christian's sanctification. Understanding God's glory in terms of moral excellence is a key ele-ment in developing a holy pattern of living. Paul reminded the Corinthians, "And we, who with unveiled faces all reflect the Lord's glory are being transformed into his likeness with ever increasing glo-ry, which comes from the Lord, who is the Spirit" (II Cor. 3:17-18).

We cannot originate glory. We can only reflect God's greater glory. Pratney observed,

> What is the *essence* of the tragedy of sin and rebellion? Why is sin so bad and human disobedience so disappointing to God? Because he had in his heart so much to share with us; He carried a "pressure of love" when He came unto His own, and His own did not receive him (John 1:9-11). Man's awful failure is that we have all, without exception, become active participants in a world that has broken off friendship with the ultimate lovely Person: "All have sinned and come short (fallen, failed) of the glory of God" (Rom. 3:23). All are "without excuse" because "when they knew God, they did not give him glory as God, neither were thankful . . . changed the glory of the uncorruptible God into an image made like to a corruptible man" (Rom. 1:20).[11]

WHAT DOES GOD'S GLORY MEAN TO US

If we think of glory in human terms, we may end up asking superficial questions such as "Does God have an ego problem?" We have to remember that "glory" in the Biblical sense is not the same thing as "fame" in the earthly sense. He does not actually need us to "rise and shine and give God the glory." He is self-sufficient. "The God who made the world and everything in it is the Lord of heaven and earth and does not live in temples built by hands. And he is not served by human hands, as if he needed anything because he himself gives all men life and breath and everything" (Acts 17:24-25). Pratney sums the matter up well when he says, "God has no intrinsic or extrinsic needs. He is happy in himself and knows fully who He is."[12]

Nevertheless we are urged to glorify God. The church is urged to seek unity "so that with one heart and mouth you may glorify the God and Father of our Lord Jesus Christ" (Rom. 15:6). Glorifying God extends to all of our lives. Paul wrote the church in Corinth, "So whatever you eat or drink or whatever you do, do it all for the glory of God" (I Cor. 10:31).

But how does attempting to live a life that reflects the glory of God benefit the Christian?

Perhaps the most profound way of answering that question is to say that to seek the glory of God is to pursue the inward desire that many of us have for intimate fellowship with him. During our Lord's last hours upon the earth, Philip raised the universal question, "Lord, show us the Father and that will be enough for us" (John 14:8). Philip's inquiry was not wrong. His mistake came in not recognizing the fact that God's nature had been fleshed out for him day by day in the person of Jesus.

As we are able to recognize God's glory and then respond by reflecting his glory in the way we live and think, we approach finding satisfaction for man's deepest questions concerning his origin, purpose and destiny. It is in this respect that I am most impressed with what I see in the current generation of devoted Christian young people. Many of the controversial issues that have preoccupied us in our recent history have had the effect of getting us off track from the business of knowing a glorious God. I see many young people in the church today who neither understand nor care about the issues which have preoccupied us and divided us. They have a tendency to go right to the heart of things. Sometimes I have the feeling that they need to be a little more careful about doctrinal matters, but they have a way of seeing the relationship between God and his people much more clearly than some of us have in the past.

I would also suggest that we need to respond to the glory of God, because it's only in developing fellowship with a glorious God that life's ultimate purpose is clarified. Many philosophers of both the past and the present have been terribly cynical about the purpose of life. J. I. Packer noted,

Once you become aware that the main business that you are here for is to know God, most of life's problems fall into place of their own accord. The world today is full of sufferings from the wasting disease which Albert Camus focused as Absurdism ('life is a bad joke') and from the complaint which we may call Marie Antoinette's fever, since she found the phrase that describes it, ('nothing tastes'). These disorders blight the whole of life; everything becomes at once a problem and a bore, because nothing seems worthwhile.[13]

162

Contemporary society has devised various ways of describing the frustration which characterizes life among people who have not learned to make the glorious God the object of all their hopes and desires. Gail Sheehy's book, *Passages,* was a popular expression of this frustration during the seventies.[14] Sheehy spoke of the frustrations which some women feel when they have invested their entire lives in caring for their husbands and children. The frustration comes in the realization that death awaits them at some point in the future and none of life has been lived in preparation for that event. Anthony Campolo graphically describes their ultimate fate.

> The time comes for each woman to be put into a black hearse, driven out to a cemetery, dropped in a hole, and have dirt thrown into her face. And after it is over, the crowd of mourners will return to the church and eat potato salad and chicken in the fellowship hall. Middle-aged women sense this fate approaching and become increasingly sad.[15]

Such a cynical view of mid-life is understandable among people whose view of life is limited to what takes place between the experiences of what we commonly call birth and death. But according to the Biblical view, the Christian will not only survive death but live in a state of perpetual glory. We have been granted the privilege of participating in the divine nature. The person who basks in God's reflected glory can say, "I consider that our present sufferings are not worth comparing with the glory that will be revealed in us" (Rom. 8:18).

CONCLUSION

During a visit to Yosemite National Park, my wife and I decided to take a bus tour to Glacier Point. On our way up to the 8,000 foot level, the bus driver gave us a geology lecture detailing the naturalistic version of the formation of Yosemite Valley. He proclaimed uniformitarian geological theory as if it were an undisputed fact and left no room for God to have formed this scenic wonder. He announced that he would be available for questions when we reached the top. I was curious about the height of the mountains in the Sierra Nevadas which lie beyond Yosemite, so I asked him about them. He gave me the information I was asking for and said, "It gives you an idea of how insignificant we really are, doesn't it?"

I took the trip to admire scenery, not to engage in theological warfare, but I've since wished that I would have developed some kind of intelligent reply to his remark about our insignificance. I can think of no better one than these words from the hymn, "How Great Thou Art."

> When through the woods and forest glades I wander
> And hear the birds sing sweetly in the trees;
> When I look down from lofty mountain grandeur
> And hear the brook and feel the gentle breeze.
> Then sings my soul my Savior God to thee,
> How Great Thou art.

But that would only negate his claim that Yosemite is the result of natural causes. He said it was a succession of three glaciers, but he never did tell us what caused the glaciers. But if he conceded that God may have been the cause of the glacial action which created the park, he still might be able to get away with the claim that we are insignificant. That's why the last verse of the song is so meaningful.

> When Christ shall come with shout of acclamation
> And take me home, what joy shall fill my heart!
> Then I shall bow in humble adoration
> And there proclaim, My God, how great thou art.

Endnotes

1. J.B. Phillips, *Your God Is Too Small.* (New York, The Macmillan Company, 1961), p. 8.

2. J.I. Packer, *Knowing God.* (Downers Grove, Illinois: Intervarsity Press, 1973), p. 74.

3. W.A. Pratney, *The Nature and Character of God.* (Minneapolis, Minnesota: Bethany House Publishers, 1988), p. 109.

4. M.R. Gordon, "Glory," *Zondervan Pictorial Bible Encyclopedia.* (Grand Rapids, Michigan: Zondervan Publishing House, 1976), Vol. 2; p. 731.

THE GLORY OF GOD

5. S. Aalen, *"Doxa," New International Dictionary of New Testament Theology.* Colin Brown, ed. (Grand Rapids, Michigan: William B. Eerdmans Company, 1971), Vol. 2; p. 44.

6. Ibid., p. 45. Aalen comments, "Behind this new meaning lies the Heb. OT concept of *kabod,* glory, honour. The LXX represents this by *doxa* and gives it essentially the same meaning. When it is used of God, it does not mean God in his essential nature, but the luminous manifestation of his person, his glorious revelation of himself" (p. 45).

7. W.E. Vine, *Expository Dictionary of New Testament Words.* (Old Tappan, New Jersey: Fleming H. Revell, 1940; rp 1966), Vol. 2; p. 153.

8. Ibid.

9. Pratney, *The Nature and Character of God.* p. 115.

10. Ibid.

11. Ibid., p. 116.

12. Ibid., p. 113.

13. J.I. Packer, *Knowing God.* p. 129.

14. See Gail Sheehy, *Passages.* (New York: Bantam Books, 1977).

15. Anthony Campolo, *A Reasonable Faith.* (Waco, Texas: Word Books, 1983), p. 115.

13
Jesus, the Holy One of God

The Old Testament contains primary reference material on the subject of God's holiness. From the summit of Sinai, a holy God declared that Israel, his chosen nation, would be holy (Exod. 19:6). National holiness was inseparably linked to the character of God. He instructed Moses to "Speak to the entire assembly of Israel and say to them, 'be holy because, I the Lord your God, am holy' " (Lev. 19:2). Later Isaiah, the prophet gasped in self-condemnation during his visionary sighting of the throne of God. He was devastated by guilt when he beheld the throne and listened to the melodious chant of the seraphim - "Holy, Holy, Holy is the Lord Almighty, the whole earth is full of his glory" (Isa. 6:3). Most Bible students recognize that the vast majority of Old Testament references to the holiness of God refer either to God, the Father or the Trinity as a whole.

The idea that God has a Son is indeed projected in the Old Testament, but the concept was not fully explained until "the Word became flesh and dwelt for awhile among us" (John 1:14). The careful student

167

of holiness recognizes the fact that the New Testament writers did not often employ the usual words in the holiness vocabulary when they talked about Jesus. The great emphasis is on the third person in the Godhead, the Holy Spirit.[1] This observation is not meant to suggest that the concept of holiness is overlooked in the New Testament or that the idea of holiness is lacking in emphasis. It does, however, suggest that we must look for more subtle indications of our Lord's holiness.

EVIDENCE FOR THE HOLINESS OF JESUS

The Primary Passages Making Use of Hagios and Hosios.
Luke 1:35
   This is the first reference to the holiness of Jesus. When Gabriel announced the birth of Jesus to Mary, he said "The Holy Spirit will come upon you, and the power of the Most High will overshadow you. So the holy one to be born will be called the Son of God." This verse contains enormous implications concerning the needs of the human race. In his pre-existent state Jesus possessed the divine nature and was therefore in possession of the same degree of holiness as God, the Father. He was chosen to enter the world of people through a human birth, but he did not lose his holy status in so doing. Geldenyhus observed,

> The angel in these words does not merely announce that the incarnation of Jesus will take place through the direct influence of the Holy Ghost, but also expressly declares that He who will through Him be begotten as Man will be free from all taint of sin – He will be the Holy One. It was necessary for the Redeemer to be "born of woman" (Gal. iv.4) so that He should be of the same nature as those whom he came to save. But it was just as imperative that He should be perfectly holy since no sinful being can accomplish reconciliation for the sins of others. The angel, as God's messenger emphasizes the glorious fact that both these requirements will be fulfilled in the case of Jesus.[2]

Mark 1:24; Luke 4:34
   In these parallel passages the demonic powers actually admitted

their awareness of our Lord's holy nature. According to Mark's account, a demon-possessed man observed Jesus entering the synagogue and cried out, "What do you want with us, Jesus of Nazareth? Have you come to destroy us? I know who you are - the Holy One of God." It is significant that his position as the "Holy One of God" is so clearly marked out that even the demons recognize it. We should never forget that the demons believe "and shudder" (Jas. 2:19).

John 6:69; Acts 2:27; Acts 3:14; Acts 13:34,35.

At a time when the multitudes were beginning to become disillusioned with Jesus because it became apparent that he had something spiritual in mind, not physical loaves and fishes or reigning over an earthly kingdom, Peter affirmed his belief in Jesus as "the Holy One of God."

The expression, "Holy One of God," usually has messianic implications. In Psalm 16:10, David wrote, "You will not abandon me to the grave, nor will you let your Holy One see decay." In his sermon on Pentecost, Peter quoted from the 16th Psalm and applied it to Jesus (Acts 2:27). In his sermon at the temple, Peter again placed emphasis on his recognition of Jesus as "the Holy and Righteous One" in Acts 3:14. Paul used the same Psalm when he lectured at the synagogue in Acts 13:34,35.

Acts 3:13, 4:27, 30

In these three passages, Jesus is identified as God's "holy servant." Acts 3 gives the record of the healing of a lame man at the entry way to the temple. The miracle produced an astonishing crowd reaction and Peter used it as a bridge to dialogue with the people about Jesus, whom he described as God's glorified servant (13).

Later Peter and John were taken into custody by officers of the Sanhedrin and subsequently released after being warned not to preach in the name of Jesus anymore. They returned to the relative safety of their fellowship with the church and offered prayer. During the course of their prayer, they twice referred to Jesus as the "holy servant" of the "Sovereign Lord." It has been suggested that this use of the term "holy" as applied to Jesus, "significantly identifies Jesus with the Suffering Servant of Isaiah and at the same time asserts his divine Sonship. Both as Servant and Son, he is holy."[3]

When Isaiah the prophet predicted the coming Messiah, he related the "Suffering Servant" concept (Isa. 52:13-53:12). Among the attributes of the Suffering Servant are the following:

1. He acts wisely (52:13).
2. He will be raised, lifted up and exalted (52:13).
3. His appearance will not be desirable in the eyes of many, but kings will shut their mouths because of him (52:14-15).
4. He was despised and rejected by men and familiar with suffering (53:2-3).
5. He bore human infirmities as our sins were placed upon him (53:4-6).
6. Although he was afflicted, he raised no voice of protest (53:7-9).
7. Although it was the Lord's will to crush him, he will find satisfaction (53:10-11).
8. He bore the sins of many transgressors (53:12).

I John 2:20

John wrote, "But you have an anointing from the Holy One, and all of you know the truth." Most commentators believe this anointing or "unction" (KJV) is the Holy Spirit. However, the scriptures portray Jesus, the "Holy One," as the one who does the anointing (John 15:26).

Revelation 3:7

In the Lord's letter to the church at Laodicea he is identified as "him who is holy and true."

The Use of Hagiazo as Applied to Jesus

Hagiazo is usually translated "consecrate," "sanctify" or "make holy." "Its basic connotation is to consecrate or sanctify by contact with the one who alone is holy."[4] It is often used with regard to acts of worship (Matt. 23:19; I Tim. 4:5), with regard to the church (Eph. 5:26) and with reference to the individual Christian (I Cor. 6:11). There are a few references to the sanctification of Jesus in the scriptures.

170

John 10:36

The occasion was the feast of dedication in Jerusalem. The Jews were pressuring him about his identity. In verse 24, they demanded, "How long will you keep us in suspense? If you are the Christ, tell us plainly." He responded that his miracles spoke for him, whereupon they became so enraged that they accused him of blasphemy and threatened to stone him. In verse 36, he identified himself as ". . . the one whom the Father set apart as his very own, and sent into the world."

The *hagaizo* references clearly establish the fact that Jesus possesses holiness in a notably higher degree than the church or individual Christians. In II Peter 3:2, the writers of Old Testament scriptures are described as "the holy prophets," but Jesus is not to be thought of as a holy being on the same plane with the prophets. Jean De Vaux observed,

> The holiness of Christ is . . . of a different order from that . . . of the holy personages of the OT; it is identical with that of God, his Holy Father (Jn 17,11): the same spiritual power, the same prodigious manifestations, the same mysterious profundity; it makes Him love His own even to communicating to them the glory He has received from the Father and even sacrificing himself for them. . . .[5]

John 17:19

John 17 consists of an intercessory prayer that Jesus prayed on the night before his crucifixion. He was praying about the future welfare of his followers. It included a petition for the sanctifying of those who would believe on him. In verse 19 he said, "For them I sanctify myself, that they too may be truly sanctified." If Jesus was already the Son of God, how then could he come to sanctify himself? The answer seems to be that he voluntarily chose to participate in God's program for the redemption of the human race. In verse 24, he said, "Father, I want those you have given me to be with me where I am, and to see my glory, the glory you have given me because you loved me before the creation of the world." Dottie Rambo has poetically captured the thought of Jesus' sanctification of himself,

He left the splendor of heaven,
Knowing His destiny
Was the lonely hill of Golgotha,
There to lay down his life for me.[6]

Hebrews 2:11; 10:10, 14, 29

The writer of Hebrews saw Jesus both as the sanctified one and the one who sanctifies the children of God. In 2:11 he said "Both the one who makes men holy and those who are made holy are of the same family. Jesus is not ashamed to call them brothers." This introduces the possibility of our becoming holy. We have not acquired holiness through our own endeavors. We are made holy by the grace of God and our performance of holiness will always be flawed by our human weakness. Still, in another sense, we are treated as holy persons because we are declared to be positionally holy by one who is holy in all respects. John MacArthur commented,

> From our own perspective and experience, of course, it is difficult to think of ourselves as holy. Sin is too much with us. In thought and practice, we are far from holy. But in the new nature we are perfectly holy. Before God those who are in his Son are holy.[7]

In chapter 10, the sanctifying work of Jesus is contrasted with the attempt to atone for sins through animal sacrifice. "We have been made holy through the sacrifice of the body of Jesus Christ once for all" (10:10). ". . . by one sacrifice he has made perfect forever those who were being made holy" (10:14). It is through the "blood of the covenant that we are sanctified" (10:29). The writer is explaining how Jesus is both the one who is holy and the one who makes men and women holy. It was through the laying down of his life on the cross of Calvary, as a one-time sufficient sacrifice for the entire human race that human sanctification becomes a possibility.

IMPLICATIONS OF CHRIST'S HOLINESS

To regard Jesus as a holy personage on the same level with God the Father implies certain conclusions about his nature and the way we should regard him.

He is Unique.

There are no valid comparisons between the holiness of Jesus and the holiness of any other being in history. He is the only God-man who ever lived. Sometimes people claim to honor Jesus by making statements, like "He was the greatest man who ever lived." The term "greatest" is an adjective of comparison, but Jesus should not be thought of in comparison to important personages. As a leader, he's not to be viewed as a greater leader than Lincoln or Churchill. He's in a class by himself, an incomparable Divine Being. When portraying Jesus as a servant, it would not be appropriate to compare him to Francis of Assisi or Florence Nightingale. Charles Lamb once commented on the unique nature of Jesus when he observed that if Shakespeare were to come back to life and enter the room, we would all rise to shake his hand, but if Jesus were to enter the room, we would all bow down and worship him. That's the difference.[8] It is highly inappropriate to compare him to men and women; contrast is the better communication technique.

His deity makes him unique. Paul said "For in Christ all the fullness of the deity lives in bodily form" (Col. 2:9). His unique birth, his unique mission and his victory over the grave all attest to the fact that he stands alone as a holy personage.

He is Morally and Spiritually Pure.

It is one thing to make the claim that Jesus is uniquely holy, but it is quite another to make a credible defense of that assertion. John R. W. Stott noted, "Now the Christian's conviction about Christ is greatly strengthened by the fact that He did appear to be what he said he was. There is no discrepancy between his words and his deeds."

Stott mentions four ways in which the holy character of Jesus may be discerned.

1. It is discerned in what he thought about himself. Jesus made it clear that he had come to this earth to do the will of the Father. He boldly asserted that he had indeed done precisely that. In John 5:19, he said, ". . . whatever the Father does, the Son does also." On another occasion, he silenced his critics when he challenged them to prove any allegation of sin on his part. "Can any of you prove me guilty of sin?" he asked (John 8:46).

2. It is discerned in what the friends of Jesus said about him. The disciples lived in close proximity to Jesus for about three years. During the course of that time, they exposed their own human frailties and shortcomings, but their consistent reaction to him was a recognition of his sinless life. Peter, who regarded himself as a sinful man, summarized the life of Jesus in the words of the prophet Isaiah. "He committed no sin and no deceit was found in his mouth" (I Pet. 2:22). John was another one of the apostles who was in the inner circle of three. He had access to his most intimate thoughts and saw him in unguarded moments, yet John concluded, "and in him is no sin" (I John 3:5). Stott observed,

> . . . the apostolic testimony to the sinlessness of Jesus is the more credible because it is indirect. They do not set out to establish the truth that He was without sin. Their remarks are asides. They are discussing some other subject, and add almost as a parenthesis a reference to his sinlessness.[10]

3. It is discerned by the comments of his enemies. The enemies of Jesus were constantly looking for flaws in both his teaching and his life. The lawyer who asked Jesus what to do in order to have eternal life was testing him (Luke 10:25). Mark tells of a time when "Some of them were looking for a reason to accuse Jesus, so they watched him closely" (Mark 3:2). Has there ever been a life that was more critically examined?

In the end the best they could do was argue over trivialities like harvesting grain and healing on the Sabbath. When it came time to present their evidence in a court of law, they found nothing that would stand up in court. Pilate told the chief priest, "I find no basis for a charge against this man" (Luke 23:4). Even Pilate's wife said, "Don't have anything to do with this innocent man" (Matt. 27:19). The Roman centurion who witnessed the crucifixion conceded, "Surely, this was a righteous man" (Luke 23:47).

4. It is discerned by our own estimate of Christ. Everything that we know about him is good and pure. No one is damaged in any way

174

by living according to the way he taught. The person who practices his way of life sacrifices for others, makes love the basic principle by which life is lived, practices kindness, serves the needs of others and approaches life as a privilege. Who can fault that? He was a man approved of God who went about doing good.

He is Awesome.

There is a paradox here. On the one hand we are invited to enter into the intimacy of God's fellowship through Christ. It is even possible to "participate in the divine nature" (II Pet. 1:3). Because we have received the Spirit of sonship, we can cry "Abba, Father" (Rom. 8:15) and we are co-heirs with him of God's inheritance (Rom. 8:16). Through Jesus, our high priest, we are permitted to approach the very "throne of grace with confidence, so that we may receive mercy and find grace to help in time of need" (Heb. 4:16). He speaks in our defense when we have sinned (I John 2:1).

On the other hand, those who have been the closest to him, have come away with a feeling of personal distance when they came to understand his holy nature. In the gospel accounts of the life of Jesus, it appears that the disciples only gradually came to realize that they were dealing with the "Holy One of God." At times, they treated him as we would treat any human leader – with a sort of casual respect. They would listen to him. They would follow his directions to a point, but when he began to ask something of them that went against what they thought was conventional wisdom, they argued and resisted.

At these very moments, he broke into their lives with a new and deeper revelation of his nature. It always made them aware of their sinfulness and his holiness. Mark tells of the night when the decision was made to take an evening boat ride across the Sea of Galilee. A storm arose while Jesus was asleep. After a few moments of panic, they woke him up and he calmed the storm. After the storm died down, he rebuked the disciples for their lack of faith. At that point – after the physical danger was gone – Mark says, "They were terrified and asked each other, 'Who is this? Even the winds and the waves obey him!" (Mark 4:41). R. C. Sproul noted, "In the power of Christ they met something more frightening than they ever met in nature. They were in the presence of the holy."[11]

175

Another lake incident demonstrates the kind of distance that a person feels when he begins to recognize that he is dealing with Jesus as "the Holy One." Peter and a group of fellow fishermen were doing some night fishing. They had worked all night and the nets had all been empty. Peter apparently didn't consider Jesus to be much of an expert on fishing, so he only half-heartedly obeyed this carpenter who was trying to tell veteran fishermen how to catch fish. "Master, we've worked hard all night and haven't caught anything. But because you say so, I will let down the nets," was his half-hearted response (Luke 5:5). The catch strained the capacity of their equipment. "When Simon Peter saw this, he fell at Jesus' knees and said, 'Go away from me Lord, for I am a sinful man' " (Luke 5:8). Sproul noted, "Sinful men are not comfortable in the presence of the holy."

Sometimes, in my travels, I have occasion to fly to some distant destination. I have learned that many people don't want to talk to me if I tell them I'm a minister of the gospel. Why does that fear exist? I don't bite and I never have taken a fellow passenger kicking and screaming into the church baptistry. Actually the person who doesn't want to talk to me doesn't really know anything about me. So why doesn't he want to talk with me? There are probably many reasons. Maybe he's been burned by an overzealous soul winner or perhaps he's afraid I'm going to preach to him. He might even be afraid that he'll use some language that will be too coarse for my sensitive ears. In many instances, I'm convinced that my status as a minister of the gospel is threatening because in his mind I represent holiness. I may not be as holy as he thinks I am, but in his mind, that's what I represent. If he can't say three words without using profanity, my presence reminds him that he shouldn't be doing that. He has a little bit of the Isaiah complex. He's thinking "I'm a man of unclean lips and I'm in the presence of someone who reminds me that I have a dirty mouth."

CONCLUSION

All of us – preachers, elders, Bible school teachers, ordinary Christians – are sinful people. If we only think of Jesus as "the friend next to you," then we may well miss the awesomeness of his holiness. To see the holy Jesus is to see that there is a separation between him and us and that line is crossed only in our relationship to him through the blood he shed on the cross.

Endnotes

1. J. Muilenburg postulates possible reasons for the scarcity of references to the holiness of Jesus, "One reason for this may be the large place assumed by the activity of the Holy Spirit in the thought and worship of the early Christians; perhaps, too, other titles and appellations drawn from traditional Messianic phraseology were felt to be more immediately apposite." (J. Muilenburg, "Holiness" *Interpreter's Dictionary of the Bible.* Vol. 2; p. 624.

2. Norval Geldenhuys, *The International Commentary on the New Testament – The Gospel of Luke.* (Grand Rapids, Michigan: Wm. B. Eerdmans Publishing Company, 1979), p. 77.

3. S. Barabas, Holiness." *Zondervan Pictorial Bible Encyclopedia.* (Grand Rapids, Michigan: Zondervan Publishing House, 1975), Vol 3. p. 180.

4. Ibid., p. 179.

5. Jean de Vaux, "Holy" *Dictionary of Biblical Theology.* 2nd ed. (New York: The Seabury Press, 1973), p. 238.

6. Dottie Rambo, "If That Isn't Love." (Nashville, Tennessee: Heartwarming Music Co., 1969).

7. John MacArthur, Jr., *The MacArthur New Testament Commentary – Hebrews.* (Chicago: Moody Bible Institute. 1983), p. 67.

8. Reported by John R.W. Stott, *Basic Christianity.* (Grand Rapids, Michigan: William B. Eerdmans Publishing Company, 1958, r.p. 1966), p. 35. Stott also quotes P. Carnegie Simpson who said, "When one reads his name in a list beginning with Confucius and ending with Goethe we feel it is an offence less against orthodoxy than against decency. Jesus is not one of the group of the world's great. . . . He is not the Great; He is the Only. He is simply Jesus. Nothing could add to that. . . . He is beyond our analyses" (Ibid., pp. 34-35).

9. Ibid., p. 34.

10. Ibid., p. 39.

11. R.C. Sproul, *The Holiness of God.* (Wheaton, Illinois: Tyndale House Publishers, 1987), p. 74.

12. Ibid, p. 79.

14
The Spirit Is Holy

Several years ago Billy Graham visited in the home of the late Karl Barth, a noted Swiss theologian. The two men discussed various theological issues and at one point Graham asked, "Dr. Barth, what do you think will be the next great emphasis in theology?" Without hesitation Barth replied, "The Holy Spirit."[1]

Barth was not a prophet but time has proven that his prediction was on target. Discussion and controversy over the Holy Spirit has absorbed the minds of theologians and Bible students throughout most of the last quarter century.

Much of the discussion has centered on the "Charismatic Renewal" or "Neo-Pentecostal Movement." Charismatics emphasize the miraculous gifts of the Holy Spirit and they insist that supernatural empowerment from the Holy Spirit is still available today, especially the gift of tongues. Earlier in this century the charismatic viewpoint was pretty much confined to traditional Pentecostal churches, but in the last few years, Neo-Pentecostalism has significantly altered the religious landscape. Dissatisfaction with the staleness of traditional religion altered the attendance patterns of many church-going Americans as they left traditional churches in droves. They have identified with churches which, from their point of view, did not attempt to inhibit the activity of the Holy Spirit. Every major religious fellowship has been affected to some degree.

A 1980 Gallup Poll indicates the numerical strength of the charismatic phenomenon. Eighteen per cent of the Roman Catholic population admits to being charismatic; 22 per cent of all Baptists; 18 per cent of the Methodists; 20 per cent of the Lutherans, and 16 per cent of the Presbyterians.[2] No figures are available for the Churches of Christ and Christian Churches, but it is well known that the Restoration Movement has not been exempted from charismatic influences. A few churches openly practice the speaking of tongues in their assemblies, while many members privately hold charismatic views. Others have left the fellowship to identify with groups which are more openly oriented toward Pentecostal practices. In many cases the desire for a more intense experience with the Holy Spirit has overshadowed all other theological concerns.

Without a doubt the charismatic renewal has encouraged people from all kinds of religious backgrounds to engage in a more serious study of the Holy Spirit's personality and work. Unfortunately, much of this emphasis has been concentrated on the supernatural acts of the Holy Spirit, while very little study has been devoted to the personality of the Holy Spirit. Consider the questions that are most frequently asked. Does the Holy Spirit personally dwell within the Christian? Is the Spirit's indwelling confined to the presence of the written word in a Christian's heart? Is the gift of tongues available today? Does modern day revelation take place through the leading of the Spirit? How does one receive the gift of the Spirit? What is the gift of the Spirit? All these are important questions, but they should never be the *first* questions that we ask about the Spirit.

How can we speculate about the Spirit's work if we have no clear concept of the Spirit's identity? While this chapter will not attempt to settle all the questions concerning the Spirit's activity, it will concentrate on the fundamental question of identity. It is absolutely essential to know why the Spirit is said to be *holy*. Charismatics usually don't address that question, but then neither do the traditionalists. The subject of the Spirit's holiness is not a conversational piece for informal living room Bible study groups. Preachers never even get close to it in their pulpits and educational ministers don't include it in the adult Sunday School curriculum. Such neglect is inexcusable among people who seriously follow after holiness.

It is not for nothing that the NT describes him predominantly as the Holy Spirit. This title occurs only three times in the OT (Ps. 51:11; Isa. 63:10,11), but it is found no less than ninety-one times in the NT. In the OT He is usually designated as "the Spirit," "the Spirit of the Lord," or "the Spirit of God." In the NT, he appears as "the Spirit" forty-six times, as the "Spirit of God" eighteen times and as "the Spirit of the Lord," forty-two. The title "Holy Spirit" is by far the most common.[3]

The term *holy* is frequently combined with the term Spirit in the New Testament but *holy* is rarely used to describe either the Father or the Son. It can legitimately be claimed that the New Testament era is the "Age of the Holy Spirit." Such a claim is not meant to reflect negatively on the position of our Holy Father or Jesus, the Holy One of God. It is to say that the Spirit assumes a more visible role in the divine plan of things.

The Holy Spirit has been active since the creation, but during the personal ministry of Jesus, a time was envisioned when the Spirit's activity would increase. "But the Counselor, the Holy Spirit, whom the Father will send in my name will teach you all things and will remind you of everything I have said to you" (John 14:26). His work consists of convicting the world of sin (John 16:8), guiding men and women into all truth (John 16:13) and bringing glory to Christ (John 16:14). Baptized believers are promised the gift of the Holy Spirit (Acts 2:38; Acts 5:32) and some early day Christians were miraculously endowed with supernatural spiritual gifts which enabled them to perform miracles. The Holy Spirit intercedes for us and aids us in prayer (Rom. 8:26). Furthermore we are assured that the written word is inspired by the Holy Spirit (Heb. 3:7; II Pet. 1:20-21).

But why is the Spirit so frequently declared to be holy? The question deserves thoughtful insight. Religionists who get caught up in

181

trying to figure out the extent of the Spirit's activity, without ever pausing to study the holy nature of the Spirit, run the danger of developing a lopsided picture of the third person in the Godhead. Perhaps it will serve a useful purpose among truth seekers, if some of the more popular aspects of the Spirit's work can be set aside temporarily and attention given to the implications of the use of the word, "holy" in connection with the Spirit.

THE HOLY SPIRIT IS GOD

To identify the Spirit as the *Holy* Spirit, is to assert the conviction that the Spirit is a divine being and has all the prerogatives, power, privileges and purposes which belong to Deity. The Biblical evidence for the divinity of the Holy Spirit cannot be successfully denied. Charles Swindoll succinctly stated a fundamental truth concerning the Spirit's identity when he wrote, "The Holy Spirit is not a substitute for God, but He is deity."[4]

1. Old Testament Evidence of the Spirit's Divinity.

The deity of the Spirit is discernible in both the Old and the New Testaments. The concept of deity is openly declared in certain passages while the finer points concerning the nature of the Godhead remain shrouded in mystery in the Old Testament.

> There are no single Old Testament passages which make clear the complete New Testament doctrine of the Trinity and the distinct personality of the Spirit in the full New Testament sense.[5]

The existence of plural persons in the Godhead is implied in Genesis 1:26. Several Old Testament passages suggest a distinction between God and the Spirit of God. The distinction can be seen in Psalm 139. In verse 1, the Psalmist declares his belief in the omniscience of God – "O LORD you have searched me and you know me." In verse 7 that same omniscience is applied to the Spirit, who is associated with the LORD (Yahweh), but is also distinct from him.

"Where can I go from your Spirit? Where can I flee from your presence?"

This same kind of affiliation between God and the Holy Spirit is indicated in Isaiah 63:10, "Yet they have rebelled and grieved his Holy Spirit." In Ezekiel 36:27, God promised, "And I will put my Spirit in you and move you to follow my decrees and be careful to keep my laws."

At other points, the Old Testament indicates that the Spirit engages in the same kind of activity that God engages in, has the same kind of power and exercises the same amount of authority. According to Genesis 1:1, "In the beginning God created the heavens and the earth." Then in verse 2, "the Spirit of God was hovering over the waters." Another indication that the Spirit possesses divine prerogatives comes to light in Nehemiah 9:20, when the people of God celebrated the rebuilding of the Jerusalem wall. In offering praise to God, the Levites said, "You gave your good Spirit to instruct them."

Although the trinitarian concept is not presented in the Old Testament, many passages do harmonize with the doctrine. One example of this is seen in the following statement from the pen of Isaiah. "And now the Sovereign LORD has sent me with his Spirit" (Isa. 48:16). God assured Judah, through the prophet Haggai, "And my Spirit remains among you. Do not fear" (Hag. 2:5). Through Zechariah, he said to Zerubbabel, " 'Not by might, nor by power, but by my Spirit,' says the Almighty" (Zech 4:6).

2. New Testament Evidence for the Holy Spirit's Deity.

The Holy Spirit is clearly identified as deity in the New Testament and the trinitarian concept is assumed. The inclusion of the term *holy* in the various passages which name the Spirit is strong evidence indicating the Spirit's status as a member of the Godhead. Barabas commented,

> The qualitative aspect of the title cannot be overlooked. It implies that the third person of the Trinity shares the holiness of the Godhead. The essential nature of the deity belongs to the Spirit as well as to the Father and the Son.[6]

Although there is no explicit declaration of the Godhead's trinitari-

183

an existence, the concept is unmistakably presented in the New Testament scriptures. Objections to the idea of the Trinity are not usually based on arguments from the Biblical text, except when the disputant wants to make an attempt at disproving the trinitarian idea.

Objections to trinitarian belief are most frequently grounded in philosophical reasoning. To the thinking of Western man, three and one don't add up to the same thing. Those who dispute the Trinity fail to understand the fact that our reasoning process in the Western world has been refined from principles of rhetoric originally taught by the Greek philosopher, Aristotle. It should be pointed out that Aristotelian logic and the teaching of the Bible are not always one and the same. Aristotelian logic is especially deficient when it attempts to explain the God whose nature is not confined to humanly constructed categories.

"For my thoughts are not your thoughts, neither are my ways your ways," declares the LORD. "As the heavens are higher than the earth, so are my ways higher than your ways and my thoughts than your thoughts" (Isa. 55:8-9).

God is God and we are not. He is not required to explain himself in accordance with our demands and on our terms. G. W. Bromiley noted,

Rationalist objections to the Trinity break down on the fact that they insist on interpreting the Creator in terms of the creature, i.e. the unity of God in terms of mathematical unity. More scientifically, the Christian learns to know God from God himself as he has acted for us and attested his action in the Holy Scriptures. He is not surprised if an element of mystery defies ultimate analysis or understanding, for he is only man and God is God. But in the divine word as recorded in the Bible, the one God is self-revealed as Father, Son and Holy Ghost and therefore in true faith he must "acknowledge the glory of the Trinity."[7]

The New Testament offers evidence for the Holy Spirit's place in the Trinity in many different ways. The Holy Spirit is mentioned in connection with the baptism of Jesus. "At that moment, heaven was opened and he saw the Spirit of God descending like a dove and lighting on him" (Matt. 3:16). In the Great Commission Jesus instructed the apostles to ". . . go and make disciples of all nations, baptizing them in the name of the Father, and of the Son and of the Holy Spirit" (Matt. 28:19). In Paul's benediction, given at the end of II Corinthians, he invokes the names of the Trinity – "May the grace of the Lord Jesus Christ, and the love of God, and the fellowship of the Holy Spirit be with you all" (II Cor. 13:14). In the salutation of I Peter, the apostle addresses the letter to those ". . . who have been chosen according the foreknowledge of God the Father, through the sanctifying work of the Spirit, for obedience to Jesus Christ and sprinkling by his blood" (I Pet. 1:2).

The deity of the Holy Spirit is also observed in the fact that the authority of the Holy Spirit is equated with the authority of God in the Scriptures. When the gift of tongues was conferred on the apostles at Pentecost, it was the Spirit who enabled them to speak (Acts 2:4). In Acts 4:8, Peter is said to have been "filled with the Holy Spirit." In Acts 5:3, Ananias was accused of lying to the Holy Spirit. In verse 4, Peter said, "You have not lied to me but to God." Stephen spoke by the Spirit (Acts 6:10). He is said to have been "full of the Holy Spirit" when he saw the glory of God and Jesus standing at the right hand of God" (Acts 7:55). In rehearsing his experience at the household of Corneilus, Peter said, "The Spirit told me to have no hesitation about going to them" (Acts 11:12). At Antioch the Holy Spirit spoke to the church, "Set apart for me Barnabas and Saul for the work to which I have called them" (Acts 13:2). In explaining their position on circumcision during the meeting at Jerusalem, the apostles and elders said "It seemed good to the Holy Spirit and to us not to burden you . . . " (Acts 15:28). Paul and his companions were kept by the Holy Spirit from preaching the word in the province of Asia (Acts 16:6). In his meeting with the Ephesian elders, Paul said that he was " . . . compelled by the Spirit . . . " to go to Jerusalem and that " . . . the Holy Spirit warns me that prison and hardship are facing me" (Acts 20:23). In all these passages the Holy Spirit is assumed to have divine prerogatives. When the Spirit speaks concerning a matter, the issue is considered settled; the Spirit's word is the spiritual supreme court.

THE HOLY SPIRIT IS A HOLY PERSON

Perhaps one of the most convincing indications of the Holy Spirit's status as a member of the Godhead is the New Testament's depiction of the Holy Spirit as a divine person.

It has been suggested that the Holy Spirit is an influence and others prefer to describe the Holy Spirit as a power. A few even equate the Holy Spirit with the written word, but they confuse the identity of the Spirit with the instrument he developed (Eph. 6:17). The Holy Spirit is never an "it" in the Scriptures.[8] Charles Swindoll has observed,

> The Holy Spirit is not a glorified "it." Neither is he merely an influence. He is not a vague and impersonal force and he is far more than the mind, temper or disposition of God or Christ. The Holy Spirit is a divine person.[9]

He added, "Nowhere in any reliable version of the Scriptures is the Spirit of God referred to as an 'it'."[10]

One of the earliest principles of language that a student learns in school is the concept that pronouns take the place of nouns. In our language pronouns may appear as masculine, feminine or neuter. In the scriptures, the pronoun which describes the Holy Spirit is masculine, not neuter. Observe the pronouns in John 16:13-14. "But when *he*, the Spirit of truth is come, *he* will guide you into all truth. *He* will not speak on *his* own; *he* will speak only what *he* hears and *he* will tell you what is yet to come. *He* will bring glory to me by taking what is mine and making it known to you." (I have italicized the pronouns to emphasize how frequently they occur in this text.)

Everything the Bible tells us about the nature and the character of the Spirit suggests personality.

> We see from the Bible that the Holy Spirit has intellect, emotions and will. In addition to this, the Bible ascribes to him acts which we would expect from someone who is not a force, but a real person.[11]

In Garth Black's excellent study of the Holy Spirit, he presents an

186

extensive list of the Holy Spirit's personality traits. The following represents only a portion of these attributes.[12]

1. The Spirit speaks (I Tim. 4:1).
2. The Spirit testifies (John 15:26).
3. The Spirit teaches and reminds (John 14:26).
4. The Spirit guides (John 16:12-13).
5. The Spirit leads and forbids (Acts 16:6-7).
6. The Spirit searches (I Cor. 2:10).
7. The Spirit has a mind (Rom. 8:27).
8. The Spirit has knowledge (I Cor. 2:11).
9. The Spirit expresses love (Rom. 15:30).
10. The Spirit has a will (I Cor. 2:11).
11. The Spirit is capable of goodness (Neh. 9:20).
12. The Spirit can be grieved (Eph. 4:30).
13. The Spirit can be despised (Heb. 10:29).
14. The Spirit can be blasphemed (Matt. 12:30-32).
15. The Spirit can be resisted (Acts 7:51).
16. The Spirit can be lied to (Acts 5:3).

Surely, by now, we can see that the Holy Spirit is to be thought of as a person. The question is what kind of person? He's a *Holy* Spirit. He's referred to with the masculine pronoun, but he's clearly not a man. He's not an angel. So what is he? He is God.

This is evidenced by his work. He was involved in the creation of the world. "Now the earth was formless and empty; darkness was hovering over the surface of the deep and the Spirit of God was hovering over the waters" (Gen. 1:2). The new birth takes place as a result of the activity of the Spirit. Jesus said, "Unless a man is born of the water and the Spirit, he cannot enter into the kingdom of God. Flesh gives birth to flesh, but the Spirit gives birth to Spirit" (John 3:5-6). It is through the power of the Spirit that the Christian is strengthened in the inner being (Eph. 3:16), and becomes capable of resisting temptation. Paul said that we "put to death the misdeeds of the body by the Spirit" (Rom. 8:13).

On top of all that, the Holy Spirit, like God the Father, is without beginning and without end. Hebrews 9:14 calls him "the eternal Spirit." "These attributes and works which are ascribed to the Holy Spirit could only belong to a person. Hence, he is like God and Christ, an individual person."[13]

Why is it important to think of the Holy Spirit as a divine person? It is important because it is only as we come to recognize his personality as a full-fledged member of the Godhead that we maintain the kind of reverence and respect He justly deserves. Billy Graham made an important point when he wrote,

> Of all the essential aspects of deity belonging to the Holy Spirit, we can say of Him exactly what has been said of Jesus Christ in the ancient Nicene Creed; He is very God! So we bow before Him, we worship Him, we accord him every response Scripture requires of our relationship with the almighty God.[14]

HIS HOLINESS SEPARATES HIM FROM EVERY EVIL SPIRIT

John wrote, "Dear friends, do not believe every spirit, but test the spirits to see whether they are from God, because many false prophets have gone out into the world" (I John 4:1). To say that the adjective *holy* identifies the Spirit as a divine being only communicates a part of what the Spirit's holiness is about. There is also a sense in which the Scriptures speak of the Spirit as maintaining a holy *quality* of existence.

Steven Barabas spoke of an "adversative" use of the word *holy*.[15] "Adversative" isn't exactly the kind of word that rolls off the tongue of a person who prefers to communicate only in "shirt sleeve" English. If I knew a good synonym, I would use it here, but the King's English has certain limitations. *Adversative* means to be opposed to. The idea boils down to saying that the Spirit is the opposite of everything that is unholy, profane or defiled.

The Holy Spirit is the antithesis of the demons or the evil spirits. To understand the seriousness of that point, one needs only to examine the texts which explain the mysterious subject of the blasphemy against the Holy Spirit. In Matthew 12:24, the writer of the first gospel tells of the time when Jesus was accused of driving out demons by the power of Satan. One must remember that the demons were evil spirits – willing conspirators of the prince of the power of the air. When Jesus challenged his accusers, he was saying that according to their claims, the Holy Spirit is aligned with the evil spirits. This would place Satan in the position of working against himself. Furthermore, it amounts to blaspheming the Holy Spirit and that sin is more serious than blaspheming the Son. A more severe penalty is also attached (Matt. 12:31).

It is important for the Christian to recognize the holiness of the Spirit because he is our ultimate weapon in the war against the wiles of the devil. We must understand that we are locked in mortal combat with a powerful and vicious enemy. The enemy has enlisted the support of numerous evil agents, known as demons or evil spirits. These representatives of Satan aid him in the life and death struggle that is being fought on a daily basis in the battlefield of human hearts.

Paul reminds us that "our struggle is not against flesh and blood, but against the rulers, against the authorities, against the powers of this dark world and against the spiritual forces of evil in the heavenly realms" (Eph. 6:12). Note particularly that last category of opponents – *"the spiritual forces of evil in the heavenly realms."* On our own we would be powerless against this unholy alliance, but we have access to the Holy Spirit – an even more powerful ally. When Paul describes the Christian battle plan in the famous "Put-on-the-armor-of-God" section, he alludes to the Spirit twice. The Christian warrior is exhorted to use the "sword of the Spirit" (Eph. 6:17) and he is to "pray in the Spirit." (Eph. 6:18).

In I Timothy 4:1, Paul warned about "deceiving spirits." He said they have influence over human teachers. Their influence is so powerful that the teachers become "hypocritical liars." Barabas noted, "Gentile Christians in particular were in danger of not confusing him with other spirits, but at least of not comparing him with these."

Don DeWelt asked,

Are we to understand that those who fall away from the truth do so because they have been influenced by supernatural evil powers? We believe it is even so. Satan has his power and his preachers; and in this sense, he is counterpart as well as counterfeit of the true. The "seducing spirits" are from beneath and are in contact with "lying teachers." The teaching of such men proceeds from and through "demons." The tragedy is not that

189

we have such hypocrites, for they have always been with us, but that multitudes will give heed to their Satan inspired doctrines.[17]

To counteract the deceptiveness of these Satanic influences, the Christian must depend on the resources provided by the Spirit. By becoming completely familiar with the Spirit inspired Word we can recognize the difference between truth and error; identify the line of demarcation between what's right and what's wrong; distinguish between what is moral and what is immoral and see the contrast between the earthly and the spiritual. James was talking about a Holy Spirit inspired message when he wrote, "Therefore get rid of all moral filth and the evil that is so prevalent, and humbly accept the word planted in you, which can save you" (James 1:21). "To refuse to hear the teachings of the Word is to reject the Spirit and refuse his guidance"[18]

The written word can only provide correct information about truth and error. It can encourage us to live the right kind of lives, but it cannot provide the strength necessary for Godly living. That power is provided through the Holy Spirit in us. Paul promised that God will "strengthen you with power through his Spirit in your inner being" (Eph. 3:16). Spiritual strength is a primary and most fundamental need of human nature on its way to God. Without this strength through the indwelling of the Spirit, no one would be able to live the Christian life.

CONCLUSION

It is unfortunate that we have failed to emphasize the Holy in the Holy Spirit. To say the Spirit is Holy is to say that the Spirit is God. It is to say that the Spirit is the antithesis of everything that's evil. According to the Scriptures, the Spirit plays an essential role in both our justification and sanctification. His resources, which enable us to maintain our walk with Christ, are limitless. He is "able to do immeasurably more than all we ask or imagine according to the power that is at work within us" (Eph. 3:20).

What does that mean in practical terms? It means that because the

Spirit is holy, you can handle every adversity, every trial, and every disappointment. Consider the following observation of Charles Swindoll.

> You think you can't handle the lure of temptation. Well you certainly could not if you were all alone. You - alone - can't do that anymore than I can alone. But with the right kind of power put into operation, the very power and presence of God, you can handle it. You can do it. As a matter of fact all the pressure will be shifted and the weight transferred from you to Him. It is a radically different way to live. Because he is God, he can handle it.[20]

Endnotes

1. Billy Graham, *The Holy Spirit.* (Waco, Texas: Word Books, 1978), p. 7.

2. Kenneth S. Kantzer, "The Charismatics Among Us." *Christianity Today.* (February 22, 1980), p. 25.

3. S. Barabas, "Holiness." *Zondervan Pictorial Encyclopedia of the Bible.* (Grand Rapids, Michigan: Zondervan Publishing House, 1975), Vol. 3, p. 181.

4. Charles R. Swindoll, *Growing Deep in the Christian Life.* (Portland, Oregon: Multnomah Press, 1986), p. 179.

5. Garth Black, *The Holy Spirit.* (Abilene, Texas: Biblical Research Press, 1967), p. 10.

6. Barabas, "Holiness" p. 181.

7. G.W. Bromiley, "Trinity." *Evangelical Dictionary of Theology.* p. 1112.

8. "The fact that the Greek noun for spirit (*pnuema*) is neuter need have little bearing on this, no more than, let us say than the fact that the German word for young lady is neuter should cause us to think that a young lady is not of the female sex." Samuel J. Mikolaski, *The Triune God.* (Washington, D.C.: *Christianity Today.* n.d.), p. 16.

9. Garth W. Black, *The Holy Spirit.* p. 6.

10. Swindoll, *Growing Deep in the Christian Life.* p. 178.

11. Graham, *The Holy Spirit.* p. 17.

12. Black, *The Holy Spirit.* p. 6.

13. Ibid.

14. Graham, *The Holy Spirit.* p. 23.

15. Barabas, "Holiness" p. 181.

16. Ibid.

17. Don DeWelt, *Paul's Letters to Timothy and Titus.* (Joplin, Missouri; College Press, 1961), p. 78.

18. Black, *The Holy Spirit.* p. 58.

19. Ibid., p. 69.

20. Swindoll, *Growing Deep in the Christian Life.* p. 180.

15
The Holy Church

The New Testament never speaks of the "Holy Church," but there can be no doubt that the church is holy. We can be as certain about the doctrine of the holiness of the church as we can the substitutionary atonement of Christ, the existence of the Trinity, the necessity of baptism and the finality of the judgment.

The holiness of the church is rarely addressed in any form of Christian teaching. Adult Sunday School literature avoids the subject altogether. It is not a popular topic at seminars, conferences, workshops and lecture programs. Occasionally some authors refer to it in scholarly writings, but when they do so, it receives scant mention. The people who write about holiness normally avoid discussing the holiness of the church in the corporate sense. If the Christians who comprise the church are holy people (See I Cor. 6:11; I Pet. 1:15-16), then it follows that the church itself must be holy.

WHY IT'S IMPORTANT TO CONSIDER
THE HOLINESS OF THE CHURCH

Many people have adopted a "take it or leave it" attitude toward the visible church. An extensive study of American attitudes toward churches was undertaken by the Gallup organization in cooperation with the Princeton Research Center in 1978. According to the poll, 61 million people were regarded as non-churched.[1] The survey also indicated that eight of ten Americans " . . . believe that one can be a good Christian or Jew and not attend any church or synagogue."[2]

If the polls are to be accepted at face value, we are led to the conclusion that the majority of those who stay away from the church have not reached negative conclusions concerning the Christian faith and they hold to conservative values. The Princeton\Gallup survey discovered the following faith commitments among the unchurched.

68 % believe in the Resurrection of Christ.
64 % believe that Jesus Christ is God or the Son of God.
4 of 5 have "made a commitment to Christ."
57 % believe in life after death.
20 % believe the Bible to be an ancient book of fables.
76 % pray.
45 % pray frequently.[3]

These professing Christians who have no time for the church call to mind the college student who was caught up in the "Jesus Movement" of the sixties. He said, "Jesus is my kind of guy, but I loathe the church." Somehow we have failed to communicate the message that those who reject the church have spurned a holy body.

Some treat the church as an object of ridicule. Even members of the church make it the butt of jokes, the object of severest criticism and reduce it to caricature. Somehow we must understand that to make light of the church is to belittle an organism that God has sanctified.

Some leave the church over the slightest offense. The church didn't serve them in the way they thought they should have been served. Its leaders refused to adjust the program to suit their opinions and desires. The members accepted leaders whom the self-appointed critics thought were "the wrong people." Disgruntled members leave in disillusionment hoping to find some other flock that will cater to their whims or perhaps they elect to cease regular church attendance altogether. Those who contemplate dropping out should understand they are leaving God's *holy* church.

THE IMAGES OF THE CHURCH

Perhaps the best place to start a study of the holiness of the church is to consider the various images of the church. Several different words and phrases are used to designate the people of God in the scriptures. There is no official "name" for the church, but each descriptive word or phrase enhances our understanding of its nature. Some of the terms which depict the holiness of the church will be discussed in this chapter.

Church

The term "church" is derived from the Greek term, *kyriakos*, which means "of the Lord."[4] However, *kyriakos* never means "church" in the New Testament. The English translators chose instead the term "church" as the rendering of a different Greek word – *ekklesia*. Although some authorities claim that *ekklesia* refers to a body of people who have been called out, Everett Ferguson notes that "in spite of its root meanings, the word itself does not mean 'called out.'" Essentially, the term *ekklesia* refers to an assembly. It can either mean a secular assembly or a religious assembly.

In the New Testament, *ekklesia* sometimes has reference to the church when it is gathered in an assembly. In I Corinthians 11:18, Paul writes, "I hear that when you come together as a church, there are divisions among you and to some extent I believe it." Paul has reference to the gathered assembly in I Corinthians 14:23 when he says, "So if the whole church comes together. . . ." In verse 34 he says "women must remain silent in the churches." These are references to local assemblies called together at a given point in time. In sending his list of personal salutations in Romans 16, Paul says to "Greet Priscilla and Aquila" in verse 3 and then in verse 5, he said, "Greet also the church that meets at their house." In Colossians 4:15, he writes, "Give my greeting to the brothers at Laodicea, and to Nympha and the church in her house."

There are other occasions when *ekklesia* refers to a local body of Christians. They are the church when they are assembled, but they do not cease being the church when they leave the assembly. When Gentile conversions began to multiply in the early church, "News of this reached the ears of the church at Jerusalem, and they sent Barnabas to Antioch" (Acts 11:22). "Church" here does not mean the gathering of the Christian community into one location at a prescribed time, but it is a way of identifying those who belonged to Christ in Jerusalem. It is precisely this meaning of the term that Paul had in mind when he addressed his letters to "the church of God in Corinth" (I Cor. 1:2), "the churches of Galatia" (Gal. 1:1), and "the church of the Thessalonians in God the Father and the Lord Jesus Christ" (I Thess. 1:1).

The church does indeed become a "called out" body of people in these references. Note how the greeting to the church in Corinth and the one to the church in Thessalonica connects the church to God or Christ. As Ferguson has suggested, "The word has thus early become a technical term in Christian usage of the new people of God in a given locality."[7]

There is also a sense in which *ekklesia* has reference to the universal church. In Ephesians 1:23, "the body" is equated with the church and in 5:23, Christ is declared to be the savior of the body. Consequently, "church" became the word which was used to describe the people of God wherever they might be in the world – the body of the saved. The church is holy because its people maintain a special relationship to God.

The church sustains the same kind of relationship to God in the New Testament that the nation of Israel had with God in the Old Testament period. "The New Testament church is successor to the worshipping community of the Old Covenant and sets its beginnings in its memories and expectations."[8] On several occasions it is actually referred to as "Israel." Paul had the church in mind when he wrote to the Galatians, "Peace and mercy to all who follow this rule, even the Israel of God" (Gal. 6:16).

What kind of nation was Israel? In Exodus 19:6, God instructed

Moses to say "you will be for me a kingdom of priests and a holy nation." In I Peter 2:9, Peter said, "But you are a chosen people, a royal priesthood, a holy nation, a people belonging to God." When Peter described the church in those terms, he borrowed the language of Sinai. The same kind of holiness that God attached to the nation of Israel at Sinai is applied to the church in I Peter 2.

The Building.

The comparison of the church to a physical body is one of the best known New Testament analogies. It was the construction metaphor that Jesus had in mind when he proposed to build the church (Matt 16:18). In I Corinthians 3:9, Paul noted that "we are God's building."

In Ephesians 2:20-22 Paul confirmed the holiness of the church by his use of the building metaphor. He declared that the church is

> built on the foundation of the apostles and prophets, with Christ Jesus himself as the chief cornerstone. In him the whole building is joined together and rises to become a holy temple in the Lord. And in him you too are being built together to become a dwelling in which God lives by his Spirit.

Peter used the building metaphor when he suggested that church members are actually "living stones" in God's building (I Pet. 2:5). His analogy challenges us to make use of our imagination. Have you ever seen a living stone? Stones are made of inert material which cannot move under their own power and lack the capacity to growth. Our culture was subjected to a "pet rock" craze a few years ago, but no one seriously thinks of a stone as having life. Peter simply asked his readers to turn their thoughts inside out and imagine what it would be like to have all the stability of a stone and yet be alive.

The Body of Christ.

The figure of the body, on the other hand, works exactly the opposite way. When Paul wrote, "If one part suffers, every part suffers with it; if one part is honored, every part is honored with it" (I Cor. 12:26), he was tapping into the experience that every person has with their own physical body. He was saying that the church functions

197

the way your body functions and he did not have to explain that the body is a living organism.

In addition to explaining how the church functions and grows, the figure of the body suggests some significant concepts with regard to the church's holiness. "It may be argued that the 'body of Christ' is more than a figure of speech in that it describes a real relationship."[9]

In our day and time, we have a tendency to think of the church as an ecclesiastical bureaucracy, an organized institution with a political structure that maintains its existence. Charles Colson challenges us to rid ourselves of such lifeless thinking about the church.

> . . . biblically the church is an *organism* not an organization – a *movement*, not a monument. It is not part of the community; it is a whole new community; it is not an orderly gathering; it is a new order with new values often in conflict with the values of surrounding society.[10]

But the church is not just *a* body, it is *the* body of Christ (Eph. 1:22-23; 5:23; Col. 1:18, 24). Christ is the head of the body, which means that he is both its life source and its ruler. Just as there can be no human life when the head is severed from the body, neither can there be any Christian life apart from Christ's body, the church. As members of the body, we share a unique oneness with Christ. "The body is a unit, though it is made up of many parts; and though all its parts are many, they form one body. So it is with Christ" (I Cor. 12:12). "Paul uses the metaphor of the body to express the oneness of the church with her Lord."[11]

The implications for the holiness of the church from the figure of the body are enormous. W. E. Vine pointed out,

> An essential truth laid down in this first chapter (of Ephesians), amplified in the course of the Epistle, and conveyed in the symbolism of the head and the body is that the Church, instead of being an earthly organization built up and established in the world is heavenly in its design, establishment and destiny. Its individual members necessarily become incorporated into it in this life, according as each one received eternal life through faith in Christ and is born of God.[12]

If the church is to be identified with Jesus as closely as a human head is identified with its body, it must share the holiness of Jesus. There is simply no way that Christ can be "the Holy one of God" (Mark 1:24) while his body remains unholy. The Hebrew writer insisted "Both the one who makes men holy and those who are made holy are of the same family" (Heb. 2:11).

The Bride of Christ

In several places, the New Testament employs the use of the bride and bridegroom metaphor to make a spiritual point. John the Baptist spoke along the lines when he introduced Jesus. He said in John 3:28-30, "You yourselves can testify that I said, 'I am not the Christ, but am sent ahead of him. The bride belongs to the bridegroom. The friend who attends the bridegroom waits and listens for him, and is full of joy when he hears the bridegroom's voice. That joy is mine, and it is now complete. He must become greater; I must become less."

In Romans 7:4, Paul wrote, "So, my brothers, you also died to the law through the body of Christ that you might belong to another. . ." (KJV "married to another"). In II Corinthians 11:2, Paul said, "I am jealous for you with a godly jealousy. I promised you to one husband, to Christ, so that I might present you as a pure virgin to him." The wedding metaphor appears in Revelation 21:2, when John wrote, "I saw the Holy City, the new Jerusalem, coming down out of heaven from God, prepared as a bride beautifully dressed for her husband." It occurs in Revelation 22:17, "The Spirit and the bride say, 'Come!' And let him who hears say 'Come!' Whoever is thirsty, let him come; and whoever wishes, let him take the free gift of the water of life."

The allusion to the church as the bride of Christ occurs in Ephesians 5:22-33. Paul alternates between discussing husbands and wives and Christ and the church. He also intertwines the subjects together, although he says in verse 32, "This is a profound mystery, but I am talking about Christ and the church." In the midst of a series of admonitions directed to Christian husbands and wives, Paul spoke of the relationship between Christ and the church. Notice especially verses 25-27.

Husbands, love your wives, just as Christ loved the church and gave himself up for her to make her holy, cleansing her by washing with water through the word, and to present her to himself as a radiant church, without stain or wrinkle or any other blemish, but holy and blameless.

"It is in keeping with the New Testament perspective which affirms both a 'now' and a 'not yet' that the bride of Christ is presented to Christ at baptism in Ephesians 5:26f., but from another standpoint is not thought of as being presented to him until the end of time (Rev. 19:7-8; 21:2)."[13]

Paul may have been thinking about the Greek wedding customs when he spoke of the church being cleansed by "washing with water." A Greek bride was bathed in a stream which was thought to be sacred before she was taken to the wedding. This sacred water was thought to cleanse her from any impurity.[14]

Most scholars agree that the "washing of water" is an allusion to baptism. "The 'word' which accompanies the washing with water is probably the confession of faith."[15] This fits exceptionally well with the Hebrew writer's thought in Hebrews 10:22-23, "Let us draw near to God with a sincere heart in full assurance of faith having our hearts sprinkled to cleanse us from a guilty conscience and having our bodies washed with pure water. Let us hold unswervingly to the hope we profess, for he who promised is faithful."

Even if we are unable to formulate satisfactory solutions to the technical difficulties in these verses, the main thing for us to see is that the figure of the bride concentrates on the purity and the holiness of the church. Paul refers to the holy nature of the church twice in these two verses.

THE PRESENT HOLINESS OF THE CHURCH

While there is a sense in which the church will never be holy until we reach the close of the age, holiness is also presented in the New Testament as a present reality. The church is holy because of the relationship it sustains to Christ. It is made holy through the process of grace even though many imperfections still exist within its fellowship.

Christ Makes it a Holy Church.

The images of the church which were considered in the previous section of the chapter all indicate that the church sustains an intimate relationship with Christ. The church is not to be thought of as a club for Christians. It was not organized by a group of people who decided to start a movement because they liked some of the things they heard Jesus say. The church has always been in the plan of God. Paul wrote "His intent was that now, through the church, the manifold wisdom of God should be made known to the rulers and authorities in the heavenly realms, according to his eternal purpose which he accomplished in Christ Jesus our Lord" (Eph. 3:10-11). "The church then was decreed from eternity and destined for eternity."[16]

The church was designed and planned by Jesus. In the region of Caesarea Philippi he promised, "I will build my church and the gates of Hades will not overcome it" (Matt. 16:18). It is presented as a blood-bought entity in Acts 20:28. Paul reminded the Corinthians in I Corinthians 6:20, "you were bought with a price."

Sustained Through the Power of the Holy Spirit.

Jesus sent the Holy Spirit to empower the church. He made several promises along this line just prior to his death on the cross. In John 14:26, he said, "But the Counselor, the Holy Spirit, whom the Father will send in my name, will teach you all things and will remind you of everything I have said to you." In the next chapter he said, "When the Counselor comes, whom I will send to you from the Father, the Spirit of truth who goes out from the Father, he will testify about me"(John 15:26). In John 16:7, he said, "But I tell you the truth: It is for your own good that I am going away. Unless I go away, the Counselor will not come to you; but if I go I will send him to you."

The church is the beneficiary of the Spirit's power and is made up of people who have received the gift of the Holy Spirit (Acts 2:38; 5:32). God has poured his love into the hearts of the church's members by the Holy Spirit (Rom. 5:5). Members of the body are enabled to gain victory over our fleshly nature by the Spirit (Rom. 8:13). Our prayers are assisted by the Holy Spirit according to Romans 8:26-27 and members of the church are marked in Christ with the seal of the Holy Spirit, possessing the Spirit as an earnest or deposit of our eter-

201

nal inheritance according to Ephesians1:12-13.

These divine resources are not made available to any kind of secular body. They are present only in the church where holiness is the standard.

The Presence of Weakness in the Church Does Not Make it Unholy.

Paul addressed his first letter to the church in Corinth "to those sanctified in Christ Jesus and called to be holy" (I Cor. 6:11). He reminded his readers of their position before God as holy people in I Corinthians 6:11, "But you were washed, you were sanctified, you were justified in the name of the Lord Jesus Christ and by the Spirit of our God."

It doesn't take a Rhodes scholar to figure out that some unholy things went on among the members of the Corinthian church. There was quarreling in the church (I Cor. 1:10; 3:3), sexual immorality (I Cor. 5:1), brother going to law against brother in the secular courts (I Cor. 6:1-2), divorce (I Cor 7), insensitivity (I Cor. 8), abuses of the Lord's Supper (I Cor. 11:17-22) and other sins. The unholy actions of certain people in the church did not, however, render the church unholy in the corporate sense.

There does seem to be a point at which God will reject a local church for its refusal to conform to his will. In the seven letters to the churches of Asia (Rev. 2 and 3), many of the churches were told "I have a few things against you." Of all seven churches only the churches in Ephesus and Laodicea were threatened with expulsion from God's favor. The church at Ephesus was warned, "If you do not repent, I will come and remove your lampstand from its place" (Rev. 2:5). Laodicea was told, "I am about to spit you out of my mouth" (Rev. 3:16). God threatened disciplinary action against guilty parties in other churches, but only at Ephesus and Laodicea did he contemplate corporate rejection.

Many attempts have been made to reconcile the disparity between the church being regarded as holy in principle and yet finding itself engaging in unholy actions in practice. From time to time certain groups make the claim that theirs is the only pure and holy church. Their solution to the lack of holiness in the church is to withhold fellowship from those who fail to measure up to their standards, while insisting that they alone constitute the pure and undiluted church. This approach is faulty on two grounds. First, those who insist they have an "exclusive franchised dealership" for God have assumed the prerogatives which belong to God alone. God is the final judge of the human condition. For any human to assume that role is to presume that he has total and complete knowledge of God's will, and that he has been privileged to know just exactly how God is going to judge the world. Such a person forgets that God alone is responsible for the final determination of the spiritual condition of people.

Second, those who think they are the only holy people in the world have over-estimated their own strength. No one is completely holy in terms of our actual practice. John wrote, "If we claim to be without sin, we deceive ourselves and the truth is not in us" (I John 1:8). John was a great apostle, whom we believe to have been about 100 years of age at this time. He had walked and talked with Jesus and lived a life of commendable faithfulness, but even a man as exemplary as John still continued to commit acts of sin.

Others have sought to explain the difficulty by claiming that the members of the church are sinful, but the church itself is holy. We have to understand the truth that the church does not exist as some kind of abstract, ethereal entity. The church is made up of people – the people of God. To the extent that the people of God are lacking in holiness, the church is lacking in holiness.

It is best to see the church the same way we see individual Christians. We occupy a position of holiness by the grace of God even though we do not always practice actual holiness.

OUR RESPONSE TO THE CALL TO BE HOLY

Grace should never become an excuse for us to be lax in our pursuit of holiness. The church – the corporate body of believers – is called on to make the development of holiness a priority item on its spiritual agenda.

Paul expressed concern that the church might forget its position as the bride of Christ. He wrote, "But I am afraid that just as Eve was deceived by the serpent's cunning, your minds may somehow be led astray from your sincere and pure devotion to Christ" (2 Cor. 11:3). When the bride forsakes the wedding vows, the result is physical adultery. It is only as the church pursues the agenda of holiness that it is kept from being a spiritually adulterous bride. Francis Schaeffer observed,

> No one is perfect. None of us is totally faithful to our divine bridegroom. We are all weak. Many times we are unfaithful in a positive or a negative way in our thoughts and actions. But the scripture makes a clear distinction between the imperfection of all Christians and the spiritual adultery which results when those who claim to be God's people stop listening to what God has said and turn to other gods.[17]

While we enjoy a position of holiness, by the grace of God, it is clearly God's will for us to pursue the practice of holiness in both the corporate life of the church and in the private lives of individual Christians. It must be pointed out that the holy brethren in Corinth were also encouraged to engage themselves in an active program of holiness development. "Since we have these promises, dear friends, let us purify ourselves from everything that contaminates body and spirit, perfecting holiness out of reverence for God" (II Cor. 7:1). How do we go about living up to that challenge?

It Calls for a Life of Separation.

We live in an era when the line that separates right and wrong, truth and error often gets blurred. We're better educated and more sophisticated that we used to be. We have learned that some of our ideas about right and wrong were nothing more than biased traditions. We need to get rid of our legalism, our provincialism and our opinionated standards of right and wrong. But we can also throw the baby out with the bath water. Peter warned, "Live as free men, but do not use your freedom as a cover up for evil" (I Pet. 2:16).

The holy life is a life of separation. Paul warned of forming unequal yokes with unbelievers in II Corinthians 6:14. The passage has often been used to warn against the danger of marrying an unbeliever. Certainly, there have been many times when a person's spiritual desire was squashed by an unbelieving spouse, but the unequal yoke is not exclusively applied to marriage. In fact Paul doesn't mention marriage anywhere in the context. The unequal yoke refers to any association, any commitment, any involvement with unbelievers that threatens to destroy your devotion to God.

Christians are different. We are called to live on a higher plane from the rest of the world. "'Therefore come out from them and be separate' says the Lord" (II Cor. 6:17). Many Christians live in circumstances in which the pressure to conform to an ungodly environment is extremely strong. They may have little or no control over being placed in that environment. A Christian teenager may live in the home of unbelieving parents. A young man may be thrust among secular companions as he serves his country in military service. It's often necessary to work among non-Christian people in order to make a living for one's family. It is not possible to leave the world and God doesn't want us to. In his intercessory prayer to the Father on the night before his crucifixion, Jesus said, "My prayer is not that you take them out of the world but that you protect them from the evil one. They are not of the world, even as I am not of it. Sanctify them by the truth; your word is truth" (John 17:16-18).

We must realize that we are engaged in spiritual warfare with the agents of Satan. Through the avenue of temptation, God's holy people are going to be pressured to abandon the faith. "Unless the Christian is prepared for such evil assaults on his mind and heart, he will have great difficulty maintaining personal holiness."[18]

It Calls for a Commitment to Purity and Love.

Francis Schaeffer was adamant in his claim that "the church must be known simultaneously for its purity of doctrine and the reality of its community."[19] The church cannot afford to slack off in its pursuit of sound doctrine and ethical behavior. When Paul wrote to Timothy in Ephesus, doctrinal soundness was in jeopardy. Thus he felt compelled to warn his young protege, "Watch your life and doctrine closely. Persevere in them, because if you do, you will save both yourself and your hearers" (I Tim. 4:16).

Peter warned Christians who were struggling under the pressure of persecution to give attention to their ethical conduct. He said, "If you suffer, it should not be as a murderer or a thief or any other kind of criminal, or even as a meddler" (I Pet. 4:15). But their resistance to a hostile world was not to be from a posture of bitterness and rancor. It was important for them to remain sweet spirited. He wrote, "Finally, all of you, live in harmony with one another; be sympathetic, love as brothers, be compassionate and humble. Do not repay evil with evil or insult with insult, but with blessing, because to this you were called so that you may inherit a blessing" (I Pet. 3:8-9).

Purity and love must be pursued side by side in the life of the church.

> If we show either of these without the other, we exhibit not the character, but a caricature of God for the world to see. If we stress the love of God without the holiness of God, it turns out only to be a compromise. But if we stress the holiness of God without the love of God, we practice something that is hard and lacks beauty.[20]

God has standards. They are stated in the Bible. It's not legalism to insist that those standards must be pursued both in our individual lives and in the corporate life of the church. But we must not forget that "God is love" (I John 4:8). It's not a sign of weakness to show compassion to people, even to be understanding to people when they have committed sin, but it is a lack of love to let people continue in their sin without bringing them to an awareness of their need for holiness and purity.

CONCLUSION

In the twentieth century, the church has often felt the frustration of rejection. The world around us has grown increasingly secular and cold. Cynicism toward religion shuts Christ out of many hearts. Today's secularist looks upon the church as a society of outdated and irrelevant religious sentimentalists who stubbornly refuse to give up their superstitious past. We have also felt the rejection of some of our own people, who have grown dissatisfied with life in the church for one reason or another.

Some have predicted the demise of the church. Some have said that it must change or die. It does need to change when its practices and principles are at variance with the Word of God and out of touch with the needs of people. But the church is going to survive. I don't necessarily mean that the addresses in the yellow pages will always be the same. God may raise up the church among some people that we know nothing about. But he will have a church, because it is his church. It is a holy church and the gates of Hades cannot overcome it!

Endnotes

1. *The Unchurched American.* (Princeton, New Jersey: The Princeton Religion Research Center, 1978), p. 1. A non-churched person is defined as a person who is "not a member of a church or synagogue or who has not attended church or synagogue in the last six months apart from weddings, funerals or special holidays such as Christmas, Easter or Yom Kippur" p. 2.

2. Ibid.

3. Ibid., p. 10.

4. S.v. "church" *Webster's Ninth New Collegiate Dictionary.* (Springfield, MA: Merriam-Webster, Inc. Publishers, 1988), p. 240.

5. Everett Ferguson, *The New Testament Church.* (Abilene, Texas: ACU Press, 1968), p. 46.

6. Arndt and Gingrich offer the following definitions of *ekklesia:* "1. assembly, as a regularly summoned political body. 2. Assemblage, gathering, meeting. 3. The congregation of the Israelites when gathered together for religious purposes. 4. Of the Christian church or congregation – a. a church meeting, b. the church or congregation as the totality of Christians living in one place, c. house churches, d. the church universal." William F. Arndt and F. Wilbur Gingrich, *A Greek-English Lexicon of the New Testament.* 2nd. ed. (Chicago: The University of Chicago Press, 1958), pp. 240-241.

7. Ferguson, *The New Testament Church.* p. 46.

8. J. Muilenberg, "Holiness" *Interpreter's Dictionary of the Bible.* Vol. 2. (Nashville: Abingdon press), p. 624.

9. Ferguson, *The New Testament Church.* p. 47. Ferguson suggests, "The background of Paul's usage is probably to be found in the Hebrew idea of 'corporate personality,' in which a whole people may be viewed as one and in which one person may stand for and embody the whole" (pp. 46-47).

10. Charles W. Colson, *Loving God.* (Grand Rapids, Michigan: Zondervan Publishing House, 1987), p. 175.

11. George Eldon Ladd, *A Theology of the New Testament.* (Grand

Rapids, Michigan; William B. Eerdmans Company, 1974; reprint eidtion, 1989) p. 545. Ladd elaborates, "We would have expected Paul to say 'so it is with the church.' Paul uses the metaphor of the body to express the oneness of the church with her Lord. The church is not a body or society of believers, but the body of Christ" (p. 545).

12. W.E. Vine, *The Church and the Churches*. (Fincastle, Virginia: Scripture Truth Book Company, 1964), p. 20.

13. Ferguson, *The New Testament Church*. p. 49.

14. William Barclay, *The Daily Study Bible. The Letters to the Galatians and Ephesians*. (Edinburgh, Scotland: The Saint Andrew Press. 1954, reprint edition, 1965), p. 206. William Hendriksen insisted that the wedding analogy is Jewish. It consisted of betrothal, the interval between the betrothal and the wedding feast, the preparation and procession and finally the wedding feast itself. He attempted to fit statements of these verses into each one of these marriage segments. In his view the "presentation here referred to must be viewed as definitely eschatological, that is as referring to the great consummation when Jesus returns upon clouds of glory." (William Hendriksen. *New Testament Commentary. Exposition of Ephesians*. (Grand Rapids, Michigan: Baker Book House, 1967) p. 253.

15. Ferguson, *The New Testament Church*. p. 49. Other possibilities concerning the use of the term "word" include, "the gospel preached prior to baptism (cf. Rom. 10:17; I Peter 1;23-25), the pronounced formula over the one baptized (cf. Matt. 28:19), the confession of the one baptized (see Col. 3:17; cf. I Cor. 1:2; Rom. 10:9) or God's word of promise attached to baptism (I Pet. 1:25)." (Michael R. Weed, *The Letters of Paul to the Ephesians, Colossians, and Philemon*. (Austin, Texas: R.B. Sweet Co., 1971), p. 180.

16. Avon Malone, "God's Eternal Purpose" *Abilene Christian College Lectures, 1969* (J.D. Thomas, ed.) (Abilene, Texas: Abilene Christian College Bookstore, 1969), p. 78.

17. Francis Schaeffer, *The Church Before the Watching World*. (Downers Grove, Illinois: Intervarsity Press, 1971), p. 78.

18. Jerry Bridges, *The Pursuit of Holiness*. (Colorado Springs, Colorado: NavPress, 1978), p. 147.

19. Schaeffer, *The Church Before the Watching World*. p. 62.

20. Ibid., p. 63.

16

The Human Struggle for Holiness

Holiness is a gift from God that we receive when we are baptized into Christ (I Cor. 6:11). However, actually perfecting the practice of holiness involves human effort. The Hebrew writer urged his readers to "leave the elementary teachings about Christ and go on to maturity" (Heb. 6:1). He clearly understood that human effort is connected with the development of a Christlike character. Otherwise there is no way to make sense of the exhortation in Hebrews 12:14, "Make every effort to live in peace with all men and to be holy; without holiness no one will see the Lord."

Like these ancient Christians, each one of us participates in the struggle. Those who have gone before us have read the same scriptures and tried to work out a program for holiness within the context of their own lives. Though they were always hindered by the cultural patterns and biases of their times, they made a serious effort to apply the Word of God to their lives. This chapter will concentrate on some of the more prominent efforts to be holy as they have been reported by church historians.

THE DESERT FATHERS AND THE MONASTICS

By the end of the second Christian century, the Christian faith had lost some of its vitality. More permissive attitudes gradually cast an ominous shadow over the church. Indeed it could be said that many people were Christians in name only. Serious minded believers pondered this erosion of devotion and concluded that an ascetic approach to living was required to revitalize the church and maintain its holy character. *Asceticism* is the practice of self-denial as a means of achieving spiritual discipline. It was introduced in an attempt to correct the excesses of secularism.

Many church members came to believe that the high ideals taught in the New Testament were too demanding for the average Christian. They proposed the introduction of a "greenhouse" spiritual environment for those who are serious about holiness, while allowing the common people to follow Christ with much less diligence. *The Didache,* a second century document, offered encouragement for this two-tiered approach to faith. "If thou art able to bear the whole yoke of the Lord, thou shalt be perfect; but if thou art not able, do that which thou art able."[1]

Hermas taught that it is possible to do more than the Lord commanded and that going beyond the minimal requirements of faith would result in maximum reward for the person who achieved a higher level of personal discipline.[2] Later on, certain church leaders began to talk about the "advice" of the gospel as opposed to the "requirements" of the gospel.

The earliest ascetics appealed to the scriptures to justify their radical approach to developing holiness. They noted that Jesus taught the principle of self-denial. He said, "If anyone would come after me, he must deny himself and take up his cross and follow me" (Matt. 16:24). His admonition to the rich young ruler was taken as a personal rule of life by many of the ascetics – "If you want to be perfect, go sell your possessions and give to the poor and you will have treasure in heaven. Then come and follow me" (Matt. 19:21.) They also took

210

note of Matthew 19:12, "For some . . . have renounced marriage because of the kingdom of heaven." This was taken to mean that those who elect poverty and choose celibacy are closer to God than those who own property and marry. Voluntary poverty and celibacy thus became marks of holiness.

Some scholars believe the practice of asceticism can be traced to John the Baptist.[3] Hermas taught that greater honor comes to the person who does not marry.[4] It has been suggested by certain historians that asceticism may have even had Essene roots.[5]

Some of the heretical sects, notably the Marcionites, certain Gnostics and the Montanists observed ascetic practices. Outstanding leaders in this early period of church history practiced asceticism. "Origen, a native of Alexandria, gave an example of extreme asceticism in self-mutilation, austerity in food and drink, and bodily comforts."[6]

Not all of the ascetic influence on these early day church figures came from their religious roots. There were powerful secular influences which pulled some of them in the direction of ascetic living. It is no accident that the monastic movement had its beginning in Egypt. "Mysticism and the contemplative life were in non-Christian circles in Egypt."[7]

Walker listed six conditions in the third and fourth centuries that paved the way for the beginning of a monastic way of life.[8] They are:

1. The low condition of the church.
2. The great influx of new members into the church.[9]
3. The cessation of martyrdom.
4. The presence of fleshly temptation, from which it seemed wise to flee.
5. The high regard that people had for the practice of contemplation.
6. The extreme formalism of public worship, which in turn led to a desire for a more personal relationship with God.

Some of the ascetics chose to live in solitude. They are known as the *Desert Fathers*, or the *Hermits*. They lived in desert regions in Egypt, Palestine and Syria. They chose to leave their communities

211

and took up residence in the desert where they devoted themselves to contemplation and the struggle against temptation. One of the most famous Desert Fathers was Simeon Stylites. He lived for 36 years atop a pillar east of Antioch. He is said to have "touched his feet with his forehead more than 1244 times in succession and to have dripped with vermin."[10]

Anthony (b. 250) is usually regarded as the father of Christian monasticism. He was so impressed with the Lord's directive to the rich young ruler that he entered into an ascetic life style at age 20. Fifteen years later he became a hermit and went into solitude, devoting himself to prayer and fasting. Many others set out to imitate him. Some of them lived in groups while others chose to remain in isolation.

Pachomius (b. 292) was the first ascetic to actually begin a monastery. The word "monk" ("monastery" is derived from monk.) means alone. Pachomius believed that the struggle against the devil could best be won by participating in the ascetic lifestyle. To him this was not best accomplished as a solo act, but needed to be carried out in a community, so he established a monastery in southern Egypt (c. 315). "Here all the inmates were but a single body, having assigned work, regular hours of worship, similar dress and cells close to one another – in a word, a life under a common abbot.[11]

In the beginning, the monastic movement attracted only lay persons with both men and women entering the cloistered environment. Convents for women were in operation during Pachomius' time. Gradually, however, the monastic life style shifted to the clergy and by the 4th century Eusebius, the bishop of Vercelli in Italy, required the clergy of his cathedral to live the monastic life.[12]

Basil the Great (b. 330) added a new dimension to monastic life. He considered it the duty of all monastics to take care of the needy members of Christian society. He insisted they " . . . care for orphans, feed the poor, maintain hospitals, educate children and even provide work for the unemployed."[13]

Benedict of Nursia (b. 480) codified monastic requirements and organized the monastic community. His famous "Benedictine Rule" became the standard set of requirements for the monastic life. An abbot was appointed to head each monastery and he was implicitly

212

obeyed. No one could become a monk until he had experienced monastery life for a year and after a person was admitted, the vows could not be reversed. Worship was the primary duty of the monk. It would occupy four hours every day with the rest of the waking hours being given over to work and reading. The Benedictine Rule demanded a life of self-denial, service, worship, study and work.[14]

FRANCIS OF ASSISI

In the late medieval period, Francis of Assisi (1182-1226) set an example of personal devotion that has seldom if ever been equaled among those who have sought holiness through the ascetic life. Walker observed, "In Francis of Assisi, medieval piety had its highest and most noble representative."[15]

He was given the name, Giovanni Bernadore, at birth, but the family preferred to call him, Francis. Francis was a member of the privileged class, the son of a wealthy cloth merchant and he soon developed a reputation as an aristocratic playboy. During his youth he became a leader among the rabble-rousing young men of his community. In early adulthood he went off to war, was taken prisoner and held for a year. Shortly after his war prison experience, he suffered a serious illness. Both experiences drastically altered Francis' outlook on life.

At some point during this time, he developed compassion for the poor and began devoting himself to their needs, but occasionally lapsed into the lifestyle of his younger days. His service to the poor placed him in contact with lepers and even though he loathed the sight of them, he devoted himself to assisting them. During this period he spent a great deal of time meditating alone in the fields.

"On a pilgrimage to Rome, he thought he heard the divine command to restore the fallen house of God."[16] He interpreted the call to mean that he should restore a ruined church building in his home town. He sold cloth from his father's business to rebuild the structure, which prompted such an angry reaction at home that Francis' father petitioned the bishop for permission to disinherit his son. To Francis, the action of his father represented freedom. He declared his independence by stripping himself of his clothing, standing naked before the bishop and declaring " . . . that henceforth he desired only to serve, 'Our Father who art in Heaven.'"[17]

Francis chose a lifestyle of poverty. He wore tunics made of the coarse brown cloth worn by peasants. He begged for his food and survived on what he could get. His life was devoted to serving the poor and the sick. His rule for life was based on three passages of scriptures. Like the Benedictines, he appropriated the Lord's statement to the rich young ruler in Matthew 19:21. The other two were Luke 9:3, "Take nothing for the journey – no staff, no bag, no bread, no money, no extra tunic," and Matthew 16:24, "If anyone would come after me, he must deny himself, take up his cross and follow me."

Like-minded idealists were drawn to him. The social conditions of the time made the ministry of Francis attractive to many people. Historian Robert Payne noted,

> The medieval church since the days of Constantine had been wedded to the pomp and power of the world. It had become a political hierarchy possessing great resources in land and property. Francis quickly assailed the earthly power of the Church by pointing to a higher purpose and a more demanding ritual. His purpose was nothing less than the imitation of Christ and his ritual was poverty.[18]

In 1210 Francis and eleven associates went to Rome seeking papal permission from Innocent III to pursue their way of life. While the pope feared that their manner of life might be too severe, he did give them permission, on the condition that they secure permission from the bishop and that they organize themselves and select a leader. They became known as the Brothers Minor and Francis quite naturally became their leader. The descendants of this group are known as the Franciscans today.

Near the end of his life, Francis believed that he received the *stigmata*. *Stigmata* is a term used to describe a phenomenon in which it is thought that the wounds which Christ experienced on the cross are felt in the human body.[19]

Francis represents the most noble effort of all those who sought to pursue holiness through the ascetic lifestyle. Latourette was most certainly correct when he wrote, "Francis is one of the most winsome figures of Christian history."[20]

THE PIETISTS

The Pietists started out as a reform movement within 17th century German Lutheranism. Although they never enjoyed majority status, even in their own denomination, they have profoundly influenced the Protestant world with such impact that it is felt even to the present day.[21]

As with the other holiness movements that have arisen on the scene during the course of human history, the Pietists responded to the pressures of their times. The Thirty Years War (1618-1648) had been costly in terms of human life, property and spiritual values. "Prosperous cities were decimated or destroyed and even greater change was suffered in the coarsening and lowering of morals."[22] By the end of the 17th century Lutheranism had become cold, ritualistic, argumentative and political. "Both clergy and laity were beset by drunkenness and adultery. The message from the pulpit said nothing about holiness."[23] "This made the Christian faith exceedingly formal and forbidding to those who rightly sensed that the New Testament emphasized justification and the new life in Christ as the basis for all Christian living and thinking."[24]

Pietism exploded on the scene in the late 17th century as a corrective to those excesses. Pietism has been defined as "a recurring tendency within Christian history to emphasize more the practicalities of the Christian life and less the formal structure of theology or church order."[25]

Philipp Jakob Spener (1635-1705) is generally acknowledged to be the father of Pietism. Born in Alsace and educated in the university at Strasborg, he assumed a pastoral position at Frankfurt-on-Main in 1666. Soon he began calling for moral reform. In 1686 he moved to Dresden. His tenure there was brief and marked by controversy, but it was in Dresden that he met *August Hermann Francke* (1663 – 1727), who would become his successor. In 1691, he went to Berlin where he lived out his remaining years. In Berlin he helped start the University of Halle, which became the center of pietistic influence.

In 1675 Spener published his most famous work, *Pia Desideria (Pious Wishes)*. In it he exposed the spiritual decline that had overtaken Protestantism in general and the Lutheran church in particular. He outlined proposals for spiritual reform. To promote his ideas, he began Wednesday night meetings to pray, discuss the previous Sunday's sermons and apply passages of scripture to individual life. Perhaps this served as the forerunner of the mid-week prayer meeting, which was later to characterize many American religious fellowships.

Francke was named to head up Halle in 1692. In addition to his work as head of the school, he started an orphanage and other charitable enterprises. Under his leadership Halle became the center for training and sending out missionaries all over the world.

The Pietist Movement was a holiness movement by design. Their leaders emphasized the priesthood of believers and they pushed for more extensive use of the Word of God, for restraint in religious controversies, for edifying sermons which people could understand and for genuineness in Christian practice.[26]

Like the monastics and Francis they emphasized asceticism and eventually became quite legalistic. They did not follow the teachings of the monastics in forbidding marriage or demanding complete poverty but Spener made it clear that Christians ought to practice moderation in food, drink and dress, while forbidding the theater, dances and playing with cards.[27]

For the most part the Pietists continued to be a subculture within the Lutheran church. The Lutheran clergy feared they would infiltrate the church with subjectivism and anti-intellectual ideas. They also worried about separatism, fearing the Pietists would organize themselves into a separate denomination.

In one significant instance separation did take place. A count from Saxony, *Nicholas von Zinzendorf* (1700-1760) studied under Francke at Halle. When a group of persecuted Bohemian Hussites fled their homeland, Zinzendorf granted them asylum on his estate, settling them at Herrnhut. Eventually he became the religious leader of the group and against his wishes the group gradually chose to break away from the Lutheran church. They became known as the

216

Moravians – a name which was derived from the region where they had previously lived. Under Zinzendorf's leadership, the Moravians promoted piety with missionary zeal. One group of them came to America and settled in Georgia and later established a colony in Pennsylvania. Zinzendorf visited the Pennsylvania colony and named it Bethlehem. It remains a center of Moravian influence in the present day.

The influence of the Pietists has been felt far beyond their sociological origins.

> Religious movements resembling pietism were active beyond Germany in the seventeenth and eighteenth centuries. In fact, German pietism was but one chord in a symphony of variations on a common theme – the need to move beyond sterile formulas about God to a more intimate experience with him. The English Puritans of the late 1500s and 1600s exhibited this. Cotton Mather, who corresponded with Francke, strove to encourage pietistic vitality in the New World.[28]

JOHN WESLEY

No historical study of the human struggle to achieve a higher level of holiness can claim any degree of credibility without discussing the spectacular career of *John Wesley* (1703 – 1791). Wesley was born in Epworth, England. He was one of 19 children born to Samuel and Susanna Wesley. His father had grown up among Puritan Nonconformists. Samuel Wesley elected to cast his lot with the Anglican church and became the rector of the small country church at Epworth.

Much of Wesley's upbringing has been attributed to his mother, Susanna Wesley. Her goal was to instill discipline and piety in her children. Her methods of child training appear somewhat harsh by contemporary standards. "His mother believed that children's wills should be subdued, that they should be whipped soundly when they misbehaved and that they should cry softly after being whipped."[30] Apparently her whippings were administered with enough frequency and force that the children soon learned that crying softly would prevent yet another whipping.

He was educated at Charterhouse, a school for boys in London, and received both BA and MA degrees from Oxford. He experienced a religious conversion in 1725 and returned to Oxford to lead an organization of students which his brother Charles had begun. The scoffing students at Oxford called it "The Holy Club." Later the club members came to be known as "Methodists" because of their prescribed method of Bible study and their rigid practice of self-denial.

During this period, Wesley met *William Law* (1686-1761). Law profoundly influenced the younger man. Law was a mystic who insisted that the person who decides to follow Jesus must follow him in every area of life including business.[31]

In 1735 Wesley went to Georgia to serve as a missionary among the Indians. On the way over, he met a small group of Moravians aboard ship. He was deeply impressed when he observed how fearlessly they sang hymns during a violent storm. They seemed to possess a level of faith which he did not have. "Georgia was a test for John who learned that he really didn't like the Indians and that his strictness was not much appreciated by the Georgians."[32] Nevertheless the combination of a strict Anglican upbringing and the impressive example of the Moravians had a life-changing effect on the missionary to America.

His contact with the Moravians was expanded on his return to England. He carried on a correspondence and had conversations with *Peter Boehler* (1712-1775), a Moravian missionary and bishop. Boehler encouraged him to reassess the nature of his religious commitment and the meaning of faith. On May 24, 1738 he attended the meeting of a Moravian group on Aldersgate Street. He was listening to a reading from the preface of Luther's commentary on Romans. Wesley claimed, "his heart was strangely warmed."[33] Wesley spoke of his earlier conversion in 1725 as a "religious" conversion, but the Aldersgate experience he regarded as an "evangelical" conversion.

Wesley later broke with the Moravians, but they left an indelible influence on him. He began preaching with a new kind of enthusiasm. Those who sought to detract from his ministry even called Wesley and his friends, "The Enthusiasts." The pulpits of the Church of England were soon closed to him, but Wesley took to the open air, often speaking to thousands. He rode over 250,000 miles on horseback and preached more than 40,000 sermons. He regularly preached three times a day. "Wesley's true genius surfaced through his ability to organize new converts into Methodist "societies" and "bands," which sustained both them and the revival."[34]

Wesley remained loyal to the Church of England throughout his lifetime, even though the church's pulpits were not open to him. It was only after his death that the Methodist Episcopal church was formed as a separate denomination.

The centerpiece of Wesley's preaching was his view of sanctification. He believed that grace is made available to the human race in three different stages. One stage of grace is active during a person's life between conception and conversion. He called this "prevenient" or "preventing" grace. He believed that this form of grace is necessary before a relationship can be established between God and an individual. Wesley claimed that prevenient grace

> . . . includes the first wish to please God, the first beacon of light concerning his will, and the first transient conviction of having sinned against him. All these imply some tendency toward life; some degree of salvation; the beginning of a deliverance from a blind unfeeling heart quite insensible of God and the things of God.[35]

In Wesley's view prevenient grace is a process, but *justifying* grace takes place instantaneously. Wesley thought of conversion in two phases, the first being the experience of having all past sins forgiven.

> This then is the salvation which is through faith, even in the present world; a salvation from sin both often expressed in the word "justification" which taken in the largest sense implies a deliverance from guilt and punishment, by the atonement of Christ actually applied to the soul of the sinner now believing on Him and a deliverance from the whole body of sin, through Christ found in his heart."[36]

Justifying grace is followed by *sanctifying* grace. To his mind the "sanctifying grace" delivers one from the power to commit sin. He equated holiness with sinless perfection, a state that one acquired subsequent to justification. Wesley believed that "entire sanctification" is a process that goes on over the course of a lifetime, but he also believed that there is an instantaneous moment when the second blessing is received. Some refer to this sanctifying moment as a "second work of grace."

> From the time of our being born again, the gradual work of sanctification takes place . . . we wait for entire sanctification, for a full salvation from our sins – from pride, self-will, anger, unbelief, or as the Apostle expresses it "go on unto perfection. . . ."
> As to the means: I believe this perfection is always wrought in the soul by a simple act of faith; consequently in an instant. But I believe in a gradual work, both preceding and following that instant.
> As to time I believe this instant generally is the instant of death, the moment before the soul leaves the body. But I believe that it may be ten, twenty or forty years before.[37]

Without a doubt, Wesley's ideas about holiness profoundly impacted the religious people of his day and time. Just as Pietism had laid the ground work for the Wesleyan view of holiness, so Wesley laid the ground work for the American Holiness Movement.

THE AMERICAN HOLINESS MOVEMENT

By the middle of the 19th century, the leaders of the Methodist church had begun to neglect Wesley's ideas about perfection. Within Methodist ranks, some people were concerned about what they regarded as a great loss of spirituality and holiness. Among those who became alarmed were two New York sisters – Sarah Worrell Lankford and Phoebe Worrell Palmer. After an experience which she interpreted as "the second blessing," Sarah began conducting Tuesday night meetings in her home for the purpose of promoting holiness. Phoebe became the leader of these meetings, which soon spread to other communities. Hawley noted,

> The constant emphasis on perfectionism and the insistence that it had to be achieved NOW provoked a strong reaction within the Methodist church and raised the specter of division. Since the holiness gatherings were outside the church jurisdiction, they challenged the tight authority of the church.[38]

While this new emphasis on holiness was being promoted, American revivalism was having a profound influence on the population, especially in the form of camp meetings. The first and most famous of these camp meetings was held at Cane Ridge, Kentucky in 1801. Barton W. Stone, who later became an outstanding leader in the Restoration Movement, preached for the church at Cane Ridge and was a prominent figure in the meetings.

Later camp meetings greatly influenced the development of the American Holiness Movement. Charles G. Finney (1792-1875) has generally been credited with establishing the forms and methods of modern American revivalism. Finney emphasized the doctrine of perfection in these meetings. He believed that "an altogether higher and more stable form of Christian life was attainable and was the privilege of all Christians."[39] He was not as extreme as some other revivalists in his view of the "second work of grace." To Finney, perfection meant "a matter of perfect trust in God and complete commitment to his way rather than complete sinlessness."[40]

By the time of the Civil War, the Wesleyan Methodists and the Free Methodists had pulled away from Methodism's main body. By the 1880's mainstream Methodists had settled into becoming a "sedate middle class American Protestantism."[41] Those who wanted to move in the direction of perfectionism and insisted on the instantaneous second blessing began to form separate fellowships. Some of these included the Church of God, Anderson, Indiana (1880), the Church of the Nazarene (1908), and the Pilgrim Holiness Church (1897).

"Pentecostalism is an offshoot of the Holiness Movement. It teaches that speaking in tongues is the evidence that one has the second blessing."[42] Some Holiness denominations reject the tongue speaking experience while others teach both the second blessing and the

221

charismatic experience. It should also be pointed out that some charismatic people do not follow the perfection viewpoint concerning the second blessing.

The core emphasis in the American Holiness Movement differed from Wesley's in that it more actively promotes the instantaneous and emotional experience as the gateway to entire sanctification. Wesley, while not rejecting the instantaneous experience, saw sanctification as a lifelong process under normal circumstances. In the American Holiness Movement, "Sanctification became an obsession overshadowing other aspects of faith."[43] Like their predecessors, the promoters of holiness in America encouraged simple living, abstinence from worldly amusements and self-denial. To them the second work of grace was necessary to the maintenance of this rigid lifestyle.

CONCLUSION

In this historical overview, the contribution of many important leaders to the struggle for holiness has not been included. The limitation of space requires brevity in this brief sketch of the struggle. It certainly would be enlightening to explore the careers of such leaders as Augustine, Thomas Aquinas, Luther, Calvin, George Fox, John Bunyan and Andrew Murray among others. Each had much to say about holiness.

From the Desert Fathers to the leaders of the American Holiness Movement, certain common denominators have been present as people struggled to live more holy lives. Meditation, prayer and scripture study are essentials in the quest for holiness. All those who have promoted holiness have emphasized self-denial and simple living. Unfortunately a tendency toward asceticism and legalism too often accompanies these emphases.

This chapter has not given attention to holiness in the Restoration Movement, largely because it has not been a major emphasis. Thus it seems fitting to close this survey of the historical quest for holiness by calling attention to a man from Restoration Movement ranks whose career paralleled that of Francis in many ways. His name was Joseph Thomas. He was first attracted to the Restoration ideal as the result of his association with James O'Kelly. O'Kelly had broken with the Methodists as the result of his Restoration ideals. Although Thomas believed that he should be immersed, O'Kelly refused to immerse him on the grounds that it was not necessary. Later Thomas came under the influence of John Mulkey and Barton W. Stone. In 1811, he was immersed into Christ but after preaching for two years, he settled on a farm in Virginia and began to reflect on his lifestyle and attitudes. After much soul searching he sold his farm and his horse, got rid of his fashionable clothes and for the rest of his life wore only a white robe. He walked to the places he preached and lived a most frugal lifestyle.[44] Perhaps we would think of him as being an eccentric kind of fellow, but in reality he was following a path which had been trod for centuries by those who have struggled to achieve a higher level of holiness.

Although the struggle for holiness has frequently led people into asceticism, legalism and eccentric behavior, the fact remains that all the people considered in this chapter made an honest effort to pursue practical holiness. Our criticism of these people should be tempered by an awareness of the fact that, unlike the subjects we have considered in this chapter, many of us have not even included personal holiness on our agendas, much less given consideration to struggling for a higher level of holiness.

Endnotes

1. Quoted by Williston Walker, *A History of the Christian Church.* (New York: Charles Scribner's Sons, 1918), p. 103.

2. Ibid.

3. Kenneth Scott Latourette, *A History of Christianity.* (New York: Harper and Row, 1953), p. 233.

4. Ibid., p. 225.

5. C.T. Marshall, "Monasticism." *Evangelical Dictionary of Theology.* (Grand Rapids, Michigan: Baker Book House), 1984. p. 728.

6. Ibid., p. 225.

7. Ibid.

8. Walker, *A History of the Christian Church.* p. 136.

9. "By the middle of the third century, thousands were pouring into the church. . . . Before the close of the fifth century the overwhelming majority of the citizens of the Roman Empire were professing to be Christians, had been baptized and were members of one or the other of the bodies which bore the Christian name." Latourette, *A History of Christianity.* p. 221.

10. Ibid., p. 228.

11. Walker, *A History of the Christian Church.* p. 137.

12. Ibid., p. 138.

13. See Marshall, "Monasticism." *Evangelical Dictionary of Theology.* p. 728.

14. Walker, *A History of the Christian Church.* p. 138.

15. Ibid., p. 255.

16. Ibid., p. 257.

17. Latourette, *A History of Christianity.* p. 429.

18. Robert Payne, *The Christian Centuries.* (New York: W.W. Norton and Company, 1966), p. 310.

19. E.A. Livingstone (ed), *The Concise Oxford Dictionary of the Christian Church.* (New York: Oxford University Press, 1977), p. 489. Of the *stigmata* it is said, "Stigmata may be either invisible or visible, in which case they normally consist of wounds or blood blisters on hands, feet and near the heart, (also on the head) (crown of thorns) or shoulders and back (carrying the cross and scourging). They do not become septic and resist treatment. The first person known to have received stigmata is St. Francis of Assisi; since then cases have been numerous. The attitude of the R.C. church has always been guarded" (Ibid).

20. Latourette, *A History of Christianity.* p. 429.

21. Don Vinzant has observed parallels between the practice of Pietism and the "discipling" phenomenon among some contemporary Churches of Christ. He said, "Study Pietism and you will find an important source of much that characterizes the discipling movement." Don E. Vinzant, "Historical Roots of the Discipling Movement Among Churches of Christ." *The Discipling Dilemma.* (Nashville, Tennessee: The Gospel Advocate Company. 1988), p. 127.

22. Latourette, *A History of Christianity.* p. 894.

23. Monroe Hawley, "The Search for Holiness" (part three). Unpublished essay, n.d. p. 1.

24. John Dillenberger and Claude Welch, *Protestant Christianity.* (New York: Charles Scribner's Sons, 1954), p. 122.

25. M.A. Noll, "Pietism." *Evangelical Dictionary of Theology.* (Grand Rapids, Michigan: Baker Book House, 1984), p. 855.

26. Ibid., p. 856.

27. Walker, *A History of the Christian Church.* p. 497.

28. Noll, "Pietism." *Evangelical Dictionary of Theology.* p. 857.

29. Nonconformists were members of the Church of England who refused to conform to the "doctrines, polity or discipline of the established church." See Livingstone, *The Concise Oxford Dictionary of the Christian Church.* p. 361; also D.F. Wright, "Nonconformity." *Evangelical Dictionary of The-*

ology. (Grand Rapids, Michigan: Baker Book House, 1984), pp. 779-780.

30. "Revival and Revolution." *Church History.* 1983. Vol. 2, No. 1. p.18.

31. N.V. Hope, "William Law." *Evangelical Dictionary of Theology.* (Grand Rapids, Michigan: Baker Book House, 1984), p. 1626. Others who came under Law's influence included George Whitefield (an early associate of Wesley), Samuel Johnson and Alexander Whyte.

32. "Revival and Resolution." *Church History.* p. 9.

33. R.G. Tuttle, Jr., "John Wesley." *Evangelical Dictionary of Theology.* (Grand Rapids, Michigan: Baker Book House, 1984), p. 1163.

34. Ibid., p. 1164.

35. T. Otto Nall (ed), *By John Wesley.* (New York: Association Press, 1961), p.48,

36. Ibid., pp. 54-55.

37. Ibid., pp. 91-92.

38. Monroe Hawley, "The American Holiness Movement." Unpublished essay, n.d. p.1.

40. Ibid.

41. R.V. Pierard, "The American Holiness Movement." *Evangelical Dictionary of Theology.* (Grand Rapids, Michigan: Baker Book House, 1984), p. 517.

42. Ibid., pp. 517-518.

43. Hawley, "The American Holiness Movement." p. 2.

44. Richard Hughes, "Christians in the Early South: The perspective of Joseph Thomas, 'the White Pilgrim.' " *Disciplinia.* pp. 33-37; 43.

17

An Evaluation of the Human Struggle for Holiness

Throughout the long history of Christendom the pendulum has been constantly swinging between the extremes of permissiveness and restrictiveness. It is significant to note that each one of the historical movements discussed in Chapter 16 came about in reaction to lapses of Christian practice within the mainstream of religious life.

The lessons of history seem to indicate that extreme laxity in spiritual matters eventually provokes a cry for some sort of reformation. Reformation (and restoration) movements have a way of hardening themselves into rigid patterns of regimentation. People begin to resent the restrictions that have been imposed on them and initiate liberation movements. At that point the pendulum begins to swing back into the other direction, but it usually does not stop until the liberation movement degenerates into lawless behavior. Men and movements are forever racing from one end of the continuum line to the other.

Truth generally lies somewhere near the midpoint of this imaginary continuum line. It is very difficult for those who are attempting to avoid extremes to see the necessity of making change, but extremists sometimes serve as the conscience of the middle. When people grow comfortable and settled in their viewpoints and practices, the extremists force them to go through the painful process of self-evaluation. A study of holiness movements in church history clearly demonstrates the prevalence of this "pendulum effect."

The movements and personalties surveyed in chapter 16 tended to become extremist movements. The monastics retreated from the mainstream of life and sought to establish holiness through personal meditation and self-denial. Francis of Assisi nobly devoted himself to service, but insisted on living in abject poverty, an approach to life that is neither practical nor possible for most people. The sectarian spirit of the Pietists left them in a position of appearing to regard themselves as elitist Christians. Wesley's views of perfection fostered the belief that one can achieve the practice of sinlessness in this life. The American Holiness Movement placed more value on experience and emotions than on the objective study of the Word. All these movements started with the intention of encouraging the development of holiness, but all ended up with ideals and practices that were actually detrimental to the cause of holiness.

THE MONASTICS

The conditions that gave rise to monasticism represented a serious departure from the original objectives of the Christian faith. Christianity added more converts and gained a greater degree of public acceptance, but public favor often meant the loss of spiritual fervor. Their moral discipline and devotion to God began to wane. "By the beginning of the third century there were many whose parents, possibly remoter ancestors, had been experiential Christians, but who, though they attended public worship, were Christians in little more than name."[1]

Monasticism was a reaction to the loosening of Christian standards. The monastics believed they could draw closer to God through the practice of self-denial. They were convinced they could overcome evil "by denying property, sexual intercourse, and interest in worldly matters."[2]

The Monastic willingness to deny themselves was indeed a noble quality. In so doing they took seriously the words of Jesus when he said, "If anyone would come after me, he must deny himself and take up his cross and follow me" (Matt. 16:24). Paul viewed self-denial as a basic requirement of the gospel. He wrote, "I have been crucified with Christ and I no longer live, but Christ lives in me. The life I live in the body, I live by faith in the Son of God who loved me and gave himself for me" (Gal. 2:20).

Dallas Willard argues that Jesus lived as an ascetic. Even though he was accused of being a glutton and a winebibber by his enemies, his lifestyle included " . . . long and regular periods of solitude, fasting and prayer as well as voluntary homelessness, poverty and chastity."[3] Even so Willard concludes that " . . . nothing in the history of the Western world has done more harm to the present day prospects of necessary asceticism than the emergence of monasticism as a form of Christian life."[4]

Unfortunately, the Monastic movement was built on the assumption that God has one set of standards for ordinary Christians and a higher set of standards for those who aspire to true holiness. Such an assumption has no Biblical foundation. All the members of the Corinthian church were expected to respond to Paul's exhortation in II Corinthians 7:1, "Since we have these promises dear friends, let us purify ourselves from everything that contaminates body and spirit, perfecting holiness out of reverence for God" (II Cor. 7:1). Likewise all the readers of Hebrews fell within the scope of the author's statement in Hebrews 12:15, "Make every effort to live in peace with all men and to be holy; without holiness no one will see the Lord."

Although most contemporary Christians would agree that there is little justification for Monastic practice, the idea that God has one set of rigid standards for some Christians and another set of rules for others still holds in the popular mind. Church members often expect their leaders to set a high spiritual tone and practice ethical purity. They have every right to demand exemplary behavior from those who lead the way, but many church members make it all too clear that they have no intention of adhering to those standards themselves. We must not lose sight of the fact that God's word has one standard of holiness and it applies to all Christians – leaders and followers.

The Monastics were also mistaken in believing that retreating from the mainstream of human society would enhance their goal of achieving holiness. In this they did not follow the example of Jesus. Jesus spent his entire ministry interacting with people and responding to their needs. Peter said "he went about doing good" (Acts 10:38). There were times when he did temporarily retreat from the fast-paced world of human society, but these periods of disengagement were brief and were always followed by more teaching, healing and helping. In his prayer for the disciples, he prayed, "My prayer is not that you take them out of the world, but that you protect them from the evil one" (John 17:15).

In terms of lifestyle Jesus openly participated in the social events of his time. He performed his first miracle at a wedding celebration (John 2:1-11). He enjoyed the hospitality of friends (Luke 10:38-41) and he defended his gregarious lifestyle when challenged. "For John the Baptist came neither eating bread nor drinking wine, and you say, 'He has a demon.' The Son of man came eating and drinking and you say, 'He is a glutton and a drunkard, a friend of tax collectors and sinners. But wisdom is proved right by all her children" (Luke 7:33-35).

There is no evidence that an ascetic lifestyle automatically promotes greater holiness. On the contrary, the New Testament warns, "Such regulations indeed have an appearance of wisdom, with their self-imposed worship, their false humility and their harsh treatment of the body, but they lack any value in restraining sensual indulgence" (Col. 2:23).

FRANCIS OF ASSISI

The example of Francis was certainly more noble than that of many of the earlier monastics. He set about to be like Christ and no one can find fault with his goal. Every person who desires to be holy must follow the same objective. Like the twentieth century lady called "Mother Theresa," Francis worked among the lepers. They were loathsome to him, yet he was willing to help them because that was what he thought Jesus would do. As modern day Christians we would do well to remember the example of Francis and his early followers as we rub shoulders with AIDS victims, the homeless, mentally ill persons and substance abusers.

Much of Francis' preaching was Biblical. His emphasis was on the core message of the gospel.

> It stressed the adoration of God, repentance, generosity, and the forgiveness of wrongs done to one by others. It makes much of love for one's neighbor and one's enemies, humility, abstention from vices, including and especially the vices of the flesh.[5]

Despite the many admirable features of Francis' ministry some of his behavior suggests that he may have been lacking in emotional stability. "One of the stories which his early disciples cherished was that of a sermon he preached to the birds exhorting them to praise and love their Creator."[6] His interpretation of the stigmata pains is open to question and certainly should not be considered the mark of genuine holiness. Donald Bloesch noted, "There is . . . a danger when religion becomes conscious of itself as religion. True sanctity is oblivious to its own merits."[7]

Francis' commitment to poverty is also open to question. He not only chose a life of poverty for himself, he required it of those who joined his group.

> Francis insisted upon absolute poverty, would not permit any of the brethren to have money, and is said on one occasion to have forbidden a brother to own even a psalter, saying that if he possessed one he would wish for a breviary, and if he owned a breviary, he would soon be haughtily commanding one of his fellow men to bring it to him.[8]

Francis misunderstood the scope of the limited commission. Under the limited commission, the objective was temporary and aimed at a specific class of people. Jesus instructed the Twelve to avoid the Gentiles and speak only to the "lost sheep of the house of Israel." The lifestyle requirements were intended for that brief period of time and were never applied to all who preach the gospel. Francis took it as a

231

rule for his ministry, yet he did not confine himself to "the lost sheep of the house of Israel." That God never intended for his preachers to be cast in the role of beggars is clearly seen in Paul's instructions to the church at Corinth. "The Lord has commanded that those who preach the gospel should receive their living from the gospel" (I Cor. 9:14).

Poverty is not a virtue within itself and was never made a requirement for pursuing holiness. It is true that the Bible says of Jesus, "Though he was rich, yet for your sake he became poor so that you might be rich" (2 Cor. 8:9). It is also true that Jesus did not have "a place to lay his head" (Luke 9:58). He urged his followers to respond with compassion to the poor (Luke 4:18). On one occasion John the Baptist sent a messenger to Jesus to find out if he really was the Messiah. Jesus told the messenger to advise John that "the poor have the good news preached to them" (Matt. 11:5). Although Jesus voluntarily became poor for our sakes and counseled compassion toward the poor, he did not require poverty of his followers.

It is clear from the New Testament record that the early church included people in its ranks who owned property and could not be accurately judged as poor. These included Lydia who was a clothing merchant (Acts 16:14), Erastus, the director of public works in his home city (Rom. 16:23), Aquila and Priscilla, who were homeowners (I Cor. 16:19). Paul owned scrolls and parchments. Such possessions were rare in his day and very expensive (II Tim. 4:13). Philemon was recognized as a "dear friend and fellow worker" even though he was a slave owner (Phile. 1).

. . . Our world could not function if all of us lived as did Francis. There still have to be farmers, manufacturers and merchants. Somebody has to earn a living! The holiness of the average Christian is not expressed in wandering from place to place begging help for the needy, but by living lives of service wherever one is. We can be like Jesus without imitating his exact lifestyle.[9]

THE PIETISTS

Like the monastics the Pietists were responding to moral and spiritual laxity. Following the death of Luther, the Lutheran church lost some of its vitality.

> Though nominally based in the Scriptures, it was practically a fixed dogmatic interpretation, rigid, exact and demanding intellectual conformity. Emphasis was laid on pure doctrine and the sacraments, as constituting the sufficient elements of the Christian life.[10]

The faith had become a mind trip for church leaders. Laymen were left with little to do beyond participating in the sacraments and ordinances of the church. The people were weary at the end of the Thirty Years war. In addition to the loss of life and property, spirituality was at a low ebb. Both laity and clergy grew lax in personal morality as drunkenness and immorality increased among both classes of people.

When Pietism entered the picture, the leaders of the Pietist Movement found a population that was ready for its emphases. "It gave the primacy to a feeling in experience, emphasized the role of the laity in the life of the church and encouraged a strict ascetic attitude toward the world."[11]

Spener, the father of Pietism earnestly set out to encourage a more serious approach to Christian living. He was distressed over the controversies which had fostered a spirit of religious division. Spener played down the importance of doctrine and emphasized experience, the warmth of fellowship and the practice of moral excellence. "By accenting the warmed heart instead of the dogmatic head, it made possible a new valuation on piety and Christian work."[12]

The Pietists were clearly on the right track when they saw the need for moral reform. Their goal of creating an atmosphere in which a person could experience a genuine relationship to God, feel a warmth in Christian fellowship and practice responsible Christian living can all be placed on the plus side of the Pietist phenomenon. Their interest in world wide missions and humanitarian service was also commendable.

There were some flaws in the Pietist Movement and those flaws tend to surface in their spiritual heirs. The Pietists partook of the spirit of mysticism. Mystics, in the theological sense, are more concerned about experiential union with God than they are doctrine, structure in worship and church government. Leaders in the Lutheran church feared that the Pietists would become so subjective in their emphasis that they would lose sight of important doctrinal truths. Their fears were well founded.

The Lutheran authorities complained because the Pietists didn't attend public worship and observe the Lord's Supper. "Spener held that if one had really been converted and had a right heart, doctrinal differences were relatively unimportant."[13]

The Pietists were not wrong in emphasizing the point that Christianity needs to be experienced, but they left themselves open to abuse when they downplayed the importance of doctrine. What a person believes does make a difference! Paul sent Timothy to Ephesus to teach doctrine. "As I urged you when I went into Macedonia, stay there in Ephesus so that you may command certain men not to teach false doctrines any longer nor to devote themselves to myths and endless genealogies" (I Tim. 1:3-4). Later the apostle said, "Watch your life and doctrine closely. Persevere in them, because if you do, you will save both yourself and your hearers" (I Tim. 4:16). Doctrinal controversies can become so heated that peace-loving people would like to side with Spener and relegate doctrine to a place of little importance, but we cannot really afford to do that in view of the fact that Paul connects sound doctrine with personal salvation.

The Pietist Movement did not formally divide the Lutheran Church. Their leaders managed to hang on under the Lutheran umbrella for the most part but the thread of unity that kept the Pietists in the Lutheran fold was a thin one. Basically, their association with the Lutherans was nominal. On the inside the division was apparent. Despite their Lutheran label, the Pietists were a sectarian sub-group. Spener and Francke organized small Bible study groups which met in private homes and these Bible study groups provided the structural framework for the development of sectarian loyalty. Their conclusions and interpretation nurtured in these small groups became the official party line. Those who did not conform were either considered non-Christian or looked down upon as inferior disciples. From the Pietists perspective, "To be in Christ meant to reject that which was not of Christ and to have no traffic with it."[14]

234

The conversion of those who did not participate in the Pietist's program was either questioned or denied. The enforcement of rigid rules concerning the theater, dancing, cards, smoking and even jesting isolated them from the intellectual community. Once the air of superiority had been established, it became very difficult for them to be self critical and to make necessary corrections within the movement.

Though the Pietists themselves denied there was such a thing as "Pietism," the outsider noticed that the friends of the movement kept together and supported each other, that the sense of union with sympathizers in other localities was a living one, that adherents of the cause evinced unusual energy in pursuit of their aims, and that they exercised a potent influence. In short, Pietism had become a "party" as early as 1691; and during its golden age at Halle it manifested every evil of factionalism: greed for power; one-sided condemnation of opponents; and failure to censure friends. It seemed, therefore, both consciously and distinctly a tendency toward separation from fellow Lutherans in religious and social life; and the very fact that its measures were designed to further the religious interests of its adherents alone caused it to be suspected of tendencies toward separation and secession.[15]

JOHN WESLEY

There is much about the ministry and teaching of John Wesley that deserves our respect and admiration. His emphasis on thrift, cleanliness, honesty, salvation and good works were much needed among the common people of England during his day. Social conditions were deplorable and morality was at such a low ebb that thievery and prostitution were common means of survival among the lower classes.

Wesley had a positive impact on England.

Swearing stopped in factories and women began to concern themselves with neat and plain dresses, extravagances like expensive tea and vices like gin were dropped by his followers. Neighbors gave one another mutual help through the societies.[16]

The last letter that Wesley wrote was a short note composed on his death bed just six days before his demise. It was addressed to William Wilberforce, the member of Parliament who led the fight for abolition of slavery in the British Empire. He wanted to encourage Wilberforce in the struggle.

Wesley's positive traits are well known and do not need further embellishment here. His views on perfection, however, should be subjected to critical analysis in the light of the scriptures. Chapter 18 will focus on the Biblical concept of perfection.

THE AMERICAN HOLINESS MOVEMENT

The American Holiness Movement was an extension of the Wesleyan emphasis on perfection. They saw themselves as Wesley's true heirs. There were some subtle differences, however. For one thing, the American Holiness Movement broadened the influence of Wesley's concept of perfection. Through the first quarter of the 19th century, the concept of a "second blessing" had usually been a unique teaching of Methodism. Sarah Lankford and Phoebe Palmer were Methodists.

Once the doctrine attached itself to the Revival Movement, the concept was no longer an exclusive Methodist belief. Charles Finney was a Presbyterian, who later became a Congregationalist after he associated himself with Oberlin College. In 1858 William E. Boardman, a Presbyterian minister, published a volume called *The Higher Christian Life,* in which he sought to "present the idea of holiness in a terminology that would be acceptable to people outside the Methodist tradition."[17] The book became a best seller and "second blessing" theology became quite popular.

The Methodist church remained firmly committed to the concept of a second blessing until the 1890's. By 1880, some members began to suspect that Methodism was not being true to its origins. Many members were concerned because growing prosperity had led to pretentiousness, to what they considered an extravagant display of formal worship in expensive church buildings, indulgence in worldly amusements and conformity to the spirit of the age. Critics thought it was enough to make John Wesley turn over in his grave, so the Methodist church began to splinter. The secessionist groups called themselves "come outers." They were coming out of a fellowship which they thought was tainted with the vices of this world.

The Methodists themselves looked upon the "come outers" as radicals who wanted to turn back the clock. One Methodist writer observed, "A company of evangelists appeared who were seemingly more intent upon Puritan standards of dress and behavior than perfect love and certainly less attached to Wesleyan tradition."[18]

The leaders of the new movement were not only separatists, they also tended to place their focus on perfection and especially the idea that it is to be received instantaneously. As noted in the previous chapter, Wesley himself believed in both gradual and instantaneous sanctification. No one really knows for sure if Wesley ever believed that he had personally received the second blessing.[19] In the American Holiness Movement, however, the second blessing became the core of their message.[20]

The movement also followed the pattern of its Pietist forbearers in that it tended to be guided more by emotions and subjective thought than by adherence to the word of God. The basic error of the American Holiness Movement was in thinking that there are two kinds of Christians – justified ones and sanctified ones. That concept will be evaluated in the light of the scriptures in Chapter 18.

CONCLUSION

The human struggle for holiness has produced both good and bad fruits. We did not become Christians in a vacuum. We cannot pretend that our generation has come to the Bible without being influenced by what has taken place before. It has been said that those who fail to learn the lessons of history are doomed to repeat it. The human struggle for holiness can be a source of encouragement to us as we "press on toward the goal to win the prize for which God has called us heavenward in Christ Jesus" (Phil. 3:14). Men like Anthony, Francis, Spener, Wesley and Finney were all quite likely well motivated to do just that. We applaud their effort and admire their courage in breaking loose from the status quo and reaching for a higher degree of Christian maturity. But these men were human and so are we. Humans are error prone. It is much easier to see their errors than our own because we are removed from their times and therefore we can look at them with a certain degree of objectivity. It is not so easy to evaluate our own struggles in the light of the Scriptures, but this we must do. A study of the past should enable us to avoid the same pitfalls.

Endnotes

1. Williston Walker, *A History of the Christian Church.* (Charles Scribner's Sons, 1918), p. 130.

2. Martin E. Marty, *A Short History of Christianity.* (Philadelphia: Fortress Press, 1959), p. 68.

3. Dallas Willard, *The Spirit of the Disciplines.* (San Francisco: Harper San Francisco, 1988), p. 137.

4. Ibid., 139.

5. Kenneth Scott Latourette, *a History of Christianity.* (New York: Harper and Row, 1953), p. 421.

6. Ibid.

7. Donald G. Bloesch, *Essentials of Evangelical Theology.* Vol. 2. (San Francisco: Harper and Row, 1978), p. 63.

8. Ibid., A breviary is a hymn book.

9. Monroe Hawley, "The Search For Holiness" part 2. Unpublished essay, n.d., p. 4.

10. Walker, *A History of the Christian Church.* pp. 495-496.

11. Robert H. Culpepper, *Evaluating the Charismatic Movement.* (Valley Forge, Pennsylvania: Judson Press, 1977) p. 42. Culpepper advances the thesis that both Pietism and the influence of Wesley were necessary antecedents to the beginning of the Pentecostal Movement.

12. Martin E. Marty, *Protestantism.* (New York: Holt, Rinehart and Winston, 1972), p. 64.

13. Latourette, *A History of Christianity.* p. 895.

14. John Dillenberger and Claude Welch, *Protestant Christianity.* (New York: Charles Scribner's Sons, 1954), p. 125.

15. Carl Mirbt, *Schaff Herzog Encyclopedia of Religious Knowledge.* Vol. IX, p. 34.

16. "Revival and Revolution." *Christian History.* Vol. II, No. 1, 1983. p. 34.

17. Gerald O. McCulloh, "The Theology and Practices of Methodism – 1876-1919." *The History of American Methodism.* (New York: Abingdon

Press, 1964), p. 610.

18. Ibid., p. 618.

19. Ibid., p. 609. "Wesley never left a complete and clear testimony to his own enjoyment of perfect love, although he recorded, studied and used as examples the experiences of hundreds of others."

20. Ibid., pp. 616-617. "Henry K. Carroll, supervisor of the Federal Census of 1890, wrote that the belief that perfection was 'obtainable instantaneously between justification and death' was a chief article of their faith."

18
Perfection

The world seems to be populated by those who demand perfection and by others who plead indulgence for their shortcomings. If the world were controlled by perfectionists, there would be no place for those who can never quite measure up to their standards. On the other hand if the world were under the domination of people who conduct life on the basis of *laissez faire* philosophy, we would probably suffocate in the accumulation of our own garbage within a week.

Fortunately, "practically perfect" people like Mary Poppins manage to get mixed up with the Dick Van Dykes of the world. A husband who is so organized that he can predict with a fair degree of accuracy when his next shoestring is going to break, inevitably gets paired with a wife who hasn't the foggiest notion what she's going to prepare for dinner at 3 o'clock in the afternoon. A wife, with such an obsession for cleanliness that she jumps out of bed at 1 o'clock in the morning because she suddenly remembers that she forgot to mop up a blob of spilled orange juice from the kitchen floor, marries a clod who comes in from a hunting trip and tracks mud all over the floor she just cleaned. So goes the struggle between perfection and the spirit of tolerance.

There's a certain amount of tension in every serious Christian's mind because in one compartment of the brain, there's a tug to live up to the absolute standards of doctrine, morality and spirituality outlined in the scriptures. But then on the other hand, our attempts to measure up to those standards are always flawed. Must we always be whipsawed between the demands of the Word on the one hand and our frail performance on the other? This question has generated serious discussion for centuries. Sincere students have not always been able to agree on a precise solution. It has been noted that "Few doctrines have created more divisiveness throughout the history of the Christian church than Christian perfection."[1]

The New Testament clearly articulates our need to "perfect holiness out of reverence for God" (II Cor. 7:1). Every serious minded Christian agrees that perfection is a desired objective, but the mere use of the term frightens us and raises questions. What is Biblical perfection? Does perfection imply sinlessness? Is perfection achievable in this life? How do we promote perfection without appearing to encourage legalism and arrogance? How do we achieve perfection? This chapter will concentrate on these important questions.

WHAT IS BIBLICAL PERFECTION?

The Old Testament

In our English translations of the Bible, the term "perfect" is most often used to translate two Hebrew words – *shalem*, which means wholeness or completeness and *tamin* which can be rendered "complete," "perfect," or "blameless."[2] Some selected usages of the term will serve to illustrate how these terms were used in the Old Testament on those occasions when they were applied to people.

Job is described as "blameless ("perfect" KJV) and upright" (Job 1:1,8). The psalmist urges his readers to "Consider the blameless, observe the upright; there is a future for the man of peace" (Psa. 37:37). These references are forms of *tamin*. The term occurs 132

242

times in the Old Testament.[3]

Shalem describes "a 'perfect heart,' i.e wholly or completely devoted to Jehovah" (I Kings 8:61; I Chron. 12:38; Isa. 38:3).[4]

Among those who are described in terms of perfection in the Old Testament are Noah (Gen. 6:9), Abram (Gen. 17:1), David (2 Sam. 22:4) and Job (Job 1:1). None of these lived before God without committing sin. Strauss correctly observes, "Neither the Torah nor the Psalms assume that the sincere Israelite can live in obedience to God's torah without atonement, without the need of forgiveness, i. e., sinless."[5] On what basis can it be said that the heroes of the Old Testament were perfect? Purely on the basis of grace. That's the gist of Paul's argument concerning Abraham in Romans 4. Paul points out, "If, in fact Abraham was justified by works (i.e sinless behavior), he had something to boast about but not before God" (verse 2). Trying to make a case for Abraham's perfection on the basis of performance is an impossibility. There were times that he lied and times that he wavered in his faith, but the direction of his total life was pointed toward God and Paul concludes, "What does the Scripture say? 'Abraham believed God and it was credited to him for righteousness' " (verse 3). Abraham could not claim perfection on his own merit, but God, in consideration of Abraham's faith, was willing to recognize him as a perfect person. Of course that was done as an act of grace.

The New Testament

"In the NT, 'perfect' is usually the translation[6] of *teleios*, primarily 'having reached the end,' 'term,' 'limit,' hence 'complete,' 'full,' 'perfect.'"[7] Its contextual usage in a number of New Testament passages often implies the concept of spiritual maturity. In I Corinthians 2:6, Paul indicates that his message could not be understood by everyone. He wrote, "We do, however speak a message of wisdom among the *mature*" ("them that are perfect" – KJV). He used the same word as a human development metaphor in I Corinthians 14:20, "Brothers, stop thinking like children. In regard to evil be infants, but in your thinking be adults *(teleios)*."

In Ephesians 4:13, the spiritual growth process was clearly in the apostle's mind when he wrote that the goal of the leadership gifts which are made available to the church is to bring God's people to the point that they "become mature." Paul declared himself to be "mature" ("perfect") in Philippians 3:15 even though he clearly stated that he had not reached perfection just two verses earlier. In Colossians 1:28, Paul verbalized his goal to "present everyone perfect in Christ."

According to Hebrews 5:14, "solid food is for the 'mature,' " but that virtue was lacking among the original readers of the Hebrew letter, so the writer urged his readers to "leave the elementary teachings about Christ and go on to maturity" ("perfection" -KJV) – Hebrews 6:1.

Moral perfection is another significant emphasis in the New Testament. In Matthew 5:48, Jesus spoke of a level of perfection that is patterned after the example of God. "Be perfect, therefore as your heavenly father is perfect." At first glance this passage troubles the discerning reader. After all, who could ever expect to measure up to God's standard of perfection? There is a sense in which the word, *teleios*, means to meet or fulfill a purpose. Barclay illustrates this use of the term,

> Suppose in my house there is a screw loose, and I want to tighten and adjust the screw. I go out to the ironmongers and I buy a screw-driver. I find the screw-driver exactly fits the grip of my hand; it is neither too large nor too small, too rough or too smooth. I lay the screw-driver on the slot of the screw, and I find it exactly fits. I turn the screw and the screw is fixed. In the Greek sense, and especially in the New Testament sense, the screw driver is *teleios*, because it exactly fulfilled the purpose for which I desired and bought it.[8]

Many scholars think that "perfect" is a confusing translation in Matthew 5:48. Jack P. Lewis suggests that " 'complete,' 'whole,' or 'mature' are nearer its meaning."[9] Although sinlessness is not the idea that Jesus taught, he was making a moral demand. The context emphasizes the love of neighbor and the love of enemies. God loves both the just and the unjust, causing the rain to fall on the crops of both. The follower of Christ must be willing to see with the same kind of compassionate eyes that God does.

Another dimension of perfection involves the disciplinary trials that

244

a Christian passes through. James points out "Perseverance must finish *(teleion)* its work so that you may be mature *(teleioi)* and complete, not lacking anything" (James 1:4).

"The concept of corporate perfection seen in a community united in love is expressed by the verb *katartizein*."[10] When Paul addressed the carnal division at Corinth, he exhorted the church to be "perfectly united in mind and thought." In Ephesians 4:12, Paul indicated that the leadership gifts in the church were given for the "perfecting *(katartismon)* of the saints" (KJV). The Hebrew author prayed that the great Shepherd of the sheep might "equip (KJV- perfect) you with every good thing for doing his will" (Heb. 13:20).

In summation it may be said that the New Testament concept of perfection

> ... does not imply absolute perfection but an unblemished character which has moral and spiritual integrity in relationship to God. The goal of spiritual maturity is set forth, and the believer is charged with making sincere and proper use of the spiritual resources available through Christ in order to attain this maturity in fellowship with Christ and the Christian community.[11]

PERFECTION THEORIES

Historically there have been two great tensions within Christendom with respect to the manner in which Christians are perfected. Bloesch was surely on target when he wrote, "Few doctrines have created more divisiveness throughout the history of the church than Christian perfection."[12] Although there are many positional variations on the theme of spiritual perfection, it can be accurately stated that Reformed theology represents perfectionism at one end of the spectrum, while Wesleyan philosophy expresses the opposite view.

Reformed Views of Perfection.

At one end of the spectrum is reformed theology. "Both the Lutheran and the Calvinist reformers reflected the Augustinian position that sin remains in humanity until death and therefore spiritual perfection is impossible in this life."[13] The emphasis in reformed thinking is on the action of God in extending grace to fallen and imperfect people who live with fleshly weaknesses on this side of eternity. Luther once observed, "Paul also calls Christians righteous, holy, and free from sin, not because they are, but because they have begun to be and should become people of this kind by making constant progress."[14] Sinclair B. Ferguson expresses the basic emphasis of reformed theology when he says, "It is rooted, not in humanity and their achievement of holiness or sanctification, but what God has done in Christ, and for us in union with him."[15]

Reformers tend to fear the concept of human perfection. To them it sounds like dragging a works theory of salvation back into the church. Gerhard Forde, a Lutheran writer, insists, "Sanctification is thus simply *the art of getting used to justification*."[16] He reminds us that justification is based on grace – unmerited favor. Thus he warns against the danger of viewing justification as "God's part" and sanctification or perfection as "our part." He sees such human attempts at being perfected as an attempt to make human performance the basis of salvation. The reformers emphasize the grace of God, fearing that emphasis on a human response to grace will result in legalism. Indeed the progress we make toward perfection can never be anything more than a response to grace, but it should be noted that our fleshly nature continues to stay with us and that progress in this life will always fall short of the desired objective to be "perfectly whole." The scriptures emphasize the principle of putting to death the "misdeeds of the body" by the Spirit. In a context that places heavy stress on justification by God's grace, Paul warns, "For if you live according to the sinful nature you will die" (Rom. 8:13).

In responding to Dr. Forde's essay on sanctification, Lawrence W. Wood, a Wesleyan theologian, conceded the importance of concentrating on the priority of grace, and even admits that too much emphasis on human perfection can lead to a simplistic list of legalistic do's and don'ts. But he sought to distance himself from the reformed view by noting, "A Christian perfection of love is a dialectical process of always growing and increasing in love, knowledge, and obedience to God."[17] Perhaps the fundamental error of those who concentrate on reformed viewpoints is a tendency to keep the subject of justification always in the foreground while neglecting sanctification altogether.

At its most dangerous extreme, the reformed view of perfection degenerates into "easy believism."[18] Obedience and discipline are only given lip service. Salvation by grace alone becomes the prominent emphasis. By the time the concept filters down to the rank and file church member, grace tends to be viewed as permission to sin without negative consequences. The scriptures clearly recognize the possibility that grace could be perverted into license and warns against such destructive reasoning. Romans 4 and 5 include some of the most profound teachings on grace to be found anywhere in the scriptures, but in 6:1,2 he warned, "Shall we go on sinning so that grace may increase? By no means! We died to sin; how can we live in it any longer?" Jude warned against " . . . godless men, who change the grace of our God into license for immorality and deny Jesus Christ our only Sovereign and Lord" (Jude 4).

The Wesleyan Theories of Perfection.

If reformed theology tends to err in the direction of accepting fleshly behavior as status quo living for the Christian, then certain Wesleyans surely err in the opposite direction in their insistence that a person can be freed from the desire to sin as the result of a second blessing.

Since the time of John Wesley, his followers have divided into many separate camps. A great deal of the division hinges on various interpretations of how one is perfected through a second blessing. Much has been written as to what Wesley meant or didn't mean by the concept of "perfect love." Wesley never actually came to believe that a person could reach a state of sinlessness in this life as is sometimes alleged, but he did believe that one can lose the desire to sin. When a person reached that plateau of spiritual development, Wesley described it as "perfect love." He said, "By sanctification, we are saved from the power and root of sin and restored to the image of God."[19] He called this experience "entire sanctification." To Wesley entire sanctification had to take place instantaneously.

It is thus that we wait for "entire sanctification," for full salvation

247

from our sins. . . . As to the means, I believe this perfection is wrought in the soul by the simple act of faith; consequently in an instant. But I believe in a gradual work both preceding and following that instant. As to time I believe the instant generally is the instant of death, the moment before the soul leaves the body. And I believe it can be ten, twenty or forty years before.[20]

The instant that one receives "entire sanctification" is often called "a second blessing" or a "second work of grace" among Wesleyan theologians. John Wesley's brother, Charles, sought to communicate the second blessing concept in his famous hymn "Love Divine." Note particularly the lyrics of the second stanza

> Breathe O breathe thy loving Spirit
> into every troubled breast;
> Let us all in thee inherit;
> Let us find the second[21] rest;
> Take away the love of sinning,
> Take our load of guilt away;
> Pray, and praise thee without ceasing,
> Glory in thy perfect love.

"Second rest," "take away the love of sinning," and "perfect love" are all Wesleyan catch phrases. It is quite possible that Charles Wesley did more to advance the concept of the second work of grace through his hymn writing than his brother did through his preaching.

One other aspect of Wesley's view of perfection needs to be noted. He had his own unique definition of sin. He did not believe that every transgression against God can properly be labeled, "sin." He made a distinction between voluntary transgression and involuntary transgressions. Shelton offers the following summary of Wesley's understanding of sin.

Wesley saw it as a perverted relationship to God....In this life the Christian does not attain absolute Christlikeness but suffers numerous infirmities, human faults, prejudices and involuntary transgressions. These however are not considered sin, for Wesley saw such sin as attitudinal and relational.[22]

As indicated in the two previous chapters, Wesley's view of holiness was initially something of a protest movement against the staid formalism and immorality of the Church of England during the seventeenth century. Two centuries later, certain Wesleyans would decide that other Wesleyans had become too worldly and sophisticated to lay any legitimate claim to holiness, thus a neo-Wesleyan movement sprang up in the late nineteenth and early twentieth centuries. When Wesley's theories are taken to an extreme, they produce self-righteousness and rigid legalism.[23]

The scriptures never speak of a dramatic, instantaneous, soul cleansing second work of grace. We are given the gift of the Spirit at baptism (Acts 2:38) and we are thus empowered to live resourceful and useful lives. We don't always use the resources that God has placed at our disposal, but they are present nonetheless. There is no need for a secondary work of grace to provide us the power for righteous living. What is needed is a willingness to use the resources God has already given us. Paul wrote to the Romans, "God has poured out his love into our hearts by the Holy Spirit, whom he has given us" (Rom. 5:8).

There is no evidence that God has created a class of "super" Christians who have shattered the "sin" barrier in a glorious instant and floated into a state of "perfect love." On the contrary Paul claimed, "You, however, are not controlled by the sinful nature but by the Spirit, if the Spirit of God lives in you. And if anyone does not have the Spirit of Christ, he does not belong to Christ. But if Christ is in you, your body is dead because of sin yet your spirit is alive because of righteousness" (Rom. 8:9-10). All such passages suggest that the Spirit resides in every faithful child of God, not just those who have received a "second blessing."

> There is nothing in Paul's teaching to suggest that sanctification is the special event of a unique experience or that there are two kinds or qualities of sanctification. All Christian living meant for him, clean, pure, right living and that was sanctification.[24]

If the reformers tend to promote a "cheap grace" kind of mindset among its rank and file advocates, then it can also be noted that those who follow the Wesleyan theories often get tangled up in pointing to superficial standards of morality as evidence of holiness. Bloesch noted, "Wesley's definition of sin as a conscious act of wrong-doing prepared the way for a surface view of sin which does not consider that sin is an essential state of being. . . . "[25] Paul wrote "For the sinful nature desires what is contrary to the Spirit and the Spirit what is contrary to the sinful nature. They are in conflict with each other, so that you do not do what you want" (Gal. 5:17-18). His readers were Christians who possessed the capacity to live by the Spirit (verse 16), to be led by the Spirit (verse 18) and to keep in step with the Spirit (verse 25). They belonged to Christ and had crucified the "sinful nature with its passions and desires" (verse 24). Paul is clearly describing a sanctified and perfected people, but they still lived with a sin nature. The "second blessing" theory ignores that important truth.

SUMMARY AND CONCLUSION

If a person walked into a church service from off the street without any prior knowledge of religious vocabulary, he would probably go away scratching his head in confusion if he happened to hear a group of Christians talking about perfection. It sounds like a strange concept to the secular person. After all, "nobody's perfect." If you've heard that cliche once, you've heard it a thousand times.

The discerning Bible reader soon comes to realize that "perfection" in the Word of God doesn't mean the same thing that it means in the common language of our time. It means something akin to "maturity," "completeness," or "wholeness." It has moral and ethical dimensions, but it is not to be equated with flawless performance.

Theologians come at the subject of perfection from different directions. Those in the reformed tradition are wedded to a doctrine of salvation by grace without any consideration of human participation. Any emphasis on humans reaching toward perfection tends to gum up their theological machinery, so they often place heavy emphasis on justification while they tip toe around sanctification and perfection. Those whose thinking about sanctification is rooted in the philosophy of John Wesley have picked up the ball which the reformers dropped. They are quite willing to admit and to promote the concept of human perfection. In doing so, they go to an unwarranted extreme when they insist that a "second work of grace" is needed to complete the first portion of grace which a person receives at conversion. Their claim that the "sin desire" is eradicated causes them to reduce sinfulness to outward, wilful acts and ignores the fleshly nature with which we all live.

We need to learn how to avoid extremes on the subject of perfection. The person who shrugs the shoulder and says, "Well, nobody's perfect," fails to face reality, but the person who says, "I no longer have to struggle with my sin nature," is fooling himself and may well fall into the trap of self-righteousness.

Endnotes

1. Donald G. Bloesch, *Essentials of Evangelical Theology.* Vol. 2. (San Francisco: Harper and Row, 1978), p. 47.

2. W.L. Walker, "Perfection" *International Standard Bible Encyclopedia.* Vol. IV. (Grand Rapids, Michigan: William B. Eerdmans Company, 1955), p. 2320.

3. James D. Strauss, *Holiness and Wholeness.* (Lincoln, Illinois: Lincoln Christian Seminary. Duplicated outline. n.d.) p. 1.

4. Walker, "Perfection." p. 2320.

5. Strauss, "Holiness and Wholeness." p. 4.

6. "tr." stands for "translation."

7. W.L. Walker, "Perfection." p. 2321.

8. William Barclay, *The Daily Study Bible – The Gospel of Matthew.* (Vol. 1). (Edinburgh: The Saint Andrew Press, 1956), p. 176.

9. Jack P. Lewis, *The Gospel According to Matthew.* Part 1. (Austin, Texas: Sweet Publishing Company, 1976), p. 97.

10. R.L. Shelton, "Perfection, Perfectionism" *Evangelical Dictionary of Theology.* (Grand Rapids, Michigan: Baker Book House, 1984), p. 839.

11. Ibid., p. 840.

12. Bloesch, *Essentials of Theology.* Vol. 2, p. 47.

13. Ibid., p. 841.

14. Martin Luther in *Martin Luther's Works.* Vol. 29, p. 139, quoted by Donald G. Bloesch, *Essentials of Evangelical Theology.* Vol. 2. (San Francisco: Harper and Row Publishers, 1978), p. 48.

15. Sinclair B. Ferguson, "The Reformed View" *Christian Spirituality.* (Downer's Grove, Illinois: InterVarsity, Press, 1988), pp. 58-59.

16. Gerhard O. Forde, "The Lutheran View" *Christian Spirituality.* p. 13.

17. Laurence W. Wood, "A Wesleyan Response" *Christian Spirituality.* p. 38.

18. John MacArthur, Jr. preaches out of a Calvinistic bias, but he has seen the fruits of "easy believism" and has raised his voice against it. He deplores the fact that "There is now an atmosphere of 'easy believism' that allows people to experience an initial happiness in encountering the gospel, but not a deep, long term joy derived from serious obedience to Christ's commands." (John MacArthur, Jr., *Kingdom Living Here and Now.* Chicago: Moody Press, 1980, p. 7). Somewhat predictably, MacArthur has been challenged by others from within the Calvinistic ranks on the ground that his demand for serious obedience reduces salvation to a matter of works. The most significant challenge to MacArthur's view of "Lordship salvation" has been mounted by Zane C. Hodges of Dallas Theological Seminary, MacArthur's alma mater.

19. John Wesley, *The Nature of Holiness.* (ed. Clare George Weakley, Jr). (Minneapolis: Bethany House Publishers, 1988), p. 161.

20. John Wesley, *By John Wesley* ed. T. Otto Nalls (New York: Association Press, 1961), pp. 91-92.

21. Many Restoration Movement hymnals inserted the word "promised" in place of "second," in an obvious attempt to change the author's original intent in composing the hymn.

22. R.S. Shelton, "Perfection, Perfectionism." *Evangelical Dictionary of Theology.* p. 842.

23. Wesley himself was narrow and legalistic according to the standards of most contemporary Christians. He thought that all frivolity and merry making was contrary to the spirit of Christ. He specifically railed against dancing, attending the theater and even the playing of games. For a discussion of his views on worldliness, see his sermon, "In What Sense We Are to Leave the World" in *The Nature of Holiness.* p. 128.

24. Rall, "Sanctification," *International Bible Encyclopedia.* p. 2684.

25. Bloesch, *Essentials of Evangelical Theology.* Vol. 2, p. 50.

19
How We Are Made Holy

The Bible contains certain statements which appear to be contradictory when viewed simplistically. In our study of the Bible we must remember that we are reading inspired communication – literature that cannot always be measured by the normal human categories of reasoning. There are times when the Word of God presents two ideas " . . . which are both true and yet both seem to contradict each other. This is called an *antinomy*."[1] Failure to recognize the existence of antinomies has often contributed to religious division. This is especially true in the realm of holiness.

In I Corinthians 6:11, Paul said that the members of the Corinthian church "were sanctified (made holy)." Later on he corresponded with that same church and discussed their need to perfect holiness (II Cor. 7:1). In one context Paul was quite willing to designate a church that contained more than a few imperfections in its membership as a "sanctified" people, but later on he would tell that same group of people that they still needed to perfect holiness. That is an antinomy.

The antinomy of holiness can best be understood by recognizing that Christians experience holiness at different levels. All Christians are holy in one sense of the term. Through the grace of God we are granted holy status at conversion. Kenneth Wuest preferred to describe this dimension of holiness as *positional holiness*,[2] while John Murray elected to use the expression *definitive sanctification*[3] to designate the same concept.

There is also a dimension of holiness which involves personal growth. This level of the holiness experience could well be characterized as *progressive holiness, maturing sanctification,* or *developmental holiness.*

There is a third level in the human dimension of holiness which cannot be achieved in this life, but will be experienced when we are no longer hampered by our fleshly nature. *Prospective sanctification* or *anticipated holiness* might be suitable terms for identifying this ultimate plateau to which all Christians aspire and will experience when they finally enter the eternal presence of God.

POSITIONAL HOLINESS

To say that all Christians are positionally holy is to affirm that God, through his eyes of mercy, is willing to see us as holy people. Holiness " . . . is what we are already by virtue of our being called by God. Every Christian is holy when he or she confesses Christ and is baptized into Christ. We are holy whether we like it or not. We are holy because we are God's."[4]

Basic Requirements for Positional Holiness.
1. The Blood of Christ. A person is not granted the status of positional holiness as the result of human effort. "When a penitent believer is baptized into Christ, he touches the blood of the Savior and in that same act, he is sanctified."[5] The author of Hebrews connected sanctification with the blood of Christ in three different places. In Hebrews 10:10 he said, " . . . we have been made holy through the sacrifice of the body of Jesus Christ once for all." The deliberate sinner is warned against walking away from the grace of God. "How much more severely do you think a man deserves to be punished who has

trampled the Son of God under foot, who has treated as an unholy thing *the blood of the covenant that sanctified him,* and who has insulted the Spirit of grace" (Heb. 10:29). In Hebrews 13:12, the writer stated, "And so Jesus also suffered outside the city gate to *make the people holy through his own blood."*

2. The impartation of God's Grace. Most theological treatises on holiness include lengthy discussions of sanctification as a separate process from justification. Actually they need to be considered together. Paul saw the two acts occurring simultaneously in I Corinthians 6:11. "But you were washed, you were sanctified, you were justified in the name of the Lord Jesus Christ and by the Spirit of our God." "Sanctification and justification are not two separate actions occurring at different times, but are part of the process of salvation."[6]

Positional sanctification occurs at the same time one is justified. Justification, which occurs as the result of grace, can never be earned by any expression of human endeavor. "This righteousness from God comes through faith in Christ Jesus to all who believe. There is no difference for all have sinned and fall short of the glory of God, and are justified freely by his grace through the redemption that came by Christ Jesus" (Rom. 3:22-24).

The grace-faith principle of justification, which enables us to become positionally holy, cannot be viewed as a benefit issuing from a program which combines grace and works. Some Christians often like to think of grace as filling in the gap created by our inadequate performance. They visualize the frail hand of man reaching up toward heaven while the powerful hand of God reaches down and makes contact, thus taking up the slack when we can't do everything just right. Christians who understand grace this way have missed the picture entirely. Justification is not based on our performance at all! Our righteousness before God is a declared righteousness and never a human achievement.

Some scoff at the idea of "imputed righteousness," but there can be no other kind! After all "There is none righteous, no not one" (Rom. 3:10). The prophet Isaiah was emphatic on this point. "All of us have become like one who is unclean and all our righteous acts are like filthy rags" (Isaiah 64:6). Justification by works and justification by grace are two mutually exclusive principles. Like oil and water they do not mix. Paul declared it to be so in Romans 11:5-6, "So too, at the present time, there is a remnant chosen by grace. And if by grace, then it is no longer by works; if it were, grace would no longer be grace."

3. Baptism into Christ. Much of the Protestant world resists the thought that baptism would be connected with positional holiness in any sense. Many people regard baptism as a work, and of course they would be right in rejecting it as a necessary ingredient in positional holiness if our own worthiness could be enhanced by baptism in any way. To view baptism in the sacramental sense would place it at odds with the principles of grace that have been stated in the previous section.[7]

It should be noted that baptism is never called a *work* in the scriptures. According to Galatians 3:26-27, it is an act of faith. In Romans 6, Paul spoke about baptism in connection with a Christian's commitment to resist sin. He anticipated the possibility that some people might twist his teachings on grace around and make it appear that sinning is the best way to tap into God's reservoir of grace. He countered that argument by reminding Christians of the purpose of their baptism. When we were baptized "into Christ" (Rom. 6:3), we died to sin (Col. 2:12-13). It is in the act of baptism that we identify with the death of Christ and begin the new life (verse 4). "What is the significance of this Spirit-wrought resurrection within our souls? Basically it is a change within us that breaks the grip of sin upon our hearts and makes it possible to live a life that is holy and pleasing to God."

Practical Effects of Positional Holiness
1. It becomes the basis of our assurance. If our position of holiness is established by the blood of Christ, then it also follows that this position is maintained by the blood of Christ, which is exactly what John said in I John 1:7. "But if we walk in the light as he is in the light, we have fellowship with one another and the blood of Jesus, his son, purifies us from every sin." From the standpoint of positional holiness, the key term in this verse is *purifies*. John R. W. Stott pointed out:

The verb suggests that God does more than forgive; He erases the stain of sin. And the present tense shows that it is a continuous process. What is clear is that if we walk in the light, God has made provisions to cleanse us from whatever sin, from what otherwise mars our fellowship with him or each other.[9]

Some Christians believe that a child of God is removed from grace (and presumably positional holiness) every time a sin is committed. If that be the case, confident Christian living is a virtual impossibility because one would almost have to die with a prayer of forgiveness on his lips in order to be assured of salvation. John insisted that we ought to be able to live with more confidence than that. He said, "I write these things to you who believe in the name of the Son of God so that you may know that you have eternal life" (I John 5:13).

It is true that a person can choose to walk away from the grace of God and the blood that sanctifies us (Heb. 10:29), but a Christian is not removed from purified status so long as he or she continues to walk in the light (I John 1:7).

Can we know when we've walked out of the light and away from our holy position in Christ? The Word of God addresses the subject of human apostasy at several different points. Consider the thoughts of the psalmist.

Who can discern his errors? Forgive my hidden faults. Keep your servant also from willful sins: may they not rule over me. Then will I be blameless, innocent of great transgression (Psa. 19:12-13).

Notice that the psalmist considered himself "blameless" and "innocent of great transgression" when willful sins did not rule over him. This same kind of thought occurs at other points in scripture. In Romans 6:14 Paul wrote, "For sin shall not be your master, because you are not under law, but under grace." When grace becomes the focal point of a person's life, the control center shifts from sin to obedience. In this text, the term "master" is crucial because it indicates the way of thinking that dominates a Christian's life. Paul does not suggest that the Christian never sins, but urges the Christian not to allow sin to take charge of his life.

James offers further insight into the progressive nature of sin. He wrote, " . . . but each one is tempted when, by his own evil desire, he is dragged away and enticed. Then, after desire has conceived, it gives birth to sin; and sin, when it is full grown, gives birth to death" (James 1:14-15). According to James, spiritual death does not occur at the time a person commits sin, but only when sin is "full grown."

In II Peter 2:20, an additional insight is offered to the concepts presented by the scriptures already cited. Peter said, "If they have escaped the corruption of the world by knowing our Lord and Savior Jesus Christ and are again entangled in it and overcome, they are worse off at the end than they were at the beginning." Please note that Peter uses the term "overcome."

When does a person leave the grace of God? A person leaves the grace of God only after committing willful sin, exchanging the mastery of Christ for the mastery of sin, allowing sin to become full grown, and becoming so entangled in sin that one is overcome by it. While this still does not define "the edge," it does give encouragement to the Christian who truly wants to do the will of God. According to I John 1:7 the blood of Christ keeps that person cleansed. It's only those people who want to see how close they can walk "to the edge" who are immediately endangered by the threat of falling away.[10]

2. It is the foundation on which a life of progressive holiness is built. Many Christians are afraid that too much emphasis on the doctrine of positional holiness will lead to a permissive attitude concerning behavior and Christian responsibility. Paul anticipated the permissive response in Romans 6:1-2 "What shall we say then? Shall we go on sinning that grace may increase? By no means! We died to sin; how can we live in it any longer?"

Paul clearly addressed I Corinthians to a group of Christians whom he considered positionally holy (1:2; 6:11). His affirmation of their sanctified status occurred in the midst of a warning against sexual immorality, idolatry, adultery, prostitution, homosexuality, thievery, greed, drunkenness, slander and swindling (I Cor. 6:9-10). He was writing to a church in which the practice of sexual immorality was even more promiscuous than it was in the pagan community. He pointed out that their continuation in such behavior could result in their exclusion from the kingdom of God. But instead of concentrating entirely on the negative consequences of such behavior, he appealed to their sense of spiritual excellence. He made them aware of

258

their positional holiness. " . . . .But you were washed, you were sanctified, you were justified in the name of the Lord Jesus Christ and by the Spirit of our God" (verse 11).

The New Testament never presents the grace of God as a license to commit sin. On the contrary grace is seen as a stimulus to responsible living. "For the grace of God that brings salvation has appeared to all men. It teaches us to say 'No' to ungodliness and worldly passions, and to live self-controlled, upright and godly lives in this present age . . . " (Titus 2:11-12).

Positional sanctification means that we have been delivered from our old life of sinful rebellion through the blood of Christ.[11] As positionally holy people we do not live our earthly lives " . . . .for evil human desires, but rather for the will of God" (I Pet. 4:2). We did not receive the gift of grace so that we could indulge ourselves in worldly lifestyles and soothe our troubled consciences with sentimental thoughts about grace. On the contrary, the same grace of God which delivers us from the burden of our sinful past, also sets in place the leadership gifts in the church, which have been given for the "perfecting of the saints" (Eph. 4:7-13). Furthermore when Jesus died for the church, his atoning blood had the effect of making the church holy (Eph. 5:26). As Given Blakely has correctly noted, "It must be recognized that grace is given for the achievement of the divine purpose in people, not to circumvent it."[12]

PROGRESSIVE HOLINESS

A Rationale for Progressive Holiness

"The scriptures do not teach self-sanctification, but they do depict man as active in realizing the fruits of sanctification in Christ."[13] Continuation in the grace of God is dependent on "walking in light" (I John 1:7-10). Contrary to the thinking of the proponents of the Calvinistic doctrine of perseverance, children of God have the capacity to walk away from their sanctified position if they so choose. Peter spoke of people who have "escaped the corruption of the world," but who nevertheless became entangled in it and overcome by it. He said, "It would have been better for them not to have known the way of

259

righteousness, than to have known it and then to turn their backs on the sacred commandment that was passed on to them. Of them the proverbs are true: 'A dog returns to its vomit' and 'A sow that is washed goes back to her wallowing in the mud' " (II Pet. 2:21-22).

Furthermore progress in the matter of holiness requires a conscious decision of the mind and willing participation in God's program of spiritual growth. Paul proposed an active agenda of spiritual enterprise among the Christians in the Colossian church. He urged them to "Set your minds on things above, not on earthly things" (Col. 3:2). This program of "heavenly mindedness" required the performance of earthly activities. Both negative and positive features characterized the spiritual development process. The Colossians were expected to "Put to death, therefore, whatever belongs to your earthly nature: sexual immorality, impurity, lust, evil desires and greed, which is idolatry" (Col. 3:6). On the positive side they were urged,

> Therefore, as God's chosen people, holy and dearly loved, clothe yourselves with compassion, kindness, humility, gentleness and patience. Bear with each other and forgive whatever grievances you may have against one another. Forgive as the Lord forgave you (Col. 3:12-13).

Progressive holiness is always a process and never an achievement. Wuest observed,

> The work of the Holy Spirit in the yielded saint in which the believer is set apart for God in his experience by eliminating sin from his life and producing fruit, a process which goes on continually throughout the believer's life is called progressive sanctification.[14]

Progressing in holiness goes beyond superficial changes in things like vocabulary, habits and lifestyles. Reading the Bible every day, setting a time for daily devotionals, attending church services on a regular basis, and getting involved in the organized ministries of the church are all excellent practices but they do not guarantee progress in holiness. R. C. Sproul recalled,

> When I first became a Christian I was introduced to the priori-

260

ties of the Christian community. I quickly learned that it was expected of me that I have a daily devotion time, a time reserved for Bible reading and prayer. I was expected to go to church. I was expected to have a kind of piety that was evident by not cursing, not drinking, not smoking and the like. I had no idea that Biblical righteousness went far beyond these things.[15]

Sproul went on to explain, "Righteousness is doing what is right in the sight of God."[16] We can only begin to make progress in holiness when we identify ourselves so completely with Christ that we begin to yearn for the things that God yearns for and we begin to value the things that God values. Paul understood this point very well. He said, "I have been crucified with Christ and I no longer live, but Christ lives in me. The life I live in the body, I live by faith of the Son of God, who loved me and gave himself for me" (Gal. 2:20).

The Mechanics of Progressive Holiness

While it's true that people who are born into the family of God are made positionally holy, the fact remains that we do not lose that part of our personality known as "the flesh" or "the sinful nature" when we become Christians. It is possible for the Christian to live according to the sinful nature (Rom. 8:13), to gratify the desires of it (Rom. 13:14), to indulge it (Gal. 5:16), to follow the corrupt desire of it (II Pet. 2:10) and to sow to please the sinful nature (Gal. 6:8). The New Testament writers advocated a program of resistance against the the seduction of the flesh. It has both positive and negative elements, known in theology as *mortification* and *transformation*.

Mortification

There is a sense in which we put to death the old nature when we are baptized into Christ. Paul noted that we died with Christ in the act of baptism (Rom. 6:3-4) and that in the same act we assumed an entirely new attitude toward sin. "For we know that our old self was crucified with him so that the body of sin might be rendered powerless, that we should no longer be slaves to sin – because anyone who has died has been freed from sin" (Rom. 6:6-7).

Because of this personal inner death and resurrection, we as

261

Christians no longer have any excuse for sin or any reason to sin. Sin's grip on our hearts is broken; we are free from its enslaving power. Holiness is no longer just a duty to be slavishly pursued, but a blessed possibility to be grasped with joy and thanksgiving. Such is the nature of our salvation.[17]

While it's true that there's no reason to sin and we are even released from our indebtedness to the sinful nature (Rom. 8:12), the fact remains that we retain the capacity to sin as long as we live in the mortal body. Vulnerability to temptation is common to the entire human race (I Cor. 10:13), including the body of the saved. We are warned, "If we claim to be without sin, we deceive ourselves and the truth is not in us" (I John 1:8).

The negative part of progressive holiness involves the act of consciously dying to sin. To avoid being controlled by the sinful nature, Paul urges the child of God to "put to death the misdeeds of the body" (Rom. 8:13). The Christian is to make a conscious effort to "Put to death, therefore, whatever belongs to your earthly nature: sexual immorality, impurity, lust, evil desires and greed, which is idolatry" (Col. 3:5).

Transformation

It must be understood however, that "sanctification involves more than cleansing from sin."[18] The Christian life involves a new way of living. "Therefore, if anyone is in Christ, he is a new creation; the old has gone, the new has come" (II Cor. 5:17). We rise from the waters of baptism to "live a new life" (Rom. 6:4). Several years ago, this author had the privilege of leading a sincere seeker to Christ. A few days after his new beginning, I visited with the man's mother-in-law. During the course of our conversation, she said, "Frank doesn't seem like the same man since he became a Christian." I responded, "That's because he isn't."

The new life isn't static, however. We all rejoice when a new baby enters the world, but at the same time we expect that new baby to continue to change and grow. The same thing is true in God's spiritual family. When Peter wrote to encourage Christians scattered throughout the Roman empire, he said, "Like newborn babies, crave pure spiritual milk, so that by it you may grow up in your salvation, now that you have tasted that the Lord is good" (I Peter 2:2-3).

"The most expressive term used in the New Testament to indicate the progression that terminates in conformity to the image of Christ is that of transformation."[19] Paul used that term in Romans 12:2 as he exhorted the brothers and sisters in Rome to respond approriately to God's mercy, "Do not conform any longer," he wrote, "to the pattern of this world, but be transformed by the renewing of your mind. Then you will be able to test and approve what God's will is – his good, pleasing and perfect will" (Rom. 12:2).

In II Corinthians 3, Paul graphically described the glorious hope of the Christian by contrasting its lasting brilliance with the fading brilliance of the glory that shone on the face of Moses after he made the long trek down the slopes of Sinai. As Paul saw it, the challenge of gradually being altered to conform to the likeness of Jesus, far surpasses the glory that Moses knew. He said, "And we, who with unveiled faces all reflect the Lord's glory, are being transformed into his likeness with ever increasing glory, which comes from the Lord, who is the Spirit" (II Cor. 3:18).

How Progressive Holiness Takes Place

1. It is accomplished through our exposure to the Word of God. In his intercessory prayer just prior to his arrest, Jesus prayed, "Sanctify them by the truth; your word is truth" (John 17:17). Both mortification and transformation require knowledge. Paul recalled, " . . . .For I would not have known what it was to covet if the law had not said, 'do not covet'"(Rom. 7:7). The written word provides the Christian with indispensible guidance. It is, in fact, impossible to distinguish truth from error without a knowledge of the word. It must be remembered that the ancient people of God drifted away from him when they neglected the word. God lamented through the pen of Hosea, "my people are destroyed from lack of knowledge" (Hosea 4:6).

2. It is accomplished through the activity of the Holy Spirit. The sinful nature has a such a strong influence on the child of God that resistance through human genius is a virtual impossibilty. Paul reminded the Romans, "For if you live according to the sinful nature, you will die; but if by the Spirit you put to death the misdeeds of the body, you will live . . . " (Rom. 8:13). Elsewhere he indicates that it is the power of the Spirit in the inner being which enables the follower of Christ to ". . . grasp how wide and long and high and deep is the love of Christ, and to know this love that surpasses knowledge – that you may be filled to the measure of all the fullness of God" (Eph. 3:18-19). In addition the Spirit is active in the Christian's prayer life making intercession "with groans that words cannot express" (Rom. 8:26).

3. It is accomplished through the activity of the Christian. "Out of deference to all the stress that falls upon God's agency in sanctification, we must not fall into the error of quietism and fail to take account of the activity of the believer himself."[20] How else do we explain the fact that the Christian life is depicted as a warfare? As children of God we are challenged to understand that we struggle against ". . . the powers of this dark world and against the spiritual forces of evil in the heavenly realms" (Eph. 6:12). God doesn't bypass human effort in this struggle, rather he equips us so that we may take the initiative to arm ourselves against the "flaming arrows of the evil one" (Eph. 6:13-18). It is in the realm of progressive holiness that "work out your salvation with fear and trembling" (Phil. 2:12) is best understood.[21] Bloesch observed, "The motivation and power come from the Holy Spirit, but it is up to us to cooperate with the Spirit in bringing this blessing to fruition."[22]

PROSPECTIVE HOLINESS

In this present life we cannot expect to achieve "maximum" holiness. Paul saw a shortfall in his own performance, but was not discouraged from pursuing the goal of perfection.

Not that I have already obtained all this, or have already been made perfect, but I press on to take hold of that for which Christ took hold of me. Brothers, I do not consider myself yet to have taken hold of it. But one thing I do: Forgetting what is behind and straining toward what is ahead, I press on toward the goal to win the prize for which God has called me heavenward in Christ Jesus (Phil 3:12-14).

There will come a time when our holiness will be complete. John promised, "Dear friends, now we are children of God, and what we will be has not yet been made known. But we know that when he appears, we shall be like him, for we shall see him as he is" (I John 3:2). Paul anticipated the day when "the perishable must be clothed with the imperishable, and the mortal with immortality" (I Cor. 15:53). Surely at that time the prospect of total holiness will be realized.

SUMMARY AND CONCLUSION

The phrase, *positional holiness,* refers to the status granted to us by the grace of God when we are born into the family of God. We can do nothing to earn this position and we are all in the position of holiness if we have been born again. *Progressive holiness* is a designation for the maturing process that takes place in every growing child of God. It does involve human effort, but it cannot be achieved through human effort alone. The challenge to make progress in holiness is not confined to superficial behavior and vocabulary changes, but involves a complete transformation of attitude and a desire to overcome the tendency toward being controlled by the sinful nature. *Prospective holiness* looks beyond the limitations that are common to our earthly pilgrimmage to the time when we will be granted a position in the throne room of God and will be transformed into the likeness of Christ.

Endnotes

1. Bill R. Swetmon, *Unlocking Mysteries of God's Word.* (Nashville, Tennessee: Gospel Advocate Company, 1985), p. 3.

2. Kenneth Wuest, *Studies in the Vocabulary of the Greek New Testament.* (Grand Rapids, Michigan: William B. Eerdmans Company, 1945), p. 31.

3. John Murray, "Sanctification (The Law)" in *Basic Christian Doctrines.* (ed. Carl F.H. Henry). (New York: Holt, Rinehart and Winston, 1962), p. 227.

4. Charles A. McNeely, "Restoring the Biblical Ideal of Holiness." *Restoration Forum VII.* (Joplin, Missouri: College Press 1989), p. 5.

5. Norman L. Bales, *How Do I Know I Am Saved?* (Nashville, Tennessee: Gospel Advocate Company, 1989), p. 149.

6. Swetmon, *Unlocking Mysteries of God's Word.* p. 99. Swetmon expanded his thought along these lines with a quotation from J.K.S. Reid. "Sanctification" in Alan Richardson (ed.) *A Theological Word Book of the Bible.* (New York: The Macmillan Company, 1950). Reid wrote, "It is tempting for the sake of logical neatness to make a clear division between the two (sanctification and justification); but the temptation must be resisted, if in the fact the division is absent from the Holy Scripture. The definition of terms at this point is eased if justification be given a declaratory, imputed or forensic character. The way is then open to regard sanctification as the real status thereby conferred, which in its turn awaits exemplification, practice or exercise, just as from the newly accoladed nobleman one expects noble deeds."

7. Sacramentalism is defined as "the doctrine that there is in the sacraments themselves by Christ's institution a direct spiritual power to confer grace upon the recipient." Clarence L. Barnhart (ed), *The World Book Dictionary.* (Chicago: Field Enterprises Educational Corporation, 1971), Vol. 2 p. 1283. Baptism is an act of faith (Gal. 3:26-27) and not a sacrament.

8. Jack Cottrell, *Baptism A Biblical Study.* (Joplin, Missouri: College Press, 1989), pp. 86-87.

9. John R. W. Stott, *Tyndale New Testament Commentaries – The Epistles of John.* (Leicester, England: Intervarsity Press, 1960; Grand Rapids Michigan: William B. Eerdmans Company, 1983), pp. 75-76.

10. I am indebted to Joe Beam for these insights concerning the way we can know a Christian walks away from grace and positional holiness. The material is available on cassette tape and may be ordered from Change Dynamics International, 119 Davis Road, Suite 7 B, Martinez, GA 30907.

11. For a discussion of the relationship between both positional and progressive holiness and the saving grace of God, see "Sanctification and Grace" in the author's book, *How Do I Know I'm Saved,* pp. 146-160.

12. Given O. Blakely, "The Tutelage of God's Grace." *The Banner of Truth.* June, 1990. p. 1.

13. Donald G. Bloesch, *Essentials of Evangelical Theology.* Vol. 2. (San Francisco: Harper and Row, 1982), p. 32.

14. Wuest, *Studies in the Vocabulary of the Greek New Testament.* (Grand Rapids, Michigan: William B. Eerdmans Company, 1954), p. 31.

15. R. C. Sproul, *Pleasing God.* (Wheaton, Illinois: Tyndale House, 1988), p. 33.

16. Ibid., p. 34.

17. Jack Cottrell, *Baptism, A Biblical Study*, pp. 87-88.
18. Murray, "Sanctification (The Law)" p. 230.
19. Ibid.
20. Ibid., p. 232.
21. Murray is correct when he suggests, "God's working is not suspended because we work. There is correlation and conjunction of both." Ibid., p. 232.
22. Bloesch, *Essentials of Evangelical Theology*, p. 32.

20
Progressive Holiness - Getting Started

Let's construct the following imaginary scenario. Jim and Charlotte Prescott grew up in an unchurched family. Early in their marriage they sensed a certain emptiness in their lives and began conducting a truth search. Their search led them to a study of the scriptures and conversion to Christ. In their sincere desire to "grow in grace and knowledge," they were confronted by the mandate of Hebrews 12:14. "Make every effort to live in peace with all men and to be holy; without holiness no one will see the Lord."

As noted in the previous chapter, there is a sense in which Jim and Charlotte have already become holy. As baptized believers they have been granted holy status in the eyes of God (I Cor. 6:11). But the Prescotts realized the need to grow in holiness. Their habits, lifestyles, attitudes, perceptions and judgments have all been molded by a lifetime spent in measuring things by secular values. Their new commitment will not allow them to follow the ways of the world and the ruler of the kingdom of the air as they did when they were "dead in . . . transgressions and sins" (Eph. 2:1).

Progressive holiness will not be easy for Jim and Charlotte, nor will they reach their goal of being like Jesus through instantaneous transformation. James Le Fan described the challenge faced by people like the Prescotts,

> The beginning of the holy life is a frail and feeble thing. Good so far as it goes, and full of hopefulness, but needing growth, culture, or in the words of Paul, "perfecting." At this point, the believer is like a crude block of marble in the hands of a sculptor; every day the sculptor chisels at the block and little by little a vague likeness begins to emerge between the model and the marble. However, it is not until the hammer has fallen again and again and the sculptor has examined the model again and again that there is a genuine likeness.[1]

Staying with the sculpture model, let's assume that Jim and Charlotte have just been given new hammers, chisels and a large block of granite. Where do they strike the first blows? The project of sculpting a holy life requires a lifetime of spiritual diligence, but it has to start somewhere. Furthermore, we do not want Jim and Charlotte to be so devastated by the massiveness of their task that they lay their tools aside in desperation. This chapter will deal with the challenge of getting started on building a holy life.

CONCENTRATING ON CONVERSION

Jim and Charlotte have undergone a genuine conversion to Christ. The conversion experience is a watershed event in the lifetime of every child of God. The day a person is born into God's family is so significant that everything which took place in one's life prior to that event is seen in one light and everything that happens afterward is seen in an entirely different light. The person who wants to make progress in holiness must comprehend the nature of the change, know when it took place and understand how it affects life.

Progress Toward the Goal of Holiness Starts with the Awareness of a New Life.

The possibility of starting life all over again both baffled and intrigued Nicodemus (John 3:1-3). In response to Nicodemus' inquiries, Jesus connected the beginning of a new life with entry into the kingdom of God. "I tell you the truth, unless a man is born of water and the Spirit, he cannot enter into the kingdom of God" (John 3:5).

All those who have established a harmonious relationship with Jesus can properly be described as "born again." The popular expression, "born again Christian" is a redundancy. Biblically speaking there are no unregenerated Christians.

The experience of the new birth enables us to see ourselves in a totally different light. A person who becomes a Christian is a "new creation" (II Cor. 5:17, Gal. 6:15). Those who have converted to Christ have adopted new attitudes in their minds (Eph. 4:23) and they have put on a new self which is "created to be like God in true righteousness and holiness" (Eph. 4:24). The new self is also "being renewed in knowledge in the image of its Creator."

Our awareness of this new status fuels the desire for holy behavior. Paul's awareness of his new position in relationship to Christ caused him to think in terms of possessing a completely new identity. He wrote, "I have been crucified with Christ and I no longer live, but Christ lives in me. The life I live in the body, I live by the faith of the Son of God, who loved me and gave himself for me" (Gal. 2:20). His new identity so consumed him that he thought of his past achievements in negative terms. He wrote, "But whatever was to my profit, I now consider loss for the sake of Christ. What is more, I consider everything a loss compared to the surpassing greatness of knowing Christ Jesus my Lord, for whose sake I have lost all things" (Phil. 3:7-8).

As these words were being written, most serious minded Americans were concerned about the Persian Gulf war and the prospects of peace in the Middle East at the end of the conflict. One of the many media "Middle East experts" offered an explanation of the religious "fanaticism" that governs the decisons made by fundamentalist Moslems. He said, "To them, their religion is everything. It affects everything they do in life. They make no decision in life without considering how it relates to their faith. By contrast, Americans refuse to take anyone seriously who allows religion to dominate life." What a tragic comment on the attitudes that prevail in so-called "Christian" America.

If Jim and Charlotte are to make progress in following after holiness, they must assume the same posture toward Christ that the news commentator said the Moslem people of the Middle East assume toward their faith. They must understand that leaving the world and entering the fellowship of Christ means a radical departure from their old ways of living.

Progress in Holiness Requires Reinforcement of the Conversion Experience.

When my youngest son entered the work force, he decided that he wanted to buy a sports car. To his way of thinking he was able to arrange favorable terms with a car dealer. There was just one catch. The dealer wanted my name on the note. Sometimes fathers go through periods of temporary insanity. That's the only excuse I can give for caving in and signing my name on the loan contract. A short time later, I began asking myself, "What on earth have I done?"

Something very similar often takes place in the life of a new Christian. The act of conversion means that "the old self was crucified with him so that the body of sin might be rendered powerless" (Rom. 6:6). Jim and Charlotte may well experience a case of "buyer's blues" a short time after their conversion. Friends may question the wisdom of their decision. Research indicates that social pressure is often the primary influence when people defect from the faith.[2]

Jim and Charlotte will need to re-examine their motives for becoming Christians in the first place. They need to restudy the scriptures on salvation and remove themselves from the kinds of outside pressures that would tilt their conclusions toward human bias. Mature Christians need to be available to help answer hard questions, but if Jim and Charlotte are to make real progress toward spiritual growth, their faith must not be a second hand one.

If we can challenge new Christians to become independent Bible students, we can make more rapid progress in helping people become fruit-bearing members of the Lord's body. Our role will likely be far more effective as facilitators and not as indoctrinators.[3]

Progressive Holiness Requires The Ability to Know When Conversion Took Place.

Knowing exactly when they were converted will be important for Jim and Charlotte because the contemporary religious world sends out mixed signals concerning the way conversion takes place. Churches that practice infant baptism insist that the new life begins at Christening. The parents of a child make the faith decision, thus bypassing the will of the individual.

Modern revivalists recognize the free will of the individual, but they tell the people who come to their meetings, "Just trust Christ as your personal savior." The only requirment for salvation is a "decision for Christ." Baptism does not figure into the salvation equation according to the thinking of many popular evangelists.

The New Testament clearly connects baptism with the new life. Paul wrote "Or don't you know that all of us who were baptized into Christ Jesus were baptized into his death? We were therefore buried with him through baptism into death in order that, just as Christ was raised from the dead through the glory of the Father, we too may live a new life" (Rom. 6:3-4). Sophisticated rhetoric, emotionally charged testimonies and exegetical fancy footwork cannot set aside the simple affirmation of this text (as well as that of Mark 16:15-16, Acts 2:38; Acts 22:16; Gal. 3:26-27 and I Pet. 3:21). G. R. Beasley-Murray, a British Baptist scholar, courageously recognized the significance of the Biblical testimony concerning baptism when he said " . . . the idea that baptism is a purely symbolic rite must be pronounced, not alone unsatisfactory, but out of harmony with the New Testament itself."[4] Baptism marks the time that the penitent believer puts on Christ (Gal. 3:27).

Progressive Holiness Requires a Sense of Assurance.

Many Christians fail to make progress in holiness because they are not able to let their full weight down on the promises of God. Their commitment to humility blocks their sense of assurance. They fear that claiming confidence in their salvation means a loss of humility and they loathe the self-righteous claims of conceited religious people. The Bible does indeed warn us to remember " . . . if you think you are standing firm, be careful that you don't fall" (I Cor. 10:12), but it should be remembered that the same writer claimed, "I have fought the good fight, I have finished the race, I have kept the faith" (II Tim. 4:7).

Our positional holiness is not assigned to us as a reward for our performance, but our progress in obedience increases in direct proportion to the amount of security we feel. John wrote, "Dear friends, if our hearts do not condemn us, we have confidence before God and receive from him anything we ask, because we obey his commands and do what pleases him" (I John 3:21-22). While it is not necessary to feel saved, to be saved, John is clearly saying that our ability to please God increases when we are able to feel saved. "John has described a supportive cycle. Obedience establishes confidence and confidence enhances obedience."[5]

When Vince Lombardi coached the championship Green Bay Packer football teams in the mid-sixties, he concentrated on developing a certain mental attitude among his players. He believed that it is possible to transform a mediocre player into a great player if you can make him believe that he is a winner. A child of God, who begins the Christian life with a lack of assurance, attempts to wrestle against the powers of spiritual wickedness with a defeatist attitude. But if the Christian life is begun with the understanding that "the old has gone and the new has come," then rapid development in progressive holiness becomes a viable objective.

GETTING INVOLVED WITH THE CHURCH

John Donne once wrote "No man is an island entire of itself; every man is a piece of the Continent, a part of the main."[6] Paul wrote, "For none of us lives to himself alone and none of us dies to himself alone" (Rom. 14:7). Our creator made us social beings. The church is a social support system designed to help in the task of spiritual development. The leaders of the church are not given their roles in order that they might be honored, but so that they might serve to provide assistance in perfecting God's people.

> It was he who gave some to be apostles, some to be prophets, some to be evangelists, and some to be pastors and teachers, to prepare God's people for works of service, so that the body of Christ may be built up until we all reach unity in the faith and in the knowledge of the Son of God and become mature, attaining to the whole of the measure of the fullness of Christ (Eph. 4:11-13).

In one sense of the term, we are added to the church, the body of Christ, when we are saved (Eph. 5:23). The new Christian, however, must select a local body as a church home. This selection is a crucial decision that one must make in order to make progress in holiness.

Factors to consider when selecting a church home.
Denominationalism
The existence of denominations is a confusing thing for most new Christians. They don't understand why there are so many of them and they know very little about the differences between them. All of them meet in buildings that are recognizable as "church buildings." They worship God, sing hymns, commune and talk about following Jesus.

People who attend denominational churches are hampered in their attempts to grow in holiness because the focus of denominational leaders is limited to the doctrinal statements which define the various denominations. Furthermore, denominations are committed to perpetuating the traditions which have developed in each sectarian heritage. Many of these traditions are at variance with the scriptures themselves.

Some churches are committed to undenominational Christianity. The Bible is their only guide and standard. As Christians only, they are not committed to perpetuating the heritage of their predecessors and their doctrinal perceptions aren't bound to the credalized statements of human leaders.

The early church was undenominational in its character. When certain church members sought to impose their own personalized version

275

of the faith on the church as a whole, the inspired spokesmen of scripture offered stiff resistance. When a group of Jewish Christians thought they ought to impose Jewish traditions upon the Gentile members of the Galatian churches, Paul wrote, "It is for freedom that Christ has set us free. Stand firm, then, and do not let yourselves be burdened again by a yoke of slavery" (Gal. 5:1). In order to make progress in holiness without the hinderance of humanly devised standards of righteousness, a new Christian should seek out a local body of believers that is firmly committed to undenominational Christianity. The American Restoration Movement represents the largest indigenous religious development in American religious history. Many churches in the movement are determined to practice undenominational Christianity.[7]

The Place of Christ in the Church

Practically all churches claim to honor Christ, but there is a significant difference in the way Christ is perceived in various churches. Many years ago, a friend said to me, "It doesn't really matter which church you attend just so long as the man in the pulpit preaches that Jesus Christ is the Son of God." I responded, "Would it surprise you to know that some ministers who preach about Christ really don't believe that he is the Son of God?" My friend looked shocked. He said, "If that's the case they lie every Sunday." I was never able to convince him that such deception actually takes place.

Some theologians have cleverly redefined the terminology of the faith. They use the familiar terms – incarnation, atonement, trinity – but they have redefined those words until they no longer mean what they have meant to orthodox Christians for centuries. Many people fill church pulpits who no longer believe in the miraculous conception of Mary, the virgin birth of Christ, the miracle stories, the resurrection or the ascension. A former college professor of mine was not far from the truth when he described them as "atheists who call themselves Christians." A "demythologized" gospel is no gospel at all and the new Christian would be well advised to steer clear of those churches which have abandoned their belief in the supernaturalness of Christ.[8]

At the other end of the spectrum, some legalistic ministers have very little to say about Jesus. They may be strong on certain doctrinal and moral issues, but they have very little to say about Jesus. Their approach to the faith is usually quite argumentative and narrow in its focus. They have difficulty seeing the "big picture," because their focus is on something besides Jesus. To Paul the faith centered in Christ – "For I resolved to know nothing while I was with you except Jesus Christ and him crucified" (I Cor. 2:2). In selecting a church home the new Christian needs to know if the preaching, teaching and ministry of the church is Christ centered. Only then can balanced, progressive holiness take place.

Involvement
Your church home should be one in which you can find involvement in ministry. There are many functions in the church and people within each local body are gifted in different ways so that God's work can be done effectively. Even the new Christian has certain gifts which can be cultivated and matured in the service of God. Paul wrote, "But to each one of us grace has been given as Christ has apportioned it" (Eph. 4:7). Peter discoursed further on the same subject in I Peter 4:10-11,

> Each one should use whatever gift he has received to serve others, faithfully administering God's grace in its various forms. If anyone speaks, he should do it as one speaking the very words of God. If anyone serves he should do it with the strength that God provides, so that in all things God may be praised through Jesus Christ. To him be the glory and the power forever and ever. Amen.

Conscientious church leaders recognize that Christians have a diversity of gifts and that the church has a diversity of ministries into which these gifts can be channeled. An alert leadership will help a new Christian identify gifts, offer training to aid in the development of those gifts and find places in which the gifts can be utilized.

Get Involved in the Life of the Church.
Once the new Christian has decided on a specific church home, progressive holiness in the life of that individual will most likely take place in direct proportion to the amount of time and energy that is

devoted to the life of the church. There are no "Lone Ranger" Christians. We grow together or not all. If Christ is truly the head of the local church then it follows that "From him the whole body, joined and held together by every supporting ligament, grows and builds itself up in love as each part does its work" (Eph. 4:16).

Regular attendance will be a major part of the new Christian's personal schedule. It's as essential as mealtime and as vital to spiritual health as exercise and rest are to physical health. Sometimes Christians, in their zeal to push for attendance, come on fairly strong to new Christians and leave the impression that church attendance is a legalistic obligation. Hebrews 10:25 was never intended to be used as a club to make sure church members take their place on the pews every Sunday. Instead every new Christian needs to understand why the Hebrew writer deplored the practice of forsaking the assembly. The assembly is the place where encouragement takes place. Just prior to lamenting laxity in attendance among the readers of Hebrews, he said, "And let us consider how we may spur one another toward love and good deeds" (Heb. 10:24). A Christian needs to be present every time the church building doors are opened for any kind of meeting which is designed for the edification of the entire body. It's not for the purpose of winning a perfect attendance medal. It's for the purpose of receiving encouragement to make progress in holiness.

It's in the church that one finds the kind of friendships which are so desperately needed to withstand the assaults of the Evil One. It's in the church that opportunities for ministry are found. It's in the church that a person will also find others who can lend a helping hand when it's needed.

DEVELOPING PERSONAL DISCIPLINE

Let me tell you about Leroy. That's not his real name, but he and I grew up in the same area. He had quite a reputation as a brawler, a boozer, a womanizer and general all around scoundrel. One Sunday Leroy showed up at church. I couldn't believe it and although I didn't expect the roof to cave in, it was a surprise. His mother was a godly woman and I suppose he came out of respect for her. I remember meeting him on the church lawn. He was clad in a freshly starched white shirt, open at the collar. Leroy probably didn't own a tie. The cuffs of his neatly pressed Western style dress trousers broke over the instep of freshly polished cowboy boots. I had never seen Leroy dressed up that nice.

I spoke to him, but the conversation was just a little bit awkward. I couldn't figure out what he was doing there and he seemed obligated to offer some explanation for his presence. In his laid back West Texas drawl, he said, "Aw, I might become a Christian someday." I don't know why he said it, because I had said nothing to put him on notice that I wanted to share the gospel with him. But then he added, "I think I'll wait 'till I'm about sixty-five years old. I'm having too much fun right now and all those rules get in the way." I had the feeling that Leroy really wanted to be a Christian, but he knew enough about lifestyle requirements to figure he couldn't handle it. He wasn't afraid to smash somebody's face in a barroom brawl, but trying to live "soberly, righteously, and godly in this present age" was a bit too much to handle. Leroy was scared of responsibility.

I lost track of Leroy a long time ago, but I think of him now and then when people say, "Oh, I would like to be a Christian, but I'm not sure I can handle the requirements of Christian living." Leroy didn't realize that everything God has asked of us is designed to bring us joy and that everything he warns against will bring us sadness. I just wish there were some way to help the Leroys in the world understand that "the way of the transgressor is hard" and that Jesus has promised that his yoke is easy and his burden is light.

Neither he nor I had any way of knowing that the time would come, many years later, when I would find myself trying to encourage another man to become a Christian. I'll call this man, Virgil. Virgil was in his seventies. His alcoholic past had taken a heavy toll on his body. He was deeply bothered by the harm he had inflicted on himself and his family. When I first met him, I wasn't much impressed because he didn't stay sober for any length of time, but I talked with him one day when alcohol no longer enslaved him. I soon realized that he was an intelligent man with a pretty fair understanding of what the Bible is about. With a quavering voice he told me, "I want to be Christian, but I'm so afraid that I can't be faithful to God." Virgil died a few years ago and if he ever became a Christian I don't know about it. I don't think he ever went back to the bottle, but he died still wishing he could be a Christian – afraid that the disciplined life would be too great a burden to endure. In a way the young man and the old man were alike. They were both afraid of the responsibility that goes with being a Christian.

Jesus said "my yoke is easy and my burden is light" (Matt. 11:30). People like Leroy and Virgil have seen only the yoke and the burden in that passage. Somehow the words "easy" and "light" have never connected in their minds. The challenge of the disciplined life can be a discouragement to the new Christian. There are so many things to learn, so many changes to make, so many behavioral expectations. The task often looks insurmountable. As we have noted in previous chapters, attempts to construct one set of Christian standards for the rank and file, and another for those who truly desire to be holy, lack both scriptural support and practicality. How can a new Christian develop a disciplined life style? How can we convince them that God's burden is both "easy" and "light?"

1. It starts by understanding that a disciplined life is a natural response to God's saving grace. As recipients of grace we are "God's workmanship, created in Christ Jesus to do good works, which God prepared in advance for us to do" (Eph. 2:10). The grace of God also "teaches us to say 'No' to ungodliness and worldly passions, and to live self-controlled, upright and godly lives in this present age" (Tit. 2:12). Leroy and Virgil had trouble with Christian responsibility because they saw it more in terms of "have to" than "get to."

It would probably have been pretty difficult to convince Leroy that Christian living is a privilege more than it is a restraint. When he spoke to me, the urges of the flesh were strong, but he had not yet begun to feel the consequences of dissipation except for an occasional hangover and a few sore knuckles after a fight. He wore those like badges of honor. Virgil, on the other hand, had lived long enough to experience the consequences of undisciplined living. No one had to convince him that "the way of the transgressor is hard" (Prov. 13:15 KJV). He gave living testimony to the accuracy of that proverb. Even so, Virgil was still seeing "duty" with a capital "D." It meant drudgery, distress and discouragement. If either of them could have understood that a loving God, who sent his Son to die on the cross for the sins of a perverse human race, wants us to behave in a certain way because his way will bring us the most happiness and joy in the end, then perhaps they would have been able to realize that his "burden" is truly "easy."

2. The New Christian Must be Helped to Understand that Discipline is the Avenue to Freedom. Some sportswriters have described Joe Montana of the San Francisco Forty-Niners, as the quarterback of the nineties. He has certainly been one of the most effective players at that position in the late eighties and early nineties. But Joe Montana doesn't just walk out on the field and start throwing spectacular touchdown passes. He has been playing football most of his life. He has studied the game, practiced it and refined it to such a degree that he is almost the standard by which other quarterbacks are measured. He makes it look effortless, but his expertise has been gained at the price of discipline. He has the freedom of being a class athlete, because he denied himself the freedom to do other things when he needed to be refining his football skills.

When Paul wrote the churches in Galatia, he urged them to assert their freedom at one point (Gal 5:1), but a few verses later he pointed out, "You, my brothers, were called to be free. But do not use your freedom to indulge the sinful nature" (Gal. 5:13). It's true that discipline sometimes requires us to forego some of the things that the flesh desires, but it's worth the temporary restraint to realize the freedom of achieving a greater goal.

> The promiscuous young woman may appear to have an advantage over the virtuous girl. If she's adept at attracting men, she may even have them competing for her affection. On the other hand, the Christian single girl may find herself sitting alone at home listening to the stereo and reading books on Saturday nights. Neither of these people may understand that what happens on Saturday nights isn't the end of the story. Persistent sin usually catches up with the sinner.[9]

The undisciplined approach to life turns out to be the hardest way of living in the long run. "To depart from righteousness is to choose a life of crushing burdens, failures and disappointments, a life caught in

281

the toils of endless human problems that are never resolved."[10] When life is viewed from beginning to end, the disciplined life brings the greatest satisfaction and exempts one from receiving the "wages of sin" (Rom. 6:23). If a new Christian can be encouraged to look beyond the existential moment to the fullness of the total life experience, the beginning steps on the road to holiness will not appear to be so insurmountable.

SUMMARY AND CONCLUSION

Sometime ago the news media told the story of a woman who thought she had entered a 5,000 meter run. She had already gone a couple of miles before she realized that she was actually running with people who had entered a marathon. At that point, she thought, "I'll just run until I get tired and quit." She couldn't quite see herself running the entire 26 mile course, but she stuck it out past the half way point and realized that she still had some strength left. The going got pretty rough toward the end, but by just taking one mile at a time and responding to the encouragement of her fellow runners, she ran her first marathon and felt she had achieved a major objective.

It is common for the person who starts out to pursue the goal of holiness to think that the holy standards we aspire to achieve are as impossible as the marathon appeared to that lady. But if we'll start the race, stay the course, listen to the encouragement of other runners and consider the alternatives of not finishing, we will eventually be able to say, "I have fought the good fight, I have finished the race, I have kept the faith." The crown of righteousness awaits the winner.

Endnotes

1. James Le Fan, "Be Ye Holy." *Abilene Christian College Lectures - 1963.* (Austin, Texas: Firm Foundation Publishing House, 1963), pp. 41-42.

2. Flavil R. Yeakley, Jr., *Why Churches Grow,* 3rd. ed. (Broken Arrow, Oklahoma: Christian Communications, Inc., 1979), p. 57.

3. Norman Bales, *A Sense of Belonging*. (Nashville, Tennessee: Twentieth Century Christian Foundation, 1989), p. 124. I included an entire chapter on "The Information Needs of the New Christian" in this volume.

4. G. R. Beasley-Murray, *Baptism in the New Testament*. (Exeter, Devon, U.K.: 1962; Grand Rapids, Michigan: William B. Eerdmans Publishing Company, 1986), p. 263.

5. Norman L. Bales, *How Do I Know I'm Saved*. (Nashville, Tennessee: Gospel Advocate Company, 1989) p. 176.

6. John Donne, "Meditation XVII" from, *The Oxford Dictionary of Quotations*. (Oxford: Oxford University Press, 1980), p. 190.

7. Jim Howard offers lists of five attractive features of the restoration concept "(1) A common ground for unity," . . . "(2) Freedom and liberty for the individual conscience," . . . "(3) A minimizing of the role of the human personality," . . . "(4) The simplicity of God's pattern," . . . "(5) Love that binds it all together." Jim Howard, "The Attractiveness of Revelation." *Server*. January 13, 1991. p.2.

8. Sometimes it is hard to tell which is which. A minister who has abandoned supernaturalism still uses Biblical terminology and often quotes scripture. Several years ago one of my college professors suggested that if you wonder where a person stands with relationship to the supernaturalness of Christ, a good question to ask is, "What do you think of blood atonement?" The idea that it was essential for Christ to shed his blood to bring about human redemption is repulsive to most modernists.

9. Bales, *How Do I Know I'm Saved?* p. 9.

10. Dallas Willard, *The Spirit of the Disciplines*. (San Francisco: Harper 1988), p. 2.

283

21
Progressive Holiness -
The Danger of Diversion

Diversionary tactics are common in carnal warfare. If a military strategist can make the enemy think that the main body of invading troops is concentrated in one locality, and is able to conceal the largest number of his warriors from the view of the enemy, the chances of victory are greatly enhanced. Battle planners make extensive use of military intelligence in an effort to learn of such diversionary attempts before they occur.

Sometimes Christians don't seem to recognize the fact that we are at war with the devil and that he is the master of diversionary tactics. Paul urged the Ephesians to "Put on the full armor of God that you may be able to stand against the devil's schemes" (Eph. 6:12) Often the devil is able to convince us that we are travelling the road to holiness, when we are really being diverted into dead-end detours.

Come take a trip with me down one of these dead-end roads. At the beginning of the trip, these first few miles on the road to nowhere often look like a legitimate highway to spiritual progress. "Christian" signs have been put up along the roadway. Their messages remind us of things we already knew like, "Jesus is Lord" and "The Wages of Sin is Death." Other travellers pass us along the way and we're encouraged by their "Honk, if you love Jesus" bumper stickers. If you pull over at the rest stops and converse with fellow motorists, you'll hear them discussing scripture and planning their future vacation trips around the next big religious event, be it a seminar, a convention, a lectureship or a crusade. In fact, you learn that some of them are on the way to a gigantic rally for "God, Country, the Home, and Saving Souls." It features ten different plenary speakers including the hottest evangelical personalities on the lecture circuit – people like Tony Campolo, Chuck Swindoll, Billy Graham and a host of others. There will be forty-eight classes from everything on "How to Lose Weight With Christian Principles" to "Unraveling the Clandestine Satanic Message in Network News Broadcasts."

When you stop for gas or for a quick bite to eat, it's amazing how Christian the atmosphere can be. Instead of hearing idle speculation about who's going to win the World Series, the conversation may center on a Jerry Falwell sermon or the great church growth conference in Seattle last week. Instead of profanity and vulgarity, the air is filled with Christian vocabulary. People don't talk about "good luck," they speak of "blessings." They don't ever directly claim to have accomplished anything on their own, but some of them will be glad to tell you "how the Lord used them" for as long as you will sit and listen. If they feel gifted in evangelism, they never talk about marketing their religion, but they freely speak of sharing their faith.

The roadway looks so different from the normal highways of American life. Christians get so excited about travelling on it because at least they have their own interstate highway system. They no longer have to see those offensive liquor and tobacco billboards, coarse language in truck stops and cigarette smoke in the restaurants. They're on the road to holiness and everybody else who travels the road is going that way too.

Keith Miller describes these inadequate approaches to holiness with a different metaphor. He calls them "invisible ladders" of growth. They are present in nearly every church, but they are harmful because, "they keep us from genuine growth and development."[1] R. C.

286

Sproul believes that popular Christian jargon is an almost meaningless form of communication, but worse yet it stands for a standard of spirituality that can become "a cheap substitute for righteousness."[2] Donald Bloesch presents an even harsher view. He claims that these diversionary approaches to holiness have contributed nothing to holiness in the world, but have succeeded in causing worldliness to be entrenched in the church.[3]

This chapter will concentrate on some of the more popular diversionary tactics in the hope that the person who desires to grow in holiness will be able to recognize them, discern their lack of genuineness and avoid them like the plague.

ISOLATION

The Monastics and more specifically, the "desert fathers" thought the key to holiness lay in isolation. If they could separate themselves from worldly influences and devote themselves more completely to Christian thoughts and principles, they assumed they would achieve a higher level of holiness. Few if any Christians would ever entertain the solution of the Monastics, but the idea that holiness can be achieved by detaching oneself from society's mainstream remains a tempting approach to holiness. What spiritually minded person wouldn't prefer to live and work in a Christian environment?

Some years ago I heard a brother propose the establishment of a Christian community, which would essentially isolate itself from most of society. He suggested that Christian real estate developers should buy up a tract of suitable residential property and set out to market the building sites to Christians. A residential sub-division could then be developed that would have no one but Christians living in it. Christians would then control the community's value system. They would either form their own Christian schools or form a power structure to influence the public schools in favor of Christian principles. They would also form a voting bloc that would have control of local politics. He was convinced that this community development project would produce an ideal environment for the development of holy life styles. With a little ingenuity, his dream could be taken a few steps farther.

Christian businessmen could be encouraged to hire only Christians and thus promote holiness in the workplace. This could even be extended into various forms of recreation and marketing. In this ideal community Christians would be able to buy their food from Christian grocers, gas up the family car at a Christian service station and even buy their cars from Christian used car lots where they would be protected from the shenanigans of unscrupulous traders. If you worked it right, you might never even have to actually contact a non-Christian in the process of normal living, unless of course you happen to get audited by the Internal Revenue Service.

British Sociologist, Os Guiness, sees a different form of isolation emerging in the evangelical community and he has a name for it. He calls it *privatization*.

Privatization is the process which insures that our faith begins and ends in our private lives. The industrial revolution has divided the private and public worlds to the extent that they now seem to work with different rules. At its extreme, the public world is that of large corporation, academic institutions, and government, while the private is the family, personal tastes, leisure time, individual fulfillment - the world of spending, not producing. Religion is practiced with magnificent freedom within the captivity of the private sphere, but our private religious preferences are not to appear, much less interfere with public life.[4]

Isolation, whether it be in the form of Monasticism, overzealous Christian networking or privatization leaves much to be desired. In the first place the history of attempts to gain holiness through isolation has been very disappointing. The standards of holiness which are selected for emphasis in these Christian "greenhouses" are usually selective and arbitrary. Like the Pharisees, the isolationists often neglect "the more important matters of the law" (Matt. 23:23). While a "Christian" motel may be entirely "smoke free," there's no guarantee that its proprietor will not succumb to the twin temptations of greed and avarice. The trouble with trying to build a holy society by shutting the world out is the fact that we still have too much of the world in our hearts when we close the door.

It is true that Christians are to separate themselves from unbelievers when their association with the people of the world results in the lowering of spiritual and moral standards. Paul warned, "Do not be yoked together with unbelievers. For what do righteousness and wickedness have in common. Or what fellowship can light have with darkness" (II Cor. 6:14). Christian isolation takes Paul's warning much farther than he ever intended. Working in the world's arena of commerce, participating in the world's system of economics and politics, attending schools operated by people in the world, and even sharing recreational activities with some of the world's residents do not necessarily constitute an "unequal yoke." It's an unequal yoke only when the world is leading the Christian instead of things being the other way around.

Jesus recognized that it is neither desirable nor possible for the Christian to become isolated from the world. In his intercessory prayer he said, "My prayer is not that you take them out of the world, but that you protect them from the evil one" (John 17:15). The Christian's influence works like yeast. "What shall I compare the kingdom of God to? It is like yeast that a woman took and mixed into a large amount of flour until it worked all through the dough" (Luke 13:20-21).

> The church does not draw people in; it sends them out. It does not settle into a comfortable niche, taking its place alongside the Rotary, the Elks and the country club. Rather the church is to make society uncomfortable. Like yeast, it unsettles the mass around it, changing it from within. Like salt it flavors and preserves that into which it vanishes.[5]

ADAPTATION

A person who promotes the adaptation theory of holiness proposes acceptance of the culture as it exists. Instead of resisting the culture, the adaptationist blends in with it. The mores and values of the secular culture are accepted and regarded as holy. H. Richard Nieburh submitted the following description of an adaptationist.

In every culture to which the Gospel comes there are men who

289

hail Jesus as the Messiah of their society. . . . These men are Christians not only in the sense that they count themselves believers in the Lord, but also in the sense that they seek to maintain community with all other believers. Yet they seem equally at home in the community of culture. They feel no great tension between the church and the world, the social laws and the Gospel, the workings of divine grace and human effort, the ethics of salvation and the ethics of social conservation or progress.[6]

The whole range of ethics and morality is defined more by public opinion than by authoritative statements from scripture. Lawrence O. Richards recalls the time he heard a young lady, who was enrolled in a seminary, argue for the practice of young people living together without being married. She said,

Morality isn't about sex. Morality is about unjust wars and poverty. Morality is about South American dictators and persecution. Morality is about politicians who lie to us. Morality is about companies that raise prices in black areas because the people can't go outside their community to shop. That's what morality is about.[7]

While Richards points out that her views did not represent the views of the seminary that he attended in the late sixties, her views were somewhat representative among activists who were prominent in effecting social change during that time.

This secular approach to holiness ends up as an assault on the moral and spiritual foundation of the Christian faith. Morality standards are defined by the culture and not by the authoritative statements of scripture.

In his critique of this approach to holiness, Bloesch noted, "When the church becomes acculturized and secularized, it can no longer penetrate the world as leaven."[8] Evidence that Christians are often lured by the temptation to adapt to curvature of the culture can be seen in the statements of the liberal clergy who argue for normalizing homosexuality and accepting abortion on demand as a fundamental human right. These same clergymen promote pacifist causes, the redistribution of wealth and environmental sensitivity as evidence of holiness. They ask no questions concerning sexual mores, substance abuse and other areas of personal morality.

One must not assume, however that adaptationism is limited to the liberal clergy. It's alive and well in the conservative religious community. Charles Colson charges that the " . . . church has been crippled from within by an invasion of barbarian values and habits."[9] Colson sees the media evangelists as the primary promoters of these barbarian values. To hype the ratings, the religious television producers look for ways to compete with "Wheel of Fortune" and in doing so, they appeal to the materialistic instincts of the viewing public.

> Isolated in front of their television sets, the utilitarian individualists find in much Christian programming what they see most – the promise of material gain – now sanctified in the name of God. Meanwhile sofa-loads of expressive individualists recline in their living rooms nibbling chocolates and reveling in TV-induced tears, testimony, and titillation.[10]

Restoration Movement people have also been affected by this cultural approach to holiness. Allen, Hughes and Weed see evidence of secularism on several different fronts within the Restoration Movements. As proof that we imbibed more deeply of the spirit of adaptationism than we should have, they point to (1) the fact that the primary concern in conducting ministry is that of attempting to determine how well a project will fare in the market place, (2) the emphasis on human effort in attempts to promote "church growth," (3) the assumption that promoting recreation is essential to evangelism, (4) the assumption that the gospel cannot stand on its own merits, but has to be packaged under the guise of meeting needs, (5) the fact that serious Bible study has often been relegated to a place of lesser importance in the educational program of the church and (6) the assumptions that missions is no longer "marketable" in the church.

Adaptationists often forget that Jesus said, "My kingdom is not of this world" (John 18:36). According to the scriptures, this present world is to be viewed as the temporary residence of the Christian. Paul taught that " . . . this world in its present form is passing away" (I Cor. 7:31). On another occasion he wrote, "But our citizenship is in heaven. And we eagerly await a Savior from there, the Lord Jesus Christ" (Phil. 3:20). The Hebrew writer echoed the same sentiment. "For here we do not have an enduring city, but we are looking for a city that is to come" (Heb. 13:14). In Romans 12:1-2, Paul distinctly established the connection between the holy life and separation from the standards of this world. J. B. Phillips translation says it best to the modern mind,

> With eyes wide open to the mercies of God, I beg you, my brothers, as an act of intelligent worship, to give him your bodies, as a living sacrifice, consecrated to him and acceptable by him. Don't let the world around you squeeze you into its mold, but let God remold your minds from within, so that you may prove in practice that the plan of God for you is good, meets all his demands and moves toward maturity.[12]

LEGALISM

Legalism is one of the most deceptive diversionary tactics in the arsenal of the devil. Legalists are so sure of their ground they never feel the need to examine themselves. They specialize in criticizing the shortcomings of others, thus elevating themselves to a position of superior spirituality. Legalists base their claim to personal holiness on their ability to take the right side of every controversy, to abstain from questionable behavior practices and to demonstrate their prowess at arranging proof texts in support of their biases. Their assurance is confirmed by their ability to show why those who do not agree with them are condemned in the scriptures.

Legalism means different things to different people. As used in this study, legalism covers a variety of attitudes toward the scriptures which concentrate more on the human response to God than what God has done for the human race. Legalists have trouble keeping the cross in perspective. They are far more interested in the Bible's rules and regulations than they are the story of redemption. The line that separates the scriptures from human tradition is blurred in the eyes of the legalist. "What we've always believed" or "What our pioneer preachers taught" carries as much weight as the Word of God in their thinking. Legalists have difficulty understanding that there's a difference between their perception of the Word of God and the Word of God itself. Legalism is nearly always divided because no two legalists are ever able to agree on which "essential matters of faith" should be bound on the church.

Legalists have a tendency to major in minors and ignore monumental issues. The decision to purchase an electric range and refrigerator to put in the basement of the church building may well result in a bitter church split. At the same time the disputants may be totally unable to see that their bitterness, hatred and malicious behavior have made them the laughingstock of the world around them.

Legalism cannot be dismissed as a harmless way of life among a few grouchy people. Donald Bloesch labels it a "worldly heresy."[13] It's a dangerous heresy, because it looks innocent enough to the simple minded folk. How can you fault anyone who quotes book, chapter and verse? That makes it doubly deceptive because legalistic teachers are using the Word of God to divert our attention away from the crucified Christ.

This is seen most clearly in Paul's letters to the Galatian churches. Back then the issue was circumcision, which no longer troubles the church, but we have managed to come up with an endless number of legalistic demand requirements. Paul reminded his readers, " . . . if righteousness could be gained through the law, Christ died for nothing" (Gal. 2:21).[14] Peace loving Christians are sometimes willing to give way to the legalists, because they want to keep unity in the church, but there comes a time when the legalists have to be resisted, because their arbitrary control of the church is stifling the progressive holiness of the members. A person who does not understand the nature of Christian freedom never really grows in Christ. Thus the great apostle wrote, "It is for freedom that Christ has set us free. Stand firm and do not let yourselves be burdened again by a yoke of slavery" (Gal. 5:1).

In Romans 14 Paul urged more mature Christians to give in to weaker Christians on matters of scruples. However, Romans 14 is not talking about the legalistic power broker who wants to control the church. The weaker brother in Romans 14 must be yielded to because the example of a stronger brother exercising liberty will cause the weaker brother to stumble and be lost. Paul warns, "It is better not to eat meat or drink wine or to do anything else that will cause your brother to fall" (Rom. 14:21). The legalists whom Paul discussed in the Galatian letter were not in danger of stumbling. They were engaged in a power struggle and their legalism was their tool for gaining control. When that's the clear motive, legalism is not to be tolerated. It contributes nothing to holiness and promotes an ungodly, sectarian spirit.

It's fairly easy to draw the line against legalism and dismiss it as one of Satan's diversionary tactics which leads people away from holiness, but it's another matter entirely to recognize it in ourselves. Philip Yancey observed, "It is easy to spot in someone else, but it is hard to avoid in yourself."[15] Some of us feel that we have put our legalistic past behind us, but we keep encountering it in ways that we had never questioned. Joseph C. Aldrich was not wide of the target when he said of all Biblically oriented people, "We are all legalists by nature"[16]

A Bible professor in a Christian College told of an experiment he conducted in his class on Romans. He asked his class members to indicate whether or not they felt they were saved. Among those who considered themselves saved, he asked for an indication of why they felt saved. He compiled their answers in two categories. Those who indicated they were saved as the result of Jesus' redemptive act on the cross were grouped under the heading "atonement" and those who gave some answer that related to their human response to Christ were listed under "achievement." He said that achievement won out by a margin of more than 2 to 1. That's just one indicator of how widely legalistic thought prevails within the body.

It is true that the pursuit of holiness deserves our best effort and it's also true that we are expected to "bear much fruit" as an indication that we are the true disciples of the Lord (John 15:4). Even so we must never lose sight of the fact that " . . . all our righteous acts are like filthy rags" (Isa. 64:6). We can never attend enough services, read the Bible through enough times, say enough prayers, win enough souls, make enough hospital visits, feed enough hungry people or do enough good works of any kind to make ourselves a truly holy people. Holiness is still a gift from God, and our holy behavior grows out of an appreciation of being made holy as the result of the sacrifice that Jesus made on the cross on our behalf.

CEREMONIALISM

Ceremonialism is another attractive looking detour away from the path to true holiness. Many people believe they can achieve a holy standing in God's sight by repeating just the right words in a worship setting, by conforming to the right rituals or by observing the right formulas. The attraction lies in the fact that ceremonial religion makes no demands in terms of heart and life. If a person can just get to the place of worship and go through the prescribed motions, holiness is assured. Bloesch observed, "Here forgiveness is assured through the sacraments without any clear call to repentance or summons to obedience."[17]

The temptation to gain God's favor through ceremonialism has afflicted people from ancient times. Saul used it as an excuse to disobey God, when he went to fight against the Amalekites. When Samuel confronted him, he responded, "The soldiers took sheep and cattle from the plunder, the best of what was devoted to God, in order to sacrifice them to the LORD your God at Gilgal" (I Sam. 15:21).

Judaizers caused great difficulty for the early church when they insisted that the circumcision rites had to be performed on the Gentiles. Instead of rejoicing over the conversion of the Gentiles, those who " . . . belonged to the party of the Pharisees stood up and said, 'The Gentiles must be circumcised and required to obey the law of Moses'" (Acts 15:5).

Ceremonialism as an approach to holiness is very much alive today, as evidenced by the importance that some attach to various liturgical rites in present day Christendom. Anyone who doubts the extent to which ceremonialism affects even non-liturgical churches will soon learn just how much it means to people when changes are made in the order of the worship. John Killinger claims that he knows ministers " . . . who shortened their tenure by acting presumptuously in shaping or reordering the liturgy, even though the congregation appeared to be largely apathetic about it before the 'tampering' took place."[18] I can recall a time many years ago when the elders of a local congregation took great care and prepared to deal with repercussions when they decided to serve the Lord's Supper before the sermon, instead of afterwards. It seems that churches are addicted to the preservation of ceremony.

While it is true that God has clearly ordained certain acts of worship to be performed in the assembly (e.g. The Lord's Supper), he has never suggested that holiness can be achieved through the rote performance of certain ceremonies. On the contrary, some of the sharpest rebukes in scripture are aimed at those who attempt to establish fellowship on the basis of ritual performance. The nation of Israel was enamored with the concept of animal sacrifice, but God said, "I have no need of a bull from your stall or of goats from your pens, for every animal of the forest is mine and the cattle on a thousand hills" (Psalm 50:9-10). Through his spokesman, Isaiah, God expressed his contempt for a nation that was obsessed with ceremony and sacrifice while practicing violence and oppression. He said

> Stop bringing me meaningless offerings! Your incense is detestable to me. New Moons, Sabbaths and convocations – I cannot bear your evil assemblies, Your New Moon festivals and your appointed feasts my soul hates. They have become a burden to me; I am weary of bearing them (Isaiah 1:13-14).

In the New Testament, more attention is given to the condition of the heart of the person who comes to worship than is given to mechanics of the act. Jesus taught,

> . . . if you are offering your gift at the altar and there remember that your brother has something against you, leave your gift there in front of the altar. First go and be reconciled to your brother; then come and offer your gift (Matt. 5:23-24).

Paul lamented the fact that the Lord's Supper had become so ceremonialized that human relations were forgotten and immorality actually invaded the assembly. To the church at Corinth, he wrote, "When you come together, it is not the Lord's Supper you eat, for as you eat, each one goes ahead without waiting for anybody else. One remains hungry, another gets drunk" (I Cor. 11:20-21).

The basic problem with ceremonialism is its tendency to bypass the heart and will of the worshiper. One must not go to the extreme of saying that God is not concerned about the way we worship him if the heart is right. God must be allowed to control the condition relationship between himself and his followers.

> Biblical worship is not left to the caprice of man. It is not controlled by arbitrary desires or contingent needs. It does not ask what things will be most helpful, or will best express the impulse to worship, from a human standpoint. It learns how to worship from the God who is the object of worship.[19]

While holiness cannot be achieved by "fine tuning" the acts of worship which are set forth in the New Testament, neither can it be achieved if we ignore the condition of the human heart. "God is spirit and his worshipers must worship him in spirit and in truth" (John 4:24). "God requires something within us that leads to outward acts of spirituality. The sacrifice of all the cattle in Kansas would avail nothing before the Lord without the inner reality of spirit and truth."[20]

SUMMARY AND CONCLUSION

On the surface some approaches to holiness appear to be legitimate avenues to personal sanctification, but there's only a thin veneer of legitimacy covering many of these maneuvers. Satan has a way of diverting our best intentioned efforts and sending us rushing headlong down some dead end alley, even while we think we are moving in the direction of deeper spiritual living.

There's a certain amount of legitimacy in each one of the "dead end" alleys and that's what makes them so dangerous. Those who think they can become holy by isolating themselves from the world can correctly point to the danger of being absorbed by the world's value system and they can find scripture to sustain their concern. On the other hand the adaptationists note that Jesus ate with publicans and sinners, that he came eating and drinking and was accused of being a glutton and a winebibber even as he set the standard by which holiness is measured. The legalists pride themselves in their knowledge of scripture and profess to uphold the Bible as the ultimate standard by which all spiritual issues are to be resolved. The ceremonialists point to the fact that God has indeed ordained certain avenues of corporate worship and that he sets the boundaries by which such worship is to be offered.

No one can or should argue with these claims, but the danger occurs when we fixate on one approach and ignore all the others. The danger is increased when attention is focused on external matters and the inward condition of the heart is ignored.

Endnotes

1. Keith Miller, *The Becomers*. (Waco, Texas: Word Books, 1977), p. 108.

2. R. C. Sproul. *Pleasing God*. (Wheaton, Illinois: Tyndale House Publishers, 1988) p. 33.

3. Donald G. Bloesch, *Essentials of Evangelical Theology*. Vol. 2. (San Francisco: Harper and Row Publishers, 1978), p. 59. Bloesch constructs a rather lengthy list of philosophies which he regards as manifestations of worldliness in the church. They include (1) syncretic mysticism, (Gnosticism was an ancient form of it. The New Age movement is a modern manifestation of the same phenomenon), (2) legalism, (3) antinomianism (claiming that salvation by grace eliminates the need of obeying commands), (4) eudaemonism (equating holiness with happiness), (5) sacramentalism (seeking to establish holiness through religious ceremony), (6) predestinarianism (asserting that salvation and holiness takes place completely outside of the human response), (7) perfectionsim (which promotes the notion that some people have "arrived"), (8) revivalism (which focuses on religious enthusiasm), (9) humanitarianism (which focuses the goal of holiness with social justice and Christian charity), and (10) technical morality (which takes many forms from the promotion of positive thinking to pastoral psychology). For a complete discussion of the weaknesses of each of these approaches see pages 59-65.

4. Dick Keyses, "The Church Up To It's Neck, A Review of *The Gravedigger File* by Os Guiness." *Pastoral Renewal*. January, 1985. p. 94.

5. Charles Colson, *Loving God*. (Grand Rapids, Michigan: Zondervan Books, 1987), p. 176.

6. H. Richard Nieburh, *Christ and Culture*. (New York: Harper Torchbooks, 1951; p. b. edition, 1975), p. 83.

7. Lawrence O. Richards, *A Practical Theology of Spirituality*. (Grand Rapids, Michigan: Academic Books, 1987), p. 195.

8. Bloesch, *Essentials of Evangelical Theology*, Vol. 2., p. 59.

9. Charles Colson, *Against the Night*. (Ann Arbor, Michigan: Vine Books, 1989), p. 102.

10. Ibid., p. 107.

11. C. Leonard Allen, Richard T. Hughes, and Michael R. Weed, *The Worldly Church.* (Abilene, Texas: ACU Press, 1988), pp. 39-40.

12. J. B. Phillips, *The New Testament in Modern English.* (New York: The Macmillan Company, 1985), p. 341.

13. Bloesch, *Essentials of Evangelical Theology.* Vol. 2. p. 60.

14. In the original language, the definite article does not precede the word, "law." In other words, there's no "the" in front of "law." Paul is saying that righteousness cannot be gained by law. That he intends to cover more than just the law of Moses is indicated by his statement in Gal. 3:21, "For if a law had been given that could impart life, then righteousness would certainly have come by that law."

15. Philip Yancey and Tim Stafford, *Unhappy Secrets of the Christian Life.* (Grand Rapids, Michigan: Zondervan Publishing House, 1979), p. 136.

16. Joseph C. Aldrich, *Lifestyle Evangelism.* (Portland Oregon: Multnomah press, 1981), p. 181.

17. Bloesch, *Essentials of Evangelical Theology.* Vol. 2, p. 62.

18. John Killinger, "Renewing the Rites of Worship." *Leadership.* (Fall, 1989), p. 82.

19. G.S. Cansdale, "Worship." *Zondervan Pictorial Bible Dictionary.* (Grand Rapids, Michigan: Zondervan Publishing House, 1975) Vol. 5, p. 976.

20. Roland Allen and Gordon Borror, *Worship: Rediscovering the Missing Jewel.* (Portland, Oregon: Multnomah Press, 1982), p. 36.

22
A Holy Way of Thinking

"What do you think about when you are alone?" I wasn't expecting the question. It came from a colleague in a staff meeting that was devoted to a routine and mostly forgettable agenda. Out of the blue he asked everyone in the room to share the kinds of subjects they concentrated on when they were on their own time and no one was expecting them to be creative.

I didn't like the question, but I disliked my answers even worse. I'm afraid that an honest answer would have revealed the superficiality of my thinking. I don't remember exactly what I said, but I know that I had to admit that I concentrated on mundane affairs that held little importance beyond the time they crossed my mind. I'm sure that holiness was not high on the agenda of my personal thoughts at that moment.

To be holy is to think holy thoughts; to cultivate a holy way of thinking. A. W. Tozer argued, "Were we able to extract from any man a complete answer to the question, 'What comes to your mind when you think about God?' we might predict with certainty the future of that man."[1] R. C. Sproul asked, "Is there any one of us who claims Jesus as Lord whose heart does not beat with a passion to hear the voice of God."[2]

All our behavioral undertakings are incubated in the mind. If the mind is allowed to concentrate on perverse things, perverted behavior will inevitably follow. If the mind is centered on holy things, holy conduct will certainly take place. To Paul the mind set of a person with respect to spiritual values is the most crucial aspect of the human personality. He said, "Those who live according to the sinful nature have their minds set on what that nature desires; but those who live in accordance with the Spirit have their minds set on what the Spirit desires" (Rom. 8:5).

A spiritually oriented mind set has been discernible throughout the ages among all people who have wanted to grow in holiness. During the reign of King Asa, the people of Judah assembled at Jerusalem and ". . . entered into a covenant to seek the LORD, the God of their fathers, with all their heart and soul" (II Chron. 15:12). The author of the 119th Psalm wrote, "I have sought your face with all my heart" (Psalm 119:58). Isaiah anticipated a time when the people of Judah would make God the desire of their hearts and people would say, "My soul yearns for you in the night; in the morning my spirit longs for you" (Isa. 26:9).

When the disciples of Jesus, who met him on the road to Emmaus, finally realized that they had been talking with the resurrected Christ, they said, "Were not our hearts burning within us while he talked with us on the road and opened the Scripture to us?" (Luke 24:32). Paul was able to reduce his own personal thoughts to one simple but overpowering desire. He said, "I want to know Christ" (Phil. 3:10). The key to living a holy life is rearranging our thinking to the point that we want to know Christ as Paul did. It is bringing ourselves to the point that our hearts burn within us for a greater understanding of Christ and our relationship to him.

A higher level of holiness is not possible if one's mind is centered on recreation and hobbies. If the cares of business and commerce consume a person's creative mental energy, little room is left for developing a higher level of personal holiness. If an individual's mind is programmed to gain power, prestige and popularity, a holy demeanor will necessarily suffer. Holiness has to become a mental priority. This chapter will concentrate on the essential elements of a holy mind set.

PROFANE WAYS OF THINKING

There has never been a Christian who has developed such complete control over the mind as to be able to claim complete freedom from profane thoughts. Even the apostle Paul recognized the existence of a constant struggle with the desires of the flesh. He wrote, "I beat my body and make it my slave so that after I have preached to others, I myself will not be disqualified for the prize" (I Cor. 9:27). He also reminded his fellow Christians in Corinth, "No temptation has seized you except what is common to man" (I Cor. 10:13).

Temptation attacks us through the mind. An evil thought is the embryo of an evil action. James taught that every person ". . . is tempted when, by his own evil desire, he is dragged away and enticed" (James 1:14). According to Jesus the inner person is responsible for "evil thoughts, sexual immorality, theft, murder, adultery, greed, malice, deceit, slander, arrogance and folly" (Mark 7:21).

We cannot realistically expect to prevent evil thoughts from entering our minds, but we do have the resources to deal with them. It may not be within our power to obstruct the entry of an evil thought, but it is well within our ability to decide whether such a thought will be welcomed and accommodated. Thoughts which frustrate the goal of holiness should be resisted. Among the thoughts which need to be curbed are the following:

Thoughts Which Promote Fleshly Appetites

The exposed indiscretions of certain well known media evangelists have made it clear that a mere profession of holy standing in God's sight does not immunize a person from the appetites of the flesh. Perhaps some of us are even more at risk as the result of our profession of faith. More than one minister has been lured into the trap of infidelity because he thought he wouldn't be vulnerable to the temptation to commit adultery. When Christians think they are no longer suscep-

303

tible to any given temptation, they would do well to remember Paul's warning in I Corinthians 10:12, "So if you think you are standing firm, be careful that you don't fall."

One day, many years ago, my wife and I went on a blackberry picking expedition. Prior to that time I had never experienced the discomforts that one endures with a poison ivy rash. I was preoccupied with harvesting blackberries and when I found a vine laden with them, my mind raced ahead to the blackberry jam that would soon grace our table and I vigorously set about the task of removing them from the vine as quickly as I could. Before I plunged into the task, my wife warned, "Honey, be careful. There's poison ivy in those vines." I said, "Aw don't worry about it, Hon. I'm immune to the stuff." I felt so secure that I had never even bothered to identify those pesky little poisonous plants. Guess who needed an "ocean of calamine lotion" the next day? Our fleshly appetites have a way of overpowering us, distorting our judgment and building a sense of false confidence. I learned of my vulnerability to poison ivy the hard way, but I also learned that sin works the same way.

A predictable pattern often occurs in the lives of those who think they have mastered the appetites of the flesh. It starts with relaxing one's defenses. Flirtation with a member of the opposite sex often starts with good natured teasing and appears harmless. A drink after dinner to relax the nervousness accumulated through a day of pressure-laden activity is certainly not going to transform one into an alcoholic. Just one piece of chocolate pie doesn't mean that you're a candidate for a weight loss clinic. No one notices when caution is being abandoned and when there is a point at which the line is crossed from innocence to lust. It's easier to cross that line when your defenses are down.

The lowering of defenses may mean nothing more than titillation – pleasant excitement, agreeable stimulation – but too often it leads to preoccupation. A man does not necessarily cross the line of sinfulness, when he notices that a woman is sexually attractive, but when he becomes preoccupied with such attractiveness, he has crossed the line. Sproul observed, "When we invite sexual thoughts into our minds and nurture them, we have passed from simple awareness into lust."[3] Jesus made it clear that lust equals adultery in God's sight.

304

"But I tell you that anyone who looks at a woman lustfully, has already committed adultery with her in his heart" (Matt. 5:28).

There's one more step in this progressive pattern of profane thinking – rationalization. I never cease to be amazed at the power of the human mind to rationalize those things that are unquestionably wrong. Not only do those who succumb to fleshly ways of thinking attempt to convince others, some have apparently convinced themselves that wrong is right. The Bible teaches that conscience can become so completely seared that no rational appeal to the life of holiness will have any affect on the person who has regressed from the faith. Paul warned,

> The Spirit clearly says that in later times some will abandon the faith and follow deceiving spirits and things taught by demons. Such teachings come through hypocritical liars, whose consciences have been seared as with a hot iron (I Tim. 4:1-2).

Thoughts Which Promote Pride

According to Proverbs 6:16 "There are six things the LORD hates, seven that are detestable to him." It comes as a shock to many people to learn that "haughty eyes" tops the list of the things God hates. Pride has so many ways of trapping us when we least expect it.

Several years ago, a state senator asked me to serve as "minister of the day" for the Iowa state legislature. I made elaborate preparation for my moment of recognition before the lawmakers of our state. I chose to wear my best suit, a grey pin striped style that was preferred by politicians and business executives at that point in time. I wrote out my prayers and practiced them. I even tried to eliminate the Texas "twang" from my voice, so the politicians would think I was "one of them." I pictured myself delivering my petitions for the state legislature in tones that would have been acceptable on the 6 o'clock news. I probably even entertained the thought that my petitions before the throne of the Almighty, might have some lasting impact on the people who made our laws. I gave very little thought to the fact that God was supposed to be the primary audience, not the Iowa house and senate.

The senator, who had invited me to commence the day's legislative business with a petition to the throne of God, met me in the chambers of the house of representatives. He introduced me to the delegation from our area and at just the right moment, we paraded down the center aisle to the podium where I shook hands with the speaker of the house. He didn't seem all that enthused about my presence, but he introduced me to the lawmakers and I dutifully invoked God's blessings on the legislative acts of the day. I probably didn't sound much like Tom Brokaw, but neither did I sound like the son of a cotton farmer from Texas (which is what I am). From there we walked to the other side of the capital building and down the aisle of the senate chambers. Just as I was about to shake the hand of the lieutenant governor, a female senator rose from her seat, ascended the rostrum and yanked my suit coat loose from my trousers. I had inadvertently tucked my suit coat inside the back of my pants along with my shirt. Just as the lieutenant governor introduced me to the Iowa senate, the horrible thought crossed my mind that I had been so careful to dress and act in just the right way, to make the best impression on these important men that I had not even noticed the position of my coat tails. I had strutted down the center aisles of both the house and the senate with my coat jammed inside my trousers looking like a man who had never even worn a suit before. I was trapped by my own vanity and I couldn't help thinking of Proverbs 16:18, "Pride goes before destruction and a haughty spirit before a fall." I have no idea what I said in the prayer for the senate, but you can be sure I had to talk with the Lord in my private praying about the way I let pride get the best of me.

My "fall" before the state legislature is hardly a matter of earth-shaking importance. I haven't been invited to be the legislature's "minister of the day" since then, but I don't imagine that will be held against me when we are called upon to "appear before the judgment seat of Christ." On the other hand I was clearly able to see the futility of human pretentiousness. As I look back on that day, the lesson I learned about the importance of humility means far more to me than the memory of having been honored by the Iowa legislature.

Pride inhibits the growth of holiness, because proud people have a tendency to elevate their own egocentric desires above the will of God. R. C. Sproul contends that the sin of pride is rooted in the desire for personal autonomy. We don't want anyone to exercise control over us, thus we stubbornly declare our independence from all kind of restraint, including the restraint that God imposes. "The temptation to be like God is greater than we think. . . . We squirm when we are placed under too much authority. We love to be free – free of restraints, free of accountability." Holy thinking cannot flourish in a mind dominated by thoughts of sinful pride.

The Jewish rejection of Jesus was rooted in pride. When Jesus promised eternal life to the Pharisees, they didn't welcome the message at all. Their pride blinded them to the truth that was being presented to them. They arrogantly responded, "Abraham died and so did the prophets, yet you say that if a man keeps your word, he will never taste death. Are you greater than our Father Abraham? He died and so did the prophets. Who do you think you are?" (John 8:52-53). The same egocentric mentality drives many people away from God even today. The requirements of the gospel appear to be demeaning to some. The idea that a bleeding, crucified Savior had to die in order to secure our salvation for us doesn't fit the image of middle class cultured America. Pride becomes a stumbling block to obedience. It's only when our pride is broken that we position ourselves to receive God's blessings.

> The sacrifices of God are a broken spirit; a broken and contrite heart, O God, you will not despise (Psalm 51:17).

Thoughts Which Promote Self-Righteousness

Self-righteousness is a particularly deadly form of pride and a mind set that renders the achievement of personal holiness virtually impossible. The worst thing about self-righteousness is the fact that it attempts to bypass grace. Once a person adopts a self-righteousness mindset, his preoccupation with self overshadows every other concern. Self-righteous people are so full of themselves they cannot see the needs of others. Their range of vision does not include their own shortcomings. In the sermon on the mount, Jesus relentlessly exposed the flaws in self-righteous behavior through the use of hyperbole. He said, "Why do you look at the speck of dust in your brother's eye and pay no attention to the plank in your own eye?" (Matt. 7:3).

Self-righteous people generally do many things right. They don't smoke, drink, wear immodest clothing, dance, play the lottery, attend X and R rated movies or participate in many of the vices that are common in the secular world. On the positive side, they give generously to the church, attend the services with predictable regularity, teach, pray, sing and witness. What could possibly be wrong with such good people? The problem is in the mind set. Many have developed an arrogant and superior attitude. Sometimes they even pray, "Lord, help us to live in such a way that the world will want to be like us." They look with disdain upon those who have failed to conform to their own personal standards of morality and righteousness.

How different is that mind set from the one the Pharisee displayed when he "stood up and prayed about himself; 'God, I thank you that I am not like all other men – robbers, evildoers, adulterers – or even like this tax collector'"? (Luke 18:11). Notice there was not a word about his own sin, or the need to bring others to repentance who had committed the sins he loathed. His prayer was consumed with the desire to elevate himself above the man beside him and his attempt to put some distance between himself and the tax collector through derogatory statements about him. The Pharisees' problem with holiness lay in the fact that they set their own standards for holiness and in doing so "They snobbishly rejected any believers who did not follow their strict rules"[5]

THOUGHTS TO CULTIVATE

Thoughts Which Promote an Awareness of God's Presence.
When David expressed remorse for his sinfulness, the heaviest burden on his heart was the threat of being denied intimacy with God. He felt the sting of emptiness because he had once known the fullness of God's presence. That's why he petitioned God to allow the bond of closeness to remain intact despite his blatant indiscretions. He said, "Do not cast me from your presence or take your holy spirit from me" (Psalm 51:11). Only those who have known the experience of God's fellowship can understand why it is so threatening for God to be absent from one's life.

308

In his book, *A Sense of Presence,* Edwin F. White lamented the fact that many contemporary Christians feel as David did because they have never actually experienced the presence of God. Many churches operate almost totally on human energy, with prayer being little more than a ceremonial function. Church leaders conduct the affairs of the kingdom as if they were operating a business enterprise. Men in the pulpit are selected for their charisma, their energy and even for their looks. They are expected to dress and talk like television personalties, but little attention is paid to how well they know God. A pulpit search committee wants to know about educational credentials, the so-called "track record" and how well the prospective minister "mixes" with the public, but rarely does a ministerial interview include questions about one's personal spiritual life.

Church success is measured in terms of budgets, buildings, baptisms and attendance records. Promotion of the inner life doesn't make the agenda of most church business meetings. Some time ago I sat in on a discussion of ways to improve the worship experience. Most of the talk concentrated on ways to streamline the worship service in order to get the whole thing over within a 60-minute period. Some discussion participants had even gone so far as to record the amount of time it takes to serve the Lord's Supper and suggested ways of shaving a few minutes off of that function. How we might draw closer to God during the communion service never received any attention at all.

Perhaps that's the reason White lamented,

> It isn't that these Christians flatly deny God's existence; rather they perceive God as impersonal and remote. God lives in their thoughts but not in their hearts. The church....as a whole is in a period of deprivation and impoverishment while totally unaware of its poverty.[6]

Most contemporary Christians are appalled at David's immorality, his insensitivity and his acts of violence. How could a man, who sometimes behaved so selfishly and lustfully, be held in such high esteem? The answer lies in the nature of David's heart. True enough, he sometimes committed atrocious sins, but David's redeeming feature is seen in the kind of heart he possessed. He yearned so for the presence of God that he is described as a man after God's own heart (I Sam. 13:14). It was this yearning that brought him back to his senses when he went too far. By way of contrast, the church is filled with people who have never come close to sinning on the scale that David did, but they have little idea of what it means to crave the presence of God.

God created us with the capacity to experience his presence. According to Acts 17:27, men and women are placed on this earth so that they might ". . . seek him and perhaps reach out for him and find him, though he is not far from each one of us." As individuals with free wills, it is within our power either to expand or reduce that capacity.

Thoughts Which Encourage Us to Duplicate the Attitudes of Christ.

Jerry Clower is a former fertilizer salesman, who developed an entertainment career by relating humorous experiences about growing up in rural Mississippi. Clower is also very serious about his relationship to Christ. When people ask him for his autograph, he signs, "Jerry Clower, John 3:30" John 3:30 says, "He must increase, but I must decrease" (KJV). That's taking the passage slightly out of context because the passage has reference to the ministry of John the Baptist, but it's on target with the kind of mindset that must characterize every person who wants to cultivate holiness.

When our attitudes are allowed to develop in response to the desires of the flesh, we mentally reverse John 3:30. We decide that we must increase and Christ must decrease, although few of us would ever say it that bluntly. The fleshly mindset is fueled by the "drum major" instinct. When a marching band takes the field, every eye takes notice of the fellow who stands at the head of the band in a plumed hat with his baton held high in the air. He arches his body backwards and moves down the field highstepping eight steps to every five yards. You won't notice the flute player unless she's your daughter, but everybody sees the drum major.

In life everyone wants to be the drum major. We demand "what's coming to us." Merchants and store clerks are expected to cater to our wants and desires. Some people even threaten church leaders with withdrawal of contributions and involvement if their wishes are not granted. Behind this spiritual grandstanding is a desire to be the center of attention.

Holiness cannot develop in a mind that's dominated by such self-centeredness. Jerry Clower's autograph indicates the only way that it can take place. In Philippians 2, Paul warned against being dominated by "selfish ambition and vain conceit" (verse 3). In contrast to the "drum major instinct," Paul urged, "Your attitude should be the same as that of Christ Jesus" (Phil. 2:5).

In the next few verses he proceeded to point his readers to certain specifics which may be observed in the Christlike attitude. (1) To have a Christlike attitude is to assume a posture of humility. Although Jesus possessed the nature of God (verse 6),[7] he voluntarily surrendered his divine prerogatives when he "made of himself nothing, taking the very nature of a servant and being made in human likeness and being found in appearance as a man, he humbled himself and became obedient to death – even death on a cross!" (Phil. 2:7-8). To assume a Christlike attitude is to be willing to empty ourselves of our privileges (and remember that we are co-heirs with Christ, according to Rom. 8:17) to advance the cause of the kingdom.

(2) To have a Christlike attitude means voluntarily accepting the role of servanthood. Jesus chose the role of a servant and so must we, when we follow in his footsteps. For him it was costly. It meant a cross. For us it may only mean sacrifice of time, energy and personal comforts.

(3) To have a Christlike attitude means letting God take care of the reward. Although Jesus assumed the posture of a suffering servant, the Father did not ignore him. "Therefore God exalted him in the highest place and gave him a name that is above every name" (Phil. 2:9). What does that have to do with our attitude? If we become too preoccupied with receiving glory in this life, we may miss it altogether. If we focus on humility and servanthood, God will take care of the glory.

Thoughts Which Concentrate on Wholesome Things.
There is a school of thought in psychology known as Behavior

Modification. An oversimplified explanation of behavior modification theory would suggest that a person who concentrates on consciously changing a certain way of doing things will eventually discover that the mindset has also been changed. It's basically the belief that it's easier to act one's way into a certain way of thinking or feeling than it is to think or feel one's way into a certain way of acting.[8]

As applied to. Christian living, behavior modification theory would say, "If your behavior is sinful, start doing what's right and you'll overcome the desire to sin." Sometimes that works, but not always. Sometimes the tug of the flesh is still there years after behavior patterns have stopped. Reformed smokers often say that nicotine cravings never leave. It's a well known fact that recovering alcoholics are just one drink away from relapse. Besides that, people sometimes go through the outward actions of holy living without internalizing the standards of Christ. Some people attend church services for political, business or family reasons. Their outward actions may be technically correct, but their hearts aren't in the right place. In such cases the major need is mind modification, not behavior modification.

Paul urged the Philippian Christians to adopt a regular program of wholesome thinking. He wrote, "Finally, brothers, whatever is true, whatever is noble, whatever is right, whatever is pure, whatever is lovely, whatever is admirable – if anything is excellent or praiseworthy – think about such things" (Phil. 4:8). What we program into our minds has a lot to do with the kind of behavior patterns we practice. If our minds feed on the values and standards promoted by contemporary television dramas, we may well find ourselves going in the opposite direction of holiness.

Fortunately, it also works the other way. During World War II, a young man was drafted into the army shortly after his wedding day. At that point in time he was only a nominal Christian, but he was sure of one thing. He was determined that he would remain faithful to his wife. Knowing the nature of temptation in the military and also being keenly aware of his own weaknesses, he decided that the best way to maintain the resolve to remain faithful to his wife was to fill his mind with worthwhile things. When he left for military service he took two items with him as a part of his plan to protect his commitment to fidelity. He took his Bible and a one volume commentary on the New

Testament. He read both from cover to cover many times during the course of the war. After the war he became an outstanding preacher of the gospel because he programmed his mind with the right kind of input. If you want to be holy, ask yourself the question, "What am I allowing to enter my mind?"

SUMMARY AND CONCLUSION

To grow in holiness a person must give attention to the kind of material that's allowed to enter the mind. No one can become holy without thinking holy thoughts. In Romans 8:5, Paul contended that our mental outlook with regard to spiritual values is the most crucial aspect of the human personality.

Even mature Christians recognize the fact that Satan is locked in a struggle with God and that the human mind is the battlefield upon which the war is being fought. While we cannot expect to keep unholy thoughts from entering our minds, we do have the power to decide whether those thoughts will be welcomed or quickly invited to depart. The difference between a holy mindset and a sensual mindset is not discerned by an absence of evil thoughts in the mind of the Christian. The sensual mind allows profane thoughts to enter, becomes preoccupied with them, gives in to the practice of sensual behavior and then rationalizes the sins that have been committed.

Some people are not attracted to such sensual acts as sexual misconduct and substance abuse, but they are hindered from growing in holiness because they fall victim to diseases of the disposition such as pride and self-righteousness.

A holy way of thinking can only become a reality when we make a deliberate effort to expose ourselves to holy ideas. Therefore, it is imperative for us to concentrate on developing a keener awareness of the presence of God. We must come to know God on a personal and intimate basis. The person who wants to be holy must identify thoroughly with the example of Jesus and adopt the attitude our Savior displayed during his life here on the earth. A Christlike attitude includes practicing voluntary humility, getting involved in a life of unselfish service and waiting to let God take care of handing out

313

rewards.

Finally, the person who wants to be holy must concentrate on wholesome thoughts. It's not enough to merely change one's outward behavior. The mind has to be thoroughly reprogrammed in the direction of holy attributes.

Endnotes

1. A.W. Tozer, *The Knowledge of the Holy.* (San Francisco: Harper and Row, 1961), p. 1.

2. R.C. Sproul, *One Holy Passion.* (Nashville: Thomas Nelson Publishers, 1987), p. 79.

3. R.C. Sproul, *Pleasing God.* (Wheaton, Illinois: Tyndale House Publishers, 1988), p.79.

4. Ibid., p. 165.

5. Phillip Yancey and Tim Stafford, *Unhappy Secrets of the Christian Life.* (Grand Rapids, Michigan: Zondervan Publishing House, 1979), p. 139.

6. Edwin F. White, *A Sense of Presence.* (Nashville: The Gospel Advocate Company, 1989), p. 11.

7. The King James Version uses the term *morphe,* which refers to the inward nature of something. With reference to Jesus it refers to the unchanging essential nature of his being. In other words it refers to his deity. He has always been God and he will always continue to be God. John quotes him in Rev. 1:8, " 'I am the Alpha and the Omega,' says the LORD God, 'who is, who was, and who is to come.' "

8. For a thorough discussion of the theories of behavior modification see B.F. Skinner, *About Behaviorism.* (New York: Knopf, 1974).

23
Disciplines
That Encourage Holiness

Personally, I think the word *discipline* is distasteful. It reminds me of "two-a-days" under the hot Texas sun during the latter part of August when I played on the high school football team. Each practice was supposed to be two hours long, but the coaches never looked at their watches. They also thought we would be tougher if we could go through the whole ordeal without drinking any water. Gatorade had not even been invented. That's the first thing I think of when I hear the term *discipline*.

The word also brings to mind certain obnoxious people who arise at 5 o'clock in the morning and run five miles before breakfast and try to make the rest of us feel guilty because we don't. It's the favorite word of the legalist who is still trying to work his way to heaven and still thinks that Grace is the name of a waitress at an all night truck stop. It's the term preferred by people who want to expel others from the church fellowship when they won't line up behind certain pet causes. Those are just some of the reasons the word discipline leaves a sour taste in my mouth.

Still I have to admit discipline is quite essential. Quite honestly, I never would have gotten this far in writing this book had I not been able to practice some degree of personal discipline. More importantly the Word of God confronts us with the realization that growth in holiness takes place only in the context of personal discipline.

WHY CHRISTIANS MUST PRACTICE PERSONAL DISCIPLINE

Spiritual discipline is not a popular concept in the contemporary religious world. No doubt there are many reasons why it is so. The abuses practiced by some who promoted the "disciplines" in the past has discouraged the practice of discipline among Christians today. No one wants to be another Simeon Stylites wasting away on a pillar of stone or an Oliver Cromwell imposing his ideas of morality on an entire nation and executing those who fail to measure up.

The general permissive environment in which middle class Americans live is consumer oriented, comfort driven and fiercely independent. Discipline cuts against the grain of that approach to living.

Dallas Willard believes that the Protestant Reformation overreacted to the Catholic error of justification by meritorious works and ended up with a theology that actually required nothing in terms of personal discipline from church members.

As a result . . . it has never been able to develop a coherent view of our part in salvation that would do justice either to the obvious directives of the New Testament for the disciple of Christ or to the facts of human psychology.

DYING TO SELF

The Biblical mandate for disciplined living is clear and unmistakable. It is discerned in the Biblical demand that we die to ourselves and to the old life of sin. In Rom. 6, Paul spoke of dying to sin and

316

living to God (verse 10). That death occurs at the time of our baptism, but just two verses later he clearly points out the fact that our human nature remains intact even though we have come to regard ourselves as dead to sin. We still have the power to act like we did when we were controlled by the sinful nature. Consequently, he appealed to his readers to exercise personal discipline to avoid being trapped by the old patterns of living. He said, "Therefore do not let sin reign in your mortal body so that you obey its evil desires"(Rom.6:12). Two chapters later, he said, "For if you live according to the sinful nature, you will die; but if by the Spirit you put to death the misdeeds of the body, you will live" (Rom. 8:13).

In his correspondence with the Galatians, Paul exposed the slavery of legalism and wrote a dynamic affirmation of justification by grace. Still he warned against giving in to the "desires of the sinful nature" (Gal. 5:16) and reminded his readers that "Those who belong to Christ Jesus have crucified the sinful nature with its passions and desires." He echoed the same theme in Colossians 3:5 when he wrote, "Put to death, therefore whatever belongs to your earthly nature: sexual immorality, impurity, lust, evil desires and greed which is idolatry." All these "put-to-death" passages are demands for discipline.

Discipline is the Fruit of Grace.

During those terrible days when the Third Reich controlled Germany, Dietrich Bonhoeffer spoke out against those members of the Lutheran clergy who chose to accommodate themselves to Hitler's program. He regarded their refusal to make waves against such a monstrous evil as a capitulation to the devil. In angry reaction he wrote, "Cheap grace is the deadly enemy of the church. We are fighting today for costly grace."[2]

When grace is properly understood it does not produce a permissive spirit, it produces a spirit of sacrifice and obedience. Paul declared that it was so in his own life. "But by the grace of God I am what I am, and his grace to me was not without effect. No, I worked harder than all of them – yet not I, but the grace of God was with me" (I Cor. 15:10).

In Philippians 2:12 Paul said, " . . . work out your salvation with fear and trembling." Quite often this verse has been offered as a

317

prooftext indicating that we are saved by our works. Actually the very opposite is true. The works that Paul has in mind are actions performed in response to the salvation that Christ has brought to our lives. John Wesley was on target in this respect when he wrote,

> Experience as well as Scripture show this salvation to be paradoxically instantaneous and gradual. It begins the moment we are justified, in the holy, humble, gentle, patient love of God for man. It gradually increases from that moment . . . until we grow up in all things to Him who is our head, until we attain the measure of the stature of the fullness of Jesus.

The Concept of Training.

The scriptures also teach the necessity of discipline through the concept of training. During my football days, I was required to observe certain rules because I was "in training." My regimen included a curfew, certain dietary restrictions, and many hours devoted to practicing the craft of playing football.

The scriptures even use the athletic metaphor to describe the discipline of the Christian. In I Corinthians 9:24-25, Paul said,

> Do you not know that in a race all the runners run, but only one gets the prize? Run in such a way as to get the prize. Everyone who competes in the games goes into strict *training.* They do it to get a crown that will not last; but we do it to get a crown that will last forever.

In I Timothy 4:7 he said "*train* yourself to be godly." In II Timothy 3:16-17, he wrote, "All scripture is God-breathed and is useful for teaching, rebuking, correcting and *training* in righteousness, so that the man of God may be thoroughly equipped for every good work." As he looked back over his life and expressed his confidence of the salvation, once again he used the sports metaphor. He said, "I have finished the race" (II Tim. 4:7). "This is what we must do if we pursue holiness: We must correct, mold, and train our moral character."[4]

The accumulation of Biblical data on the subject of personal discipline is overwhelming. No one can be serious about practicing Christianity and ignore it. While we can grant that many attempts at practicing discipline have been misguided, we can say unequivocally that discipline is not an optional exercise for God's holy people.

Some aspects of spiritual discipline are highly individualized. We have different temperaments, different gifts and different needs. We ought to be wary of anyone who requires everybody else to follow a certain prescribed regimen. Such a person may have more interest in control than in assisting people in the task of holy living. Much thought has been given to various programs of spiritual discipline. Two very good source books on the subject are Richard J. Foster's *Celebration of Discipline* and Dallas Willard's, *The Spirit of the Disciplines.* However, it should be pointed out that these two works represent the thoughts of fallible men and should be read with discretion. Neither author intended to clone himself.

DISCIPLINING OUR APPETITES

Sex

Sexual desire is not evil within itself. Within the context of scriptural marriage, the act of sexual intercourse is wholesome. "Marriage is honorable in all, and the bed undefiled: but whoremongers and adulterers God will judge" (Heb. 13:4, KJV). "God made us with the sexual need for each other. To realize that we have the need or feel within us the need is not evil."[5]

Sexual desire is one of the most powerful urges within the human body. Perhaps that's the reason the Lord warned his disciples about lust. He urged them to recognize the fact that a lustful thought precedes an adulterous act. "But I tell you that anyone who looks at a woman lustfully has already committed adultery with her in his heart" (Matt. 5:28).

The scriptures recognize the power of the sexual drive. Husband and wife are taught not to deny each other their conjugal rights (I Cor. 7:1-7). Married couples who refuse to meet each other's legitimate sexual needs place each other in temptations way (I Cor. 7:5). There is, however, a time when it would be proper to forego sexual intercourse by mutual consent. Paul suggested that his readers mutually agree to forego the exercise of their marital rights " . . . for a time, so

319

that you may devote yourselves to prayer" (I Cor. 7:5). Willard noted, "Voluntary abstention helps us appreciate and love our mates as whole persons, of which their sexuality is but one part."[6]

Food

The desire for food is an essentially neutral appetite among humans. However, if that appetite becomes an all consuming passion or if it hinders the desire to please God, it becomes a negative desire. It is also possible for our spiritual growth to be enhanced on certain occasions when food is consumed. It was within the context of the passover meal that our Lord instituted the Lord's Supper. The celebration involving the consumption of bread and the fruit of the vine continues to be a means of enhancing our spiritual growth even to this day.

Middle class America is not noted for the practice of self-control. Eating disorders are commonplace. Bridges suggests that there may be no area of life in which evangelical Christians are more susceptible to fleshly indulgence than in the area of eating without giving any thought to restraint.[7]

The Bible repeatedly notes the dangers of becoming preoccupied with food. During their wilderness wanderings, the children of Israel murmured against God because they missed the fish, cucumbers, melons, leeks, onions and garlic they had enjoyed in Egypt (Num. 11:5). Jesus counseled " . . . do not worry about your life, what you will eat; or what you will wear. Life is more than food and the body more than clothes" (Luke 12:22-23). Paul identified those whose " . . . god is their stomach . . . " as enemies of the cross (Phil. 3:19)

Those who maintain no control over food consumption, may well end up with more serious spiritual problems, because they are not bringing the body under control. "If we cannot say no to an indulgent appetite, we will be hard pressed to say no to lustful thoughts."[8]

Power

As these words are being written, war rages in the Persian Gulf. It is always difficult to sort out the reasons for war during the midst of a conflict. Theories about this one include the price of oil, stability in the Persian Gulf and stopping naked aggression among others. A power struggle lies behind all wars, whether the struggle exists in the board room or on the battlefield. James said, "What causes fights and quarrels among you? Don't they come from desires that battle within you. You want something, but don't get it" (James 4:1-2). Power can be addictive.

"If money hits us in the pocketbook, and sex hits us in the bedroom, power hits us in our relationships."[9] Anthony Campolo suggests that power is always a negative concept. He differentiates between *power* and *authority*. When an individual attempts to persuade others to act in a certain way, even though it is against the wishes of the one being persuaded, a power move is being made. When a person is able to persuade another without coercion, he has authority.[10] Authority is legitimate; power is not.

The earliest disciples of Jesus had great difficulty understanding the need to discipline their power urges. They argued about which one of them would be considered the greatest, but Jesus responded, "The kings of the Gentiles lord it over them; and those who exercise authority over them call themselves Benefactors. But you are not to be like that . . . " (Luke 22:25-26). To practice the discipline that enhances holiness, a child of God must learn to curb the desire to control human relations.

DISCIPLINING OUR MINDS

Study

A lady once approached her preacher after hearing him deliver an unusually fine sermon and said, "I'd give half my life to be able to know the Bible as well as you do." He responded, "Ma'am, that's exactly what it cost me. Half my life." In God's lament over Israel in Hosea 4:6, he sighed, "My people are destroyed from lack of knowledge." It is impossible to cultivate the requirements of holiness without spiritual knowledge and spiritual knowledge cannot be obtained without diligent study.

A serious minded college student soon learns that the difference between poor grades and good grades is the difference between haphazard study habits and disciplined study habits. It is no less true with the Word of God. The Word of God has been addressed to rational minds and some parts of it are "hard to understand" (II Pet. 3:16). The person who wants to follow after holiness will learn to develop effective study skills. Richard Foster suggests that these include *repetition, concentration, comprehension* and *reflection.*[11]

Actually a Christian never reaches the point in which study becomes unnecessary. When Paul knew he was facing execution, he wrote to Timothy and asked him to bring " . . . my scrolls, especially the parchments" (II Tim. 4:13). It has been said that William Tyndale asked someone to bring him his Greek New Testament as he awaited execution. There's no better way to die than to die with your mind engaged in the study of God's Word.

Meditation

The Desert Fathers believed meditation to be the key that unlocks the door to holiness. While some of their austere forms of meditation actually resulted in promoting behavior that works against holiness, meditation can be a helpful discipline in achieving a higher level of individual sanctification.

Although meditation and study can be viewed as disciplines that sometimes overlap, they are not quite the same. "Meditation is devotional; study is analytical. Meditation will relish a word; study will explicate it."[12] Meditation has been defined as " . . . the ability to hear God's voice and obey his word."[13] The suggestion that we meditate to "hear" the voice of God should not be taken to mean that we listen for an audible sound from the Lord. Revelation was finished with the completion of the canon! If not, the canon is yet incomplete. Meditation is a way of attuning the mind to the things of God, a way of being receptive to the Word and to the ways that God is at work in our lives.

In Biblical times great men of God gave themselves to meditation. The author of the first Psalm described the righteous man in this manner, "But his delight is in the law of the Lord and on his law he meditates day and night" (verse 2). A later Psalm echoes a similar thought, "My eyes stay open through the watches of the night that I may meditate on your promises" (Psa. 119:148).

The goal in meditation is to bring one's mind into a harmonious

322

flow with the mind of God. "'He walks with me and he talks with me' ceases to be pious jargon and instead becomes a straightforward description of daily life."[14]

Solitude

"In solitude, we purposefully abstain from interaction with other human beings, denying ourselves companionship and all that comes from conscious interaction with others."[15] Solitude by itself does not guarantee an enhancement of holiness. It has been said that "living in a hole does not make you holier." But when a person engages in solitude for the right reason, it becomes an instrument of holiness.

A minister once sought the help of the famous Swiss psychiatrist, Carl Jung. The man admitted that he was a nervous wreck and attributed his overwrought condition to 14-hour work days. Jung suggested that he shorten his work days to 8 hours and urged him to spend the evenings alone in his study.

Every night the minister went home and entered his study. Once he closed the doors behind him, he alternated between playing Chopin and Mozart on the piano and reading the literature of Herman Hesse and Thomas Mann. A few days later, he went back to see Dr. Jung and reported that his mental condition had not improved. Dr. Jung said, "I didn't ask you to spend your evenings with Hesse and Mann or even Chopin and Mozart. I wanted you to be all alone with yourself." The psychiatrist noticed a look of horror on his client's face as the minister confessed, "I can't think of worse company." Dr. Jung replied, "And yet this is the self you inflict on other people fourteen hours a day."

How much time do you spend in solitude? Solitude does not mean time reading the newspaper, books or periodicals. It does not include time spent listening to music. You're probably thinking, "Come on, Norman. You know how busy I am these days. I don't have time for solitude?" Is that really the way it is? Could it be that you fear what Dr. Jung's client feared? How well do you like the company when you spend time by yourself?

Jesus often retreated from his interaction with people to spend time alone with God. Immediately after his baptism, he went to the wilderness for forty days of solitude and fasting (Matt. 4:1-2). When he learned that Herod had taken the life of John the Baptist, " . . . he withdrew to a solitary place" (Matt. 14:13). On the eve of his crucifixion, he found the solitude of Gethsemane (Matt. 26:36-46). After his conversion, Paul left Damascus and went to Arabia (Gal. 1:17). We have no record of that three-year period in his life. It is certainly possible that he passed that time in solitude.

More than ever, serious-minded Christians need to experience solitude. Americans are geared to noise and activity. We almost dread the thought of spending time alone without music, without television, without access to the telephone and without noise of numerous appliances that whirr, buzz and growl. In such an environment, "Be still and know that I am God," is more needed than ever before. We need to find a quiet place to spend time alone with God, but we must also recognize that such quietness is not always easy to come by. We must remember that "solitude is more a state of mind and heart than it is a place."[16] Sometimes we may have to aim for the solitary state of mind in the midst of noise and confusion.

Fasting

I'm going to have to confess that I don't measure up very well on this one. My experiences with fasting have been less than satisfactory because of physical reactions. I can't say that it did that much for my spiritual frame of mind other than to give me the satisfaction of knowing that I maintained control of myself for a certain period of time. I'm sure the fault is my own and I must concede that fasting does have both scriptural and practical support.

Fasting was practiced on numerous occasions in Biblical times. Jesus addressed an abuse of fasting in Matthew 6:16: "When you fast, do not look somber as the hypocrites do, for they disfigure their faces." The hypocrites had turned fasting into a public display of their pious demeanor and Jesus saw that as unbecoming to his followers. Many scholars have suggested that the phrase "when you fast" suggests that fasting was normative practice among the disciples of Jesus, although it cannot be said that such a statement is to be taken with the force of a command.

Paul and Barnabas appointed elders in every church on their second missionary journey " . . . .with prayer and fasting" (Acts 14:23).

In II Corinthians 11:27, Paul said that he had " . . . often gone without food." There is no indication as to whether this was voluntary or involuntary fasting.

What is the purpose of fasting? Willard assigns two purposes to it. (1) "Fasting confirms our utter dependence upon God by finding in him a source of sustenance beyond food."[17] (2) " . . . fasting is one of the more important ways of practicing the self-denial required of *everyone* who would follow Christ."[18]

DISCIPLINING OUR ACTIONS

Worship

When Jesus spoke with the woman at the well in Samaria, the conversation turned to the subject of worship. The woman was confused by conflicting traditions concerning the proper place of worship. Jesus took her to a higher level of consciousness regarding worship when he said,

> Yet a time is coming and has now come when the true worshipers will worship the Father in spirit and truth, for they are the kind of worshipers the Father seeks. God is spirit, and his worshipers must worship him in spirit and in truth (John 4:23-24).

Worship is a word that we have adapted from the Old English term, "Worthship." To worship is to ascribe worth and glory to God. Regular worship, on both the corporate and individual levels, is essential to progressive holiness. Jesus said the Father seeks worshipers.

Many Christians have assumed that worship consists entirely of the structured program which takes place in the assembly on Sunday mornings. While it's true that a worship experience does take place in the assembly, it should not be thought that the worship experience is confined to a specific place and hour.

The Samaritan woman was concerned about time and place while Jesus stressed lifestyle and attitude. According to Colossians 3:16, everything a Christian does in response to God brings glory to the Creator. "The concept of worship in the New Testament is in no way restricted to special acts, but rather encompasses the believer's whole life offered in sacrifice to God."[19] Paul used the term *latreuo* in Romans 12:1, a word which is used in Romans 9:4 to describe worship in the temple under the law. In Romans 12:1 it applies to the life of devotion to Christ. "Therefore I urge you, brothers, in view of God's mercy, to offer your bodies as living sacrifices, holy and pleasing to God – which is your spiritual worship." At other times the term worship applies to an outward act of reverence which is deliberately entered into. Worship is not a question of the life versus the structured acts of praise. It includes both and must be entered into regularly by all those who aspire to reach higher levels of holiness.

Evangelism

Holiness is a virtue that was intended to be shared, thus its connection with evangelism. A person who views holiness as a quality to be developed in isolation from the rest of the human race would be a self-centered individual. Our desire to share the life we live in Christ is rooted in our love for the human race. "For the love of Christ compels us, because we are all convinced that one died for all, and therefore all died" (II Cor. 5:17).

Many Christians resist any thought that evangelistic activity might be a part of the holiness discipline. Some overzealous advocates of evangelistic fervor have sought to mobilize the church in the direction of soul winning by laying on heavy guilt trips. It usually doesn't work and if it does work, it doesn't last because people feel like they are being coerced into evangelistic enterprise. Evangelistic technique has sometimes paralleled high pressure sales technique and many people find that distasteful.

Evangelistic involvement could become a more enjoyable ministry if we would define evangelism a little bit differently. Those who think of evangelism in terms of backing people into a corner and convincing them of the error of their ways have missed the picture of genuine evangelism. Evangelism flows from the joy that holy living has brought to our lives. When our joy is real, it's contagious. Paul said, "For we are to God the aroma of Christ among those who are being saved and those who are perishing. To the one we are the smell of death; to the other the fragrance of life" (II Cor. 2:14-15). Joseph C. Aldrich notes,

> When an individual, a family or a corporate body of believers are moving together toward wholeness (holiness), a credible lifestyle emerges . . . .Because this is true, evangelism is a way of living beautifully and opening one's web of relationship to include the nonbeliever.[20]

Servanthood

Those who aspire to be holy must emulate the holy life that Jesus lived. It has been said that the footwashing incident in the upper room on the night Jesus was betrayed is a portrait in miniature of the lifestyle of Jesus. Some people have missed the point entirely and instituted footwashing as a ceremony to be performed in church services. Footwashing was a task, a menial task at that. When a host received guests into his home, he supplied a basin of water and a towel and assigned the job of washing the dirt from the feet of his guests to the least honored servant.

Jesus, whom the disciples called master, elected to perform the task himself. After they had observed the passover together, " . . . he poured water into a basin, and began to wash his disciples' feet, drying them with the towel that was wrapped around him" (John 13:5). Later on he gave the following instructions to the disciples. "Now that I your Lord and Teacher have washed your feet, you also should wash one another's feet. I have set you an example that you should do as I have done for you" (John 13:14-15). Jesus mandates servanthood as the aspiration of his disciple.

The discipline of servanthood may be the most difficult discipline of all, because we are naturally inclined to show more interest in being served than we are in volunteering for service. It sounds very "spiritual" to talk about servanthood in a church service, but when it comes to engaging in the "hands on" business of serving the needs of hurting people, we tend to think that it's beneath our dignity. One way I try to get around servanthood is to select a 'nice' clientele that I can serve gladly, but the Scriptures won't allow me to escape with such thinking. Jesus said, " . . . a servant of all."[21]

327

THE HOLY SPIRIT – OUR RESOURCE
FOR SPIRITUAL DISCIPLINE

If we set out to engage ourselves in the practice of all these disciplines, we may soon become discouraged and conclude that to dream of achieving holiness is to "dream the impossible dream." Surely God has not required something of us which we cannot practice. God has said, "Be holy because I am holy" (I Peter 1:16). As rational students of the Bible, we can only conclude that such a command can be obeyed. Otherwise God would be cruel, repressive and impossible to please.

Our discouragement stems from our failure to understand that we have divine resources at our disposal. God has not only called us to a disciplined life of holiness, he has equipped us with the ability to do his will. The equipping is made available to us through the indwelling of the Holy Spirit. The Holy Spirit supplies the strength that we need to resist temptation. "For if you live according to the sinful nature, you will die, but if by the Spirit, you put to death the misdeeds of the body, you will live" (Rom. 8:13). The Holy Spirit is also present to provide the positive power for productive living. "I pray that out of his glorious riches, he may strengthen you with power through his Spirit in the inner being" (Eph. 3:16).

A few years ago I was invited to serve as a resource speaker at a weekend retreat for a church in the Deep South. I was getting ready to pack my car and head for home, when a middle-aged gentleman approached me and asked, "Could you give me some practical tips on how I might be able to tap into the Holy Spirit when I'm facing temptation." He caught me completely off guard. His question was a valid one and I did not give him the kind of answer he deserved. After thinking about it for a long time, if I were asked that same question again, here's how I would answer.

1. Develop a conscious desire to want for yourself what God wants. Those who work with Alcoholics Anonymous and similar programs all know that recovery begins when the alcoholic admits there is a problem and desires to change. In the spiritual sense we can only make use of the Holy Spirit's help when we recognize how Satan is attacking us at the level of the flesh and when we desire to overcome

328

it. As Paul put it, "Set your mind on things above, not on earthly things" (Col. 3:2).

2. Meekness is a key ingredient. Meekness is listed as one of the components of the fruit of the Spirit in Galatians 5:22, 23. The NIV translators chose the word, "gentleness," but that really does not convey the idea the author intended. To be meek is to yield, to be brought under control, to let God have his way. Tapping into the Spirit's power involves the recognition that we are not capable of controlling our lives alone and the willingness to say, "All right Lord. I'm not handling this very well. I'm ready to try it your way."

3. Make a conscious decision to rely on the Spirit's power. Paul promised, "The Spirit helps us in our weakness" (Rom. 8:26). We must be willing to accept that promise by faith and deal with the flesh on that basis. A friend of mine insists that it's inadequate to tell people they need to practice this reliance on the Spirit's promise one day at a time. He insists that we may have to remind ourselves of the promise thirty minutes at a time. If you're struggling with weakness, ask God about it. Thirty minutes later ask him again and thirty minutes after that ask again. Maybe that's what the Bible means when it says to "pray without ceasing."

SUMMARY AND CONCLUSION

To talk about discipline as an avenue to holiness is to invite a response of spiritual inertia. That's why the discussion has been postponed until we got nearly to the end of the book. Maybe if you get this far, it won't scare you away.

If we accept the Bible as an inspired message from God, we cannot sidestep the need to live disciplined lives. God has not required us to be disciplined because he wants to spoil our fun. Discipline is an avenue of holiness and holiness the key to joy and peace. "No discipline seems pleasant at the time, but painful. Later on, however, it produces a harvest of righteousness and peace for those who have been trained by it" (Heb. 12:11). "God intends the Christian life to be a life of joy – not drudgery . . . .Only those who walk in holiness experience true joy."[22]

329

Endnotes

1. Dallas Willard, *The Spirit of the Disciplines.* (San Francisco: Harper, 1988), pp. 147-148.
2. Dietrich Bonhoeffer, *The Cost of Discipleship.* (New York: The Macmillan Company, 1963), p. 45.
3. John Wesley, *The Nature of Holiness.* (Minneapolis: Bethany House Publishers, 1988), pp. 161-162.
4. Jerry Bridges, *The Pursuit of Holiness.* (Colorado Springs, Colorado: Navpress, 1978; reprint edition, 1985), p. 99.
5. Bob Rigdon, *Happiness Explained.* (Raleigh, North Carolina: Edwards and Broughton Company, 1983), p. 42. Dr. Rigdon is a professor of psychology at Western Carolina University and also serves as a minister of the gospel in Sylva, North Carolina. Following the "hierarchy of needs" popularized by Dr. Abraham Maslow, Rigdon contends that every legitimate human need can be lawfully and scripturally fulfilled and that to satisfy those needs within the limits of scriptural regulations is both pleasing to God and personally fulfilling.
6. Willard, *The Spirit of the Disciplines,* p. 170.
7. Bridges, *The Pursuit of Holiness,* p. 112.
8. Ibid., p. 113.
9. Richard J. Foster, *Money, Sex and Power.* (San Francisco: Harper and Row, 1985), p. 175.
10. Anthony Campolo, Jr., *The Power Delusion.* (Wheaton, IL.: Victor Books, 1984), p. 11.
11. Richard J. Foster, *The Celebration of Discipline.* (San Francisco: Harper and Row, 1988), pp. 64-66.
12. Ibid., p. 64.
13. Ibid., p. 17.
14. Ibid., p. 19.
15. Willard, *The Spirit of the Disciplines,* p. 160.
16. Foster, *The Celebration of Discipline,* p. 96.
17. Willard, *The Spirit of the Disciplines,* p. 166.
18. Ibid., p. 167.
19. Ervin Bishop, "The Assembly." *Restoration Quarterly.* 4th Quarter, 1975. p. 224. Bishop commented, "Worship . . . is almost synonymous with salvation. Entering into a saved relationship with Christ is entering into a worshipping relationship with God." p. 223.
20. Joseph C. Aldrich, *Lifestyle Evangelism.* (Portland, Oregon: Multnomah Press, 1981), p. 28.
21. Gayle D. Erwin, *The Jesus Style.* (Waco, Texas: Word Books, 1983), p. 48.
22. Bridges, *The Pursuit of the Holy,* p. 15.

24

The Social Dimensions
of Holiness

Does our personal commitment to holiness require us to participate in the process of improving the quality of life in the world community? Men and women of conviction have answered the question in
different ways. To John Wesley, the commitment to holiness meant
opposing the evil of slavery. Just six days before his death, he wrote
William Wilberforce a letter urging him to work toward influencing the
British Parliament to abolish slavery.[1] To James C. Fenhagen, a holy
person is anyone who is attempting to bring social reform to the
world. He displays little regard for a person's individual ethics or doctrinal commitments.[2] At the extreme opposite end of the pendulum
are the Mennonites who ". . . not only renounce all participation in
politics and refuse to be drawn into military service, but follow their
own distinctive customs and regulations in economics and education."[3]

Christians are legitimately concerned about dealing with the world
on the redemptive level. Since the redemptive level of awareness has

clear and definite eternal consequences, we tend to attach greater importance to redemptive matters than to social matters. After all, social needs can be very transient and temporary. Still the Bible makes it clear that Christians cannot bury their heads in the sand and disengage themselves from the temporal needs of people. On the other hand our walk with God does indeed require social interaction. James said, "Religion that God our Father accepts as pure and faultless is this: to look after orphans and widows in their distress and to keep oneself from being polluted by the world" (James 1:27). Holiness does have a social dimension. In this chapter, we will attempt to set forth certain principles to help sincere Christians make decision about the kind of involvement they should have with the world at large.

ESCAPE OR ENGAGEMENT?

What should be the attitude of Christians toward social action? Should we concentrate solely on winning souls and forget about responding to the physical plight of those who suffer? Is it appropriate for a Christians to enter the political arena? If so, which political agenda can be appropriately labeled the "Christian position?" The Bible teaches that ". . . the earth and everything in it will be laid bare" (II Pet. 3:10). Does that eliminate any need on our part to work on improving the quality of life in our present environment? Is it appropriate for churches to lobby for passage of certain bills being considered by legislative bodies? These and other questions must be pondered as we make our decisions either to escape the call for social involvement or engage ourselves in the social process.

The Rationale for Escape.
  1. Christians should disengage themselves from the world because the world is hostile to Christ. To a certain extent, this assessment is accurate. In our Lord's intercessory prayer, he said, "I have given them your word and the world has hated them for they are not of the world, anymore than I am of the world" (John 17:14). According to I John 5:19, "We know that we are the children of God, and that the whole world is under the control of the evil one."

332

The "world" in these passages does not refer to the physical earth, the ground, or the earth's ecological system. When viewed from that perspective, "The earth is the Lord's, and everything in it" (Psa. 24:1). As John used the term, "world," he had reference to moral, social and spiritual orders which excluded the authority of Christ.

The world appears as a realm under the power of evil; it is the region of darkness, into which the citizens of the kingdom of light must not enter; it is characterized by the prevalence in it of lies, hatred and murder; it is the heir of Cain. It is a secular society dominated by the "lust of the flesh, the pride of life" or, in Prof. Dodd's translation of these phrases, it is a "pagan society," with its sensuality, superficiality and pretentiousness, its materialism and its egoism.[4]

Those who counsel escape from involvement with the world's social system look upon such engagement as fraternizing with the enemy. To some degree, they have a point. Holiness of life does indeed involve separation from the world. Paul reminded the Christians at Corinth, "Do not be yoked together with unbelievers. For what do righteousness and wickedness have in common? Or what fellowship can light have with darkness?" (II Cor. 6:14). There is also the danger of compromise when Christians rub shoulders with unbelievers. "Bad company corrupts good character" (I Cor. 15:33).

2. *Christians should disengage from the world because time spent in social action is time taken away from evangelism.* No one can deny the urgency of evangelism. People without Christ are lost in sin. Jesus said, "I am the way the truth and the life. No one comes to the Father except through me" (John 14:6). Nothing on the agenda of human affairs is more urgent than the business of bringing men and women to Christ. The apostle Paul said that he was willing to adjust to a variety of social conditions in order to be able to work to be redemptive with people. He said,

To the Jews I became like the Jew, to win the Jews. To those under the law I became like one under the law (though I myself am not under the law), so as to win those under the law. To the weak, I became weak, to win the weak. I have become all

333

things to all men so that by all possible means I might save some (I Cor. 9:20-22).

When our social involvement hinders our ability to work redemptively with people, then one has to question whether such social engagement is indeed a holy act. The decision to become engaged or to refrain from engagement is personal and often depends on circumstances. I personally believe that the Bible teaches against abortion and I have stated my position publicly, but I have consistently refused to sign petitions, participate in demonstrations and have not been active in lobbying efforts to repeal the effects of Roe vs. Wade. Some people in the congregation where I worship have done all those things. I respect them for their decision, but I also insist that my decision is not a cowardly one, but a decision made with a redemptive purpose in mind.

I have counseled with people who were contemplating an abortion and in at least one instance I have been successful in persuading a person not to go through with it. The incident ended satisfactorily when the baby came to full term and was adopted by a fine Christian family. I might never have had the opportunity to even engage in the conversation had I walked down the street with placards in my hand denouncing the sin of abortion.

Another incident which served to convince me that a redemptive approach to the subject might be preferable to the legislative approach, occurred during the heat of a political election. On the Sunday morning before the election, some of the pro-life people came onto our parking lot (uninvited) and placed literature on the windshields of all the automobiles parked there that day, urging voters to cast their ballots against a certain candidate because he did not favor a constitutional amendment outlawing abortion. Many of our members were offended because church property was used to openly campaign against a certain political candidate. I found myself agreeing with them. It was not the kind of tactic that I could visualize Jesus using.

While there is no hard and fast rule for involvement of this nature, it should be remembered that our mission is not to force society to adopt a pro-Christian legislative platform. Our mission is to share the good news that Jesus brings forgiveness of all kinds of sin. We do have some latitude in this respect because we live in a society that has a participatory government. The rules that govern our society are made by those who are being governed. On that basis we have the right to make our voice heard. It should be remembered however that many people live in a closed society. In a closed society any expression of dissent from the government's point of view can be viewed as an act of treason. Paul lived under such a government and he counseled conformity to government, except in those areas in which the government forbade obedience to God. (See Rom. 13:1-7).

3. *Christians should disengage themselves from the world because attempts to legislate morality have proven futile.* The eighteenth amendment of the constitution went into effect on January 16, 1920. It prohibited the manufacture and sale of alcoholic beverages in the United States. By 1924 many people in America became convinced that this "noble experiment" was a mistake and on December 5, 1933 the eighteenth amendment was officially repealed when 36 states ratified the twenty-first amendment.

Since 1976 every presidential election has been influenced by evangelicals. Jimmy Carter was a Scripture quoting, Sunday School teaching, Baptist. Soon after he entered office, however leaders from the religious right became disillusioned because they felt the new president did not advance their agenda. Ronald Reagan openly courted the favor of the evangelical community. He advocated passing a constitutional amendment to overturn Roe vs. Wade. His wife, Nancy, crusaded against drugs in the "Just say, 'No,'" campaign. He favored allowing prayers in the schools and returning to old fashioned standards of decency and morality. George Bush has pretty much favored the same things and declared war on drugs.

Even though the last three presidents have publicly claimed to be on the side of the Bible, morality and clean living, the nation's moral and spiritual standards have continued to deteriorate. There has been an increase in crime; gangs terrorize our cities and the drug problem continues to get worse. On the surface it appears that much of the political energy exerted by reform minded evangelicals has not achieved its desired effect. Some say that the evangelical cause has been betrayed by politicians who talk out of both sides of their mouth.

Charles Colson, former aide to President Nixon and prominent figure in the evangelical movement, has a different view. ". . . I think the true explanation lies in our disregard for two key truths: first, the solutions to all human ills do not lie in political structures; and second it is impossible to effect genuine political reform solely by legislation."[5]

In our enthusiasm to promote the standard of morality, we must never forget that "Righteousness exalts a nation, but sin is a disgrace to any people" (Prov. 14:34). Christians may legitimately influence society through example and persuasion, but when we cross the line to coercion, we not only tread on dangerous ground from a scriptural point of view, we run the risk of being much less effective than we might otherwise have been.

The Rationale for Engagement.

1. God upholds the principle of social justice. You can't reach any other conclusion if you read the prophets. Isaiah exhorted the people of his day, ". . . Seek justice, encourage the oppressed. Defend the cause of the fatherless, plead the case of the widow" (Isa. 1:17). Amos lamented the social injustice that permeated Israel's society in the 8th century B.C. He pleaded, "Hate evil, love good; maintain justice in the courts . . ." (Amos 5:15). Lawrence O. Richards notes,

> The law established social structures such as interest-free loans and the right to glean in harvested fields. But making these structures work depended on godly individuals willing to loan freely and to open their gates to the working poor.[6]

2. Jesus taught and modeled concern for social justice. The New Testament is not totally silent on the subject of social justice. Although it is clear that the apostles never spoke out against such an obvious evil as the institution of slavery, it must be remembered that they were living within the framework of a closed society. Dissent on the subject of slavery would neither have been taken seriously nor tolerated. Even so, the pronouncements of Jesus clearly indicate a concern for social justice. At the beginning of his earthly ministry, Jesus addressed this matter in his speech before the synagogue in Nazareth.

336

He read the following passage from the scroll of Isaiah.

The Spirit of the LORD is on me, because he has anointed me
to preach good news to the poor. He has sent me to proclaim
freedom for the prisoners and recovery of sight to the blind, to
release the oppressed, to proclaim the year of the Lord's favor
(Luke 4:18-19).

The social concern of Jesus can be observed in his example. He
identified with the poor, the sick, and the disenfranchised. It was the
powered elite and the people who were interested in protecting their
position in the religious establishment who took him to task for ignoring social propriety and meeting the needs of those who were not
thought to be "the right kind of people." When challenged about his
insensitivity to their ideas about protocol, he answered, "It is not the
healthy who need a doctor, but the sick" (Matt. 9:12).

He also made it clear that social involvement is expected among
those who choose to follow him. According to Matthew 25:31-46,
those who respond to the hungry, the thirsty, the people who are
poorly clothed, the sick and the imprisoned will be the ones welcomed into heaven and those who turn a deaf ear to such needs will
be excluded.

Jesus did not fear being contaminated with the world to the extent
that he cut himself off from those with unsavory reputations. When
the Pharisees criticized his association with sinners, he exposed their
concept of holiness as an external piety which was totally lacking in
substance. Some of the harshest words that ever came from Jesus'
lips are directed toward this error. He said to them, "You are like
whitewashed tombs, which look beautiful on the outside but on the inside are full of dead men's bones" (Matt. 23:27). How could Jesus
mix and mingle with the sinners of his day and not be affected himself? He was perfectly in tune with the mind of his Father in heaven.
The more we concentrate on fellowship with God, the less likely we
are going to be dragged into sin when we are trying to help somebody who is groping in darkness. Or to put it in the language of R. C.
Sproul, "The more we understand the mind of God, the less threatened we will be by Ernest Hemingway and Jean-Paul Sartre."[7]

337

3. The New Testament presents a mandate for Christians to respond to the needs of a hurting world. Whether I choose to march in a demonstration against abortion is an optional expedient requiring me to exercise judgment. Whether I choose to boycott a store that sells pornographic magazines is also in the realm of personal choice. Whether I decide to crusade against parimutuel gambling, the Equal Rights Amendment or evolutionary textbooks is a matter for me to decide within the boundaries of my own conscience. I would hope that other Christians would not think that my personal holiness is suspect if I do not choose to become involved in their pet projects.

On the other hand, whether I become involved in the social needs of my fellow man is not an option for me as a Christian. My commitment to pure religion requires concern for the fatherless and the widows (James 1:27). The same writer sharply rebuked flippant and uncaring responses to human suffering when he said, "Suppose a brother or sister is without clothes and daily food. If any one of you says to him, 'Go, I wish you well; keep warm and well fed,' but does nothing about his physical needs, what good is it?" (James 2:15-16). John wrote, "If anyone has material possessions and sees his brother in need but has no pity on him, how can the love of God be in him" (I John 3:17). Some might try to excuse themselves from exercising compassion toward non-Christians, since the last two passages specifically mention brothers and sisters. But the scripture will not allow us to be that selective about the people to whom we shall demonstrate compassion. Paul said, "Therefore, as we have opportunity, let us do good to all people, especially to those who belong to the family of believers" (Gal. 6:10). Peter wrote, "Live such good lives among the pagans that, though they accuse you of doing wrong, they may see your good deeds and glorify God on the day he visits us" (I Pet. 2:12). As people who desire to follow after holiness, we cannot shirk our responsibility to the needy.

HOW SHALL WE RESPOND?

Having first presented a rationale for escape and followed that with a rationale for engagement, which one is correct? The answer is that both are correct and both are incorrect. Holiness requires us to see our involvement with the world in balance. To completely disengage ourselves from the world is to withdraw into a shell and limit our influence in the world. Jesus taught,

> You are the light of the world. A city set on a hill cannot be hidden. Neither do people light a lamp and put it under a bowl. Instead they put it on its stand, and it gives light to everyone in the house. In the same way, let your light so shine before men, that they may see your good deeds and praise your father in heaven (Matt. 5:14-16).

The person who takes the escape route does not dispense light in the world and thus thwarts the mission of the Savior.

A Christian can become so obsessed with engagement that personal spirituality and doctrinal integrity are either relegated to a position of low importance or abandoned altogether. This was the mistake of the social gospel. The theological liberalism of the late nineteenth century gave birth to the social gospel. When liberalism removed supernaturalism from religion, it was left with a message that would not "play in Peoria." After all, if there's no heaven and no hell, then why should people bother to be religious? The social gospel endowed liberalism with a cause. Walter Rauschenbusch was the best known spokesperson for the social gospel cause. He defined the kingdom of God as the reconstruction of earthly society to conform to the ideals of Christianity. Concerning the kingdom he said, "It is not a matter of getting individuals into heaven, but of transforming the life on earth into the harmony of heaven."[8] To Bible-believing Christians, this radical redefinition of the kingdom of God constituted heresy. The kingdom of God is the rule of God. Furthermore, the Bible clearly says that if Christian virtues are cultivated, " . . . you will receive a rich welcome into the eternal kingdom of our Lord and Savior Jesus Christ" (II Pet. 1:11). The proponents of the social gospel made the mistake of attempting to replace the saving gospel with a gospel that was limited to expressions of social change. Such an approach goes too far, but it should never become an excuse for abandoning the legitimate needs of a hurting world.

Recent evangelical history of social involvement should be trouble-

339

some to people who are serious about the social requirements of the Bible. The "Christian agenda" tends to be quite selective. The issues include homosexuality, gambling (parimutuel, lotteries, riverboat casinos), women's liberation, pornography, profanity and obscenity in the media, abortion, evolution, public school textbooks, prayer and Bible reading in the schools, sex education in the schools and home schooling. Certainly there are some legitimate concerns in these areas.

On the other hand, the evangelical community practically ignores others areas which are clearly addressed in scripture. These include racism, hunger, poverty, the environment, care of the handicapped, the mentally ill, the aged, AIDS sufferers and the homeless. I have strong reservations about turning the church into a political action group. We are usually too poorly informed, too poorly staffed and too politically naive to make that much difference, when we go on record in favor of or in opposition to some public issue. Joe H. Foy, lawyer and businessman, addressed this troublesome tendency before a gathering of ministers in Houston, Texas. He asserted his conviction that the church should not be looked upon as a social welfare administration, a political activist agency, a legislative reference bureau or a society for the evaluation of scientific truth.

> In these areas, the church is essentially undertrained, underfinanced, undertalented, underorganized, but often overmotivated by that earnest zeal which is so often the victim of charlatans and the precursor of financial and political disaster.[9]

Mr. Foy's convictions are worthy of consideration by church leaders who are considering political activism. On the other hand, if we are limited in our ability to alter the structures of society, we do have a tremendous advantage over the world in area of character building. "This role of changing the world by indirection, by making men of such character and inclination as to build a better society for their fellows, has always been the church's most effective operating device."[10] If we can concentrate on developing a holy character among our people, some of those individuals whom we have trained may be the very ones that can make a difference in position of leadership in the world community.

We also run the danger of redefining the Christian faith to make it fit our own lifestyles, comfort zones and biases. Tony Campolo harshly criticized a portrait of Jesus that's all too common in contemporary society. "When I hear Jesus being proclaimed from television stations across our country, from pulpits hither and yon, he comes across not as a Biblical Jesus, but as a white, Anglo-Saxon Protestant Republican."[11] Campolo's language is strong, perhaps even excessively critical, but it makes me uncomfortable enough to decide against casting the first stone in his direction.

SUMMARY AND CONCLUSION

As Christians, we maintain a unique position in the world. We trade in its stores, consume its goods, and labor in its workplaces, but we are not of the world. "But our citizenship is in heaven. And we eagerly await a Savior from there, the Lord Jesus Christ" (Phil. 3:20). We must never forget where home really is, but neither can we afford to be so "heavenly minded that we are of no earthly use."

> We cannot be totally "world affirming" (as if nothing were evil) nor totally "world denying" (as if nothing were good), but a bit of both and particularly "world challenging," recognizing its potentiality as God's world and seeking to conform its life increasingly to his Lordship.[12]

As we spend our years on this earth, we must respond as best we can to the needs of those whose lives we touch. A homeless woman went to see a minister who offered to pray for her. In response, she wrote the following poem, which has received wide circulation. We close this chapter with the poem as a reminder of the social dimensions of holiness.

I was hungry,
  and you formed a humanities group to discuss my hunger,
I was imprisoned,
  and you crept off quietly to your chapel and prayed for my release.
I was naked,
  and in your mind, you debated the morality of my appearance.

341

I was sick,
    and you knelt and thanked God for your health.
I was homeless,
    and you preached to me of the spiritual shelter of the love of God.
I was lonely,
    and you left me alone to pray for me.
You seem so holy, so close to God,
    But I am still very hungry – and lonely – and cold.

Endnotes

1. "Wesley to Wilberforce – John Wesley's Last Letter from His Deathbed," *Christian History.* Vol. 2 No. 1. 1983, p. 29. In part the letter reads, "Go in the name of God and in the power of his might, till even American slavery (the vilest that ever saw the sun) shall vanish away before it."

2. James C. Fenhagen, *Invitation to Holiness.* (San Francisco: Harper and Row Publishers, 1978), p. 61.

3. H. Richard Niebuhr, *Christ and Culture.* (New York: Harper and Row, 1951, pb edition. Harper Torchbooks, 1975), p. 56. Niebuhr suggests that the Mennonites are the most extreme example of those who adopt a posture of "Christ against Culture."

4. H. Richard Niebuhr. *Christ and Culture.* p. 48.

5. Charles Colson, *Against the Dark.* (Ann Arbor, Michigan: Servant Publications, 1989), p. 117.

6. Lawrence O. Richards, *"A Practical Theology of Spirituality"* (Grand Rapids, Michigan: Academie Books, 1987), p. 212.

7. R.C. Sproul, *Pleasing God.* Wheaton, Illinois: Tyndale House Publishers, 1988), p. 69.

8. Walter Rauschenbusch, *Christianity and the Social Crisis.* (London: The Macmillan Company, 1907), p. 65. quoted by John R.W. Stott, *Involvement. Being a Responsible Christian in a Non-Christianity Society.* (Old Tappan, New Jersey: Fleming H. Revell Company, 1985) p. 25.

9. Joe H. Foy, "The Role of the Church in Houston." (Houston, Texas: photocopied manuscript, 1974), p. 1. The manuscript contains the text of remarks in an address delivered to a gathering of ministers for the Churches of Christ in Houston, Texas. At the time the speech was given, Mr. Foy was president of Houston Natural Gas and a church elder.

10. Ibid., p. 5.

11. Tony Campolo, "Will the Real Jesus Stand Up?" *World Vision.* October/November, 1988. p. 4.

12. John R. W. Stott, *Involvement: Being a Responsible Christian in Non-Christian Society.* Vol. 1. p. 49.

25
A New Way of Seeing

In 1965 I underwent surgery for the removal of a cataract which severely limited my vision. After nearly wrecking my car on a narrow two lane highway one Sunday night, I stopped denying that I was afflicted with vision problems and went to see an ophthalmologist. When I looked at the eye chart, I was unable to even read the big "E" on the chart with my right eye. I was legally blind in that eye and facing rapid deterioration in the other.

Two days later I underwent surgery for the removal of the cataract and five weeks after that I walked out of my doctor's office in Waco, Texas with a new pair of cataract glasses. From his office on Austin Avenue, I could look across the street and up the hill to a bakery several blocks away. I remember reading the letters on the sign in front of the bakery – "Rainbo Bread." In all my trips to the doctor's office I had never been able to make out the letters on that sign. That moment of visual correction has forever been etched in my memory, because it meant the beginning of a whole new way of seeing. When

343

people meet me today, they think I'm remarkable for a man in his fifties because they notice I don't wear glasses. Little do they realize that I can't see at all without the correction of my contact lens, but with visual correction, I enjoy nearly perfect vision.

To restore the Biblical ideal of holiness we need a similar correction. Surely we won't have to wreck the church to understand our need for it. In Hebrews 12:2, we are given this word of encouragement: "Let us fix our eyes on Jesus, the author and perfecter of our faith. . . ." Too long our eyes have been focused on the wrong things. We have been issue-oriented lovers of controversy, when we should have been faith-oriented seekers of holiness. Our eyes have been fixed on the things that have divided us – cups, classes, translations, women's role in the church, tongues, instrumental music. Our eyes are focused on the kinds of things we love to write into debate propositions. We need to remove the cataracts that cloud our vision and turn our eyes to Jesus. *He died to make men holy!*

When our vision turns away from ourselves and toward Jesus, we'll see the same thing that Isaiah saw. We'll see that we are unclean. You don't start the job of cleansing yourself by setting your brother straight. Most of us have such a monumental task ahead of us in simply trying to get rid of the cross tie firmly embedded in our own eyes that it's not very becoming to expend all our energy trying to remove the speck of sawdust from the eyes of our brothers.

WHAT CAUSES THE CATARACTS?

In my case the doctors never learned the cause of my cataracts. Cataracts are often caused by thyroid deficiencies, diabetes or trauma to the eye. None of that applied to me. The other explanation is old age, but they first diagnosed mine at age 22 and surgically removed the first one at age 29. With respect to the spiritual cataracts that prevent us from seeing the vision of perfecting holiness, several causes can easily be isolated.

Spiritual exhaustion
Paul wrote, "Let us not become weary in doing good, for at the

proper time we will reap a harvest if we do not give up" (Gal.6:9). If you can remember the time when you first became a Christian, you probably look back on it as one of the most exciting times of your life. The whole faith experience was new and different. There was so much to learn and do, so many changes to make and you were keenly aware of the need to make improvement.

With the passage of time, the new begins to wear off. Things that once excited you, don't hold the same attraction they once did. I can remember when a sermon on the Ethiopian Eunuch's baptism in Acts 8 really sent a burst of adrenalin through my entire body. I just don't get that excited about Acts 8 anymore. I still appreciate it, but I don't get the same warm glow that I used to.

That's not all bad because we're supposed to grow. The Hebrew writer said,

> Therefore let us leave the elementary teachings about Christ and go on to maturity, not laying again the foundation of repentance from acts that lead to death, and of faith in God, instruction about baptisms, the laying on of hands, the resurrection of the dead and eternal judgment (Hebrews 6:1-2).

There's no way to grow in holiness if we're only fed a baby food diet throughout the course of a lifetime. Sometimes we get stuck at certain levels of development. Inertia sets in and it seems too hard to get back on track. We even wonder if it's worth the effort to keep going.

The original readers of the letter to the Hebrews were a group of people whose vision of holiness had been dimmed by spiritual weariness. The author characterized them as people with "feeble arms and weak knees" (Heb. 12:12). "We know very little about the writer or the recipients of this letter. But we can ascertain enough from the letter itself to know that the readers had become weary of the Christian calling."[1]

As Christians aspiring to a higher level of holiness, we must recognize that we will inevitably pass through such periods of weariness. James Jauncey observes, "No single venture in living satisfies for long. No matter how exciting and absorbing it is at the start, its capacity to satisfy quickly wears off."[2] The secret of following after holiness is in refusing to see despair in the period of spiritual disappointment, but to remember Paul's promise, ". . . at the proper time we will reap a harvest if we do not give up" (Gal. 6:9).

The Secular Trap

Jesus identified an important hinderance to our spiritual vision in Luke 21:34, "Be careful, or your hearts will be weighed down with dissipation, drunkenness and the anxieties of life, and that day will close on you unexpectedly like a trap." If you have gone through the first 24 chapters of this book, you're probably spiritually minded enough to be aware of dangers of dissipation and drunkenness. Satan probably won't even bother laying those particular traps for you.

But the "anxieties of life" trap many of us. Jesus taught, "Therefore I tell you, do not worry about your life, what you will eat or drink; or about your body, what you will wear. Is life not more important than food and the body more important than clothes?" (Matt. 6:25). That's easy to talk about in Sunday School class, but hard to remember when your middle schooler campaigns for a pair of the $125.00 shoes recommended by a professional basketball player.

So much of our energy goes into the very things that Jesus said not to worry about. Everyone preaches about the importance of economic security. You've got to prepare for catastrophic illnesses that might strike you. You've got to be ready for the demands of retirement and financial planning experts say that a retired couple needs 70 percent of the income they had during their working years in order to get by comfortably. To some degree these concerns are well founded. No one wants to become a burden to the church, to children or to society.

We've got so many irons in the fire that some husbands seem to find it necessary to put time with their wives on their appointment schedules.

> We have a schedule that too often becomes our daily god. We get up by it, go to work by it, stop by it without any awareness of a full moon or autumn. We have surrounded ourselves almost completely with concrete, steel and plastics. Rain and autumn leaves are headaches. Spring just means hay fever.[3]

But there's something terribly wrong with our priorities, when we only give attention to our personal relationship with God after every other interest has been addressed. A little boy wanted to spend some time with his father in the evening, but Dad was working late at the office every night until well after the boy's bedtime. One day, the boy asked his mother, "Why can't my Dad come home before I go to bed? The mother said, "Well, your Dad has so much work to do at the office that he can't get it all done before your bedtime." The little boy said, "Then why doesn't Dad's teacher put him in a slower group?" Maybe that's what the Lord is telling us we need to do. Perhaps we need to live at a slower and more deliberate pace, so we can give attention to the things that really count.

Relationships

In II Corinthians 6:14, Paul urged, "Do not be yoked together with unbelievers. For what do righteousness and unrighteousness have in common? Or what fellowship can light have with darkness?" This passage has often been used to warn against the danger of marrying out of the faith. While it's hard for me to see how a person can grow in the faith while sharing the marriage bond with someone who is not interested in spiritual matters, the text is not limited to the marriage relationship. It applies to any kind of relationship that threatens to undermine spiritual growth.

It is important to remember that Paul's exhortation in II Corinthians 7:1 is given in the very same context, "Since we have these promises, dear friends, let us purify ourselves from everything that contaminates body and spirit, perfecting holiness out of reverence for God." Relationships have the power either to enhance or inhibit holiness. They will never be neutral.

Without a doubt, Paul was thinking of pagans when he referred to "unbelievers" in II Corinthians 6. However, we should not overlook the fact that there are times when relationships with some "members of the church" can be spiritually destructive.

In *Habitation of Dragons*, Keith Miller tells about conducting a seminar on the subject of spiritual renewal. The church's young minister drove Miller to the airport at the end of the seminar. During the course of that brief trip, the local minister said that he feared the kind

347

of spiritual growth that Miller had been advocating would not actually take place. He said that most of the people who turned out for the seminar were really interested in money, their social standing in the community and their ability to control other people. They attended church because they thought it would enhance their political stature. Miller left his host and took his seat on the plane, greatly troubled. As he reflected on his host's disturbing remarks, he noted, "Christian renewal will be accomplished – where it takes place in any lasting depth – through the lives of a group of desperate people who are finding irreplaceable hope and meaning in living for Christ and his purpose among men."[4] If our only association is with people who are oriented toward secular things, the urge to be holy will die. It is only as we associate with people who realize their need for the great physician that spiritual renewal takes place.

Unbelief

Unbelief was a major problem among the tired Christians who first read the epistle to the Hebrews. The writer urged, "See to it, brothers, that none of you has a sinful, unbelieving heart that turns away from the living God" (Heb. 3:12). He doesn't mean they were atheists. He means they no longer trusted God.

When I was just starting to preach, I received an urgent call from a church member to visit one of our Sunday School teachers. I found a distraught lady who collapsed in tears when she saw me. Through her sobs she said, "I have lost my faith." I started offering her intellectual arguments confirming the existence of God. That woman never read an evolutionary textbook in her life. She knew nothing of the intellectual arguments that skeptics make against the faith. If I had held a Bible in front of her face and asked, "Is this book true?" she would have answered, "yes." She was trying to tell me that she had lost her ability to trust God.

That's what happened to the children of Israel in the wilderness. There were 605,000 graves in the wilderness which stood as mute testimony to the foolishness of refusing to trust God. There was a danger that a similar experience might materialize among the ancient readers of the Hebrew epistle. The consequences of such unbelief were frightening to contemplate. They could only anticipate "a fearful

expectation of judgment and of raging fire that will consume the enemies of God" (Heb. 10:27). It may be happening to more of us than
we realize and it threatens to obliterate our vision of what it's like to
be a holy people.

HOW CAN WE CLEAR OUR VISION?

When I began losing my vision, I went from doctor to doctor in an
attempt to find some cure that would not require surgery. They fitted
me with glasses, then some stronger glasses and finally glasses that
were so strong that just wearing them made me sick. Eventually, I had
to take a radical step and that meant surgery. If we get bogged down
in the things discussed on the previous pages of this chapter, radical
spiritual change will be necessary for us to see things from the perspective of holiness. There are no instant solutions. We can't jump
start ourselves into holy living, but we do have to make some serious
decisions about life and the way we want to live it.

It Starts With Commitment.

We live in a day and time when commitment is not very popular.
During World War II, a Shakespearean actor wanted to do what he
could to encourage the troops who were fighting the war. The USO
reluctantly sent him to a group of battle weary soldiers who had just
returned from the front lines. The actor gave it his best shot as he re-
cited Hamlet's soliloquy for the soldiers. A correspondent asked one
of the soldiers what he thought of the performance. The G. I. said, "I
considered it good and let it go at that."

Perhaps that's our reaction to God's call to be holy. We are willing
to recognize that it's a good thing, but it makes no real change in our
lives.

> It is so apparent that Christians are called to live 'holy lives' that
> even a child who has been to worship once or twice would rec-
> ognize this necessity. From the very first some genuine interfer-
> ence with mere personal pleasure and fleshly desires and
> personal preference is implied if we're going to lead a holy life.[5]

349

There is simply no way to have a satisfying, genuine and rewarding relationship with Christ without commitment. Jesus came right to the point on this matter when he said, ". . . any of you who does not give up everything he has cannot be my disciple" (Luke 14:33).

Get Involved With the Body.
I've met people who would say, "I don't have a problem with being committed to Christ, but I don't like the idea of getting involved in the life of the church. I'm turned off with the prospect of attending all those services, serving on committees, being expected to show up for work days, attending the pot luck dinners and participating in the work program of the church." Besides that, every church seems to have those members who are difficult to live with. A person who doesn't want to go through all that protests, "Why can't I just stay home, read my Bible, listen to Chuck Swindoll on the radio and pray?"

I'll give two reasons why that's not a good idea. First, the church is the body of Christ. The Bible says so in Ephesians 1:22-23 and in Colossians 1:18. There is no possible way to profess commitment to Christ and disdain for the church. If you want to say that church leaders need to rethink their concept of ministry and restructure the work program, then you may well be exercising a legitimate concern. There is no way, however, that you can pursue a life of holiness and exclude the church from your life. The church is part of God's plan.

Secondly, Jesus chose to validate his claims as the Son of God by having the world observe caring relationships in the church. He said in John 13:34-35, "A new command I give you: Love one another. As I have loved you, so you must love one another. All men will know that you are my disciples if you love one another." The church consists of a body of people who practice this new command.

> The outside world looking at church people and church activities couldn't care less what we believe. People aren't interested in what we teach or the purity of our doctrine. What they want to know is how much we care, how much we love.[6]

We Must Be Willing to Seek Holiness for the Right Reasons.
Sometimes people go through the motions of holy living for the

wrong reasons. Some people serve the Lord because they've had heavy guilt trips placed upon them and they are afraid not to serve God. Guilt is an ineffective motivator for the long haul. I'll grant you that some people engage in actions which could outwardly be called, "holy," because they were manipulated by an articulate "Christian" power broker. Guilt tripping may get things done, but it never helps people enjoy serving the Lord.

The New Testament emphasizes voluntary servanthood. In II Corinthians 9, Paul urged the church in Corinth to make a contribution for needy brothers in the church. He didn't say things like, "Look, you people really have some nice things in Corinth. Some of you have more togas than you know what to do with hanging in your closet. Besides that you traded in your perfectly good old chariot for the latest model with wire wheels. Do you really need to be indulging yourself like that while your brothers in Jerusalem are having a hard time making ends meet?" Notice what he did say, "Each man should give what he has decided in his heart to give, not reluctantly or under compulsion, for God loves a cheerful giver" (II Cor. 9:7).

A preacher who gives high pressure stewardship sermons has trouble leaving it there. He's thinking, "But how am I ever going to encourage a person to be a cheerful giver if I don't make him squirm just a little bit?" But notice what Paul said in the next verse, "And God is able to make all grace abound to you, so that in all things at all times, having all that you need, you will abound in every good work" (9:8). Incredible, isn't it? Paul is saying, when you truly understand grace, it's going to affect your pocketbook. And so it is with all the holiness disciplines we talked about in chapter 23.

Put Jesus at the Center of Your Life

Too many people are afraid that a commitment to a life of holiness means losing out on something important. Nothing could be farther from the truth. Paul saw this point so clearly that even though he found himself on trial for his life because of his commitment to Christ, it meant more than anything else in the whole world.

> If anyone else thinks he has reasons to put confidence in the flesh, I have more; circumcised on the eighth day, of the people

351

of Israel, of the tribe of Benjamin, a Hebrew of the Hebrews; in regard to the law, a Pharisee; as for zeal, persecuting the church; as for legalistic righteousness, faultless. But whatever was to my profit, I now consider loss for the sake of Christ. What is more, I consider everything a loss compared to the surpassing greatness of knowing Christ Jesus my Lord, for whose sake I have lost all things (Phil. 3:4-8).

Why was Paul so willing to part with those things which most people in the world value the most? It was because he understood how much Christ had given up for him. In Romans 5:7, he said, "Very rarely will anyone die for a righteous man." That's a simple statement of fact. When men die in battle for their comrades, it's such an unusual sacrifice that our government sets aside the Congressional Medal of Honor to recognize those who give of themselves above and beyond the call of duty. But what God did, doesn't happen among men. It can't even be found among those brave men who receive the Congressional Medal of Honor. "But God demonstrates his own love for us in this: while we were still sinners, Christ died for us" (Rom. 5:8). That's love in the ultimate degree.

Francis of Assisi didn't fully understand how Jesus wants us to respond to his love, but he may have understood, much better than we do, that holiness is a response to love. It was a heart filled with gratitude to Christ that led him to express these thoughts,

> Lord, make me an instrument of Thy peace. Where there is hatred, let me sow love; where there is injury, pardon; where there is doubt, faith; where there is despair, hope; where there is sadness, joy; where there is darkness light.
> O Divine Master, grant that I may not so much seek to be consoled as to console; not so much to be understood, as to understand; not so much to be loved, as to love. For it is in giving that we receive, it is in pardoning that we are pardoned, it is in dying that we are born again to eternal life.[7]

CONCLUSION

When Isaiah saw God in the throne room, he felt dirty. He was especially concerned about his mouth. He said, "I've got a dirty mouth."

But then God cleansed him. As R. C. Sproul suggests, "Isaiah's wound was being cauterized, the dirt in his mouth was being burned away. He was refined by a holy fire."[8] But look at what happened next, "Then I heard the voice of the Lord saying, 'Whom shall I send? And who will go for us?' And I said, 'Here am I. Send me!' " (Isa. 6:8). Think about it. The man who came apart was put back together again and then he was confident and eager to speak God's message to the world.

We will not have anything worthwhile to share with a lost world until we get serious about holiness. Sheldon and Davy Vanauken considered themselves pagans when they decided to investigate the claims of Christianity; yet they were sure they would reject such a simplistic and superstitious faith.

They weren't really prepared to see the transforming effect that Christ has on the lives of people. Halfway into their study, Davy had embraced faith in Christ and Sheldon's skepticism was wavering. One night in the midst of his pilgrimage, Sheldon wrote these words in his journal,

> The best argument for Christianity is Christians; their certainty, their completeness. But the strongest argument against Christianity is also Christians—when they are sombre and joyless, when they are self-righteous and smug in complacent consecration, when they are narrow and repressive, Christianity dies a thousand deaths.[9]

Nearly twenty centuries ago Jesus entered a world corrupted by sin. He lived here for about a third of a century and then, *he died to make men holy.* How well we respond to the call to become like him in his holiness will go a long way toward determining whether people like Sheldon and Davy Vanauken give the Christian faith a favorable hearing.

Endnotes

1. James Thompson, *Our Life Together.* (Austin, Texas: Journey Books, 1977), p. 117.

2. James H. Jauncey, *Above Ourselves, The Art of Happiness.* (Grand Rapids, Michigan: Zondervan Publishing House, 1964), p. 117.

3. Paul Faulkner, "The Church, the Home and the Future." *Abilene Christian College Lectures, 1972.* (Abilene, Texas: Abilene Christian College Bookstore, 1972), p. 114.

4. Keith Miller, *Habitation of Dragons.* (Carmel, New York; Guideposts Associates, Inc., 1970), p. 180.

5. James Le Fan, "Be Ye Holy" *Abilene Christian College Lectures – 1963.* (Abilene, Texas: Abilene Christian College Bookstore, 1963), p. 44.

6. Willard Tate, *Learning to Love.* (Nashville: The Gospel Advocate Company, 1988), p. 76.

7. Francis of Assisi, "Lord Make Me an Instrument of Thy Peace." quoted by Alan Paton, *Instrument of Thy Peace.* New York: The Seabury Press, 1968), p. 9.

8, R.C. Sproul, *The Holiness of God.* (Wheaton, Illinois: Tyndale House Publishers, 1987), p. 47.

9. Sheldon Vanauken, *A Severe Mercy.* (New York: Harper and Row, 1977), p. 85.